D1242075

An Engineer in the Courtroom

William J. Lux

Published by:
Society of Automotive Engineers, Inc.
400 Commonwealth Drive
Warrendale, PA 15096-0001
U.S.A.
Phone: (412) 776-4841
Fax: (412) 776-5760

Library of Congress Cataloging-in-Publication Data

Lux, William J., 1925
    An engineer in the courtroom / William J. Lux.
      p. cm.
    Includes index.
    ISBN 1-56091-672-9
    1. Evidence, Expert--United States. 2. Actions and
defenses--United States. 3. Forensic engineering--
United States. 4. Engineers--Malpractice--United
States. I. Title.
KF8968.25.L89   1995
347.73'67--dc20
[347.30767]   95-32283
                                      CIP

Copyright © 1995 Society of Automotive Engineers, Inc.

ISBN 1-56091-672-9

Permission to photocopy for internal or personal use, or the internal or personal use of specific clients, is granted by SAE for libraries and other users registered with the Copyright Clearance Center (CCC), provided that the base fee of $.50 per page is paid directly to CCC, 222 Rosewood Dr., Danvers, MA 01923. Special requests should be addressed to the SAE Publications Group. 1-56091-672-9/95 $.50

SAE Order No. R-155

❋ ❋ ❋ ❋

In Memoriam

On January 19, 1995, when Bill Lux passed gently from this world, he left us all a legacy, in the pages of this book. For we who are his family, it has been a way to help him finish his work. It is indeed a fitting memorial to this man who provided for us so well and lived concepts like truth and justice so elegantly within our family.

For you, the readers of *The Engineer in the Courtroom*, we hope that in this book you will find the challenge to look at engineering, safety, and law in the way Bill did. They were not just fields of study and work for him. Technology, safety, and justice were means to humanize our world, and he spent his life assuring that always these fields of endeavor were applied in a way that enhanced life for the individual.

To Bill, the loving husband and wonderful father, we say in honor of this publication: "All our memories of you are happy. We are proud to be your family. The marks you left in this world are good, and they will guide our ways until we meet again."

Mary C. Lux
Jackie Lux
Kathy Lux Davis

Table of Contents

Preface

This book is based on my experiences as an engineer who spent most of his life in the earthmoving and construction machinery industry, and who has extensive experience in products liability litigation matters.

I have seen both good and bad performances by engineers in the courtroom—and all kinds of performances in between. I believe I know why some performances were good and others were bad. With my experience, I believe I can help engineers who may be in court in the future by helping them:

- lose or control their fear of the courtroom and of lawyers and litigation,

- do a better job of avoiding litigation (although they can't really prevent someone from suing), and

- perform more effectively in matters of litigation.

The engineer may become involved in litigation for several different reasons, or through several different channels. Without regard to how or why he might become involved, the suggestions in this book will help him to overcome his fear of the process and will help him to do a proper and professional job in court and in the matters leading to the courtroom.

This book was written almost entirely from personal experience and the studies I have made as a result of being involved in litigation. Therefore, you have a right to know my background.

I am a mechanical engineer, and I worked for 35 years in the industry that is described as "heavy-duty, off-road machinery design, development, and application." I worked with diesel engines as a starting point and branched out into the broader machinery industry.

Reaching a position of engineering management responsibility meant that I became familiar with claims and complaints that said, in effect, "Your machine isn't good enough and needs to be changed." Some of the complaints were lawsuits, which directly blamed the machine, in some way, as the cause of an accident that resulted in personal injury or some economic loss.

As an engineer responsible for the design, I was brought into the discussions and into the legal processes surrounding the claim. I met lawyers. In the process of this part of my work, I found that I could work with lawyers in the defense of "my" product. I found I even like the intellectual challenge of that type of work.

Moreover, I found that lawyers had a whole different language and unique ways of thinking and expressing their work. The differences made me suspect them at first, but I learned that one could expand his thinking and understanding by learning to understand the lawyer, just as one expands his horizons by learning a new language. Attorneys may be hard to understand because they use a different language. In addition, they think and reason somewhat differently. Let me try to explain the differences.

A scientist seeks to find new knowledge and understanding. He might be likened to a knight in shining armor, riding off in all directions at once in search of a dragon to slay. In the case of the scientist, he is searching for new information to add to his storehouse of knowledge.

The journey of the engineer is a little more direct. He starts out at a known point—today, for example. He has a specific assignment or goal to reach. He gets on to his horse and rides in the general direction of that goal. He varies his path to avoid or remove obstacles, but he generally searches for the shortest or easiest way to his objective.

The lawyer deals with a body of knowledge and experience which might be given the shorthand name "the law." The law is made up of two components: (1) legislated or enacted laws, and (2) law developed by practice. This practice is recorded as the decisions of courts in past cases. Where those cases have similarities to the present case under dispute or in litigation, the past experience becomes important in the thinking of the lawyer.

Dealing with a case, then, the lawyer considers these three things:

First, the lawyer deals with the existing statutes or laws. What specifically does it say? Perhaps, more importantly, what <u>doesn't</u> the enacted law say? The statutes say, "thou shall" and "thou shall not." If one acted contrary to a law, he may be in trouble.

Second, the attorney considers the body of legal experience and decisions made by other courts in similar or related cases. They may guide him in proceeding with his advocacy of his client's affairs.

Third, the attorney studies his case and looks for possible "new" law that may apply. The law is not constant; it changes in a continuum. The aim is to make the law more just and more in tune with the codes and mores of society. True, sometimes selfish interests get too much attention, but, usually, the general good of the people and the rights of the individual are balanced out in the process.

This leads to a kind of thinking that tells the attorney to look for new theories about his present subject case. In brief, the attorney's thinking is led into several paths. He follows those paths (searching the statutes, searching the common law record, and considering new theories of his activity in the present case) alternately—and frequently at the same time.

This process leads to what laymen sometimes see as confusing. The term "loopholes" may enter conversations about what the attorney is doing. Other comments and references, even less complimentary, may be spoken.

It is not my intent to critique the thought methods of attorneys. Just as engineers and scientist do, sometimes the attorney may get involved in so much detail that he fails to see the big picture. Likewise, either the attorney or the engineer may miss or lose important details as he thinks.

However, I find this "multi-channel" thought process of the attorney to be interesting and challenging for the engineer who has become accustomed to so-called "logical and scientific" thinking. The engineer who begins to work with attorneys and in litigation must necessarily expand his thinking if he is to be helpful and successful.

The dichotomy of thought is that the attorney is both using and developing the law at the same time. If you think of this as a truism, it will help you understand those things in litigation that seem unreasonable.

When I retired from industry at age 60, I decided to become a consultant in litigation matters, and in other matters also, as they presented themselves. In an eight-year period of consulting, I was involved in more than 300 incidents involving or leading to litigation. That experience, along with the earlier industry experience, became the basis for this book.

So long as one creates a product or performs a service, there is a possibility that someone else will claim that product or service to be defective. If a defect exists, there will always be, under our system of government, a possibility that someone will claim injury and demand redress for that loss. If somewhere in this book I seem to have turned against lawyers or against the law, it is only in the sense of a specific disagreement or criticism. I would still fight to retain the system we now have, including the opportunities in the system for continuous improvement.

I have worked on both sides of cases in litigation. I have developed the claim against a product to explain how a plaintiff was injured or sustained a loss. I have been called on to explain my product, one in which I had engineering involvement—how it was designed, how it was tested, how it was applied, and why the decisions were made as they were. I have explained drawings, letters, field reports, and service letters in doing that. As a testifying expert, I have given opinions about the products of others, as they related to the subject of some lawsuit.

In my experience, I have seen engineers frightened by the prospect of being deposed or testifying in court. They need not be. I have seen good work by engineers in such situations. I have also seen errors made by engineers who were not properly prepared for the experience. From that background, I have prepared this book aimed at explaining the process to the engineer. By making him aware of the requirements, the engineer will become confident that he can properly perform the tasks given to him, should he become involved in a matter of litigation.

I appreciate the experience my industry employers, Caterpillar, Inc., Cummins Engine Co., WABCO, and Deere & Company, have given me. Without that experience, there would be no reason to write.

I also owe a debt of appreciation to all of the attorneys with whom I have worked. They have given me an experience and understanding that confirms that the world is far larger than the engineering community. There are too many attorneys to name, and they all contributed.

Especially, I thank the Society of Automotive Engineers for 43 years of proving that the written and spoken information is necessary to the proper and successful growth of an industry—and of a career.

I hope this book is useful to you.

William J. Lux

Chapter 1

INTRODUCTION

The intent of this book is to introduce the engineer to what he may expect to encounter in a matter of litigation. Being so introduced, the engineer may:

- be able to avoid litigation altogether,

- know what leads to litigation,

- understand what accidents are, and how they are caused,

- learn something about the litigation process,

- realize the importance of decisions made by an engineer,

- be aware of how the engineer can assist the attorney,

- know what to expect in discovery, in deposition, and at trial, and

- know how to best conduct himself in those situations.

By exploring these subjects, the engineer will be less frightened by the prospect of litigation and more effective in assisting his company or his attorney-client. He will understand the importance of his professional work and his obligations to society.

You will probably become familiar with the courtroom and with litigation through the same means as many others—you will be asked to defend a design for which you held responsibility. You won't particularly like the idea of being told through an official-looking piece of paper that "You have been summoned to appear" before a court reporter and a group of attorneys for a deposition in a matter that involved serious injuries to a plaintiff. You will be told that you would be expected to produce certain written information, records, and other documents. You will also be told that the attorneys will ask questions of you and that you will answer those questions under oath and under penalty of perjury.

But you haven't done anything wrong! Why you? Simply because you were the engineer in charge of the product or design and because, under the rules of litigation, the plaintiff has the right to "discover" information and to question you about the product and its design.

In a nutshell, when you design a machine or a product, you have an obligation to society that the product be "reasonably safe" and "not defective or dangerous for its intended uses."

Now, that is not an unreal expectation. When a customer pays money for a product, he has a right to expect it to work properly, and the plaintiff in a matter of litigation is merely exercising his right to claim—if it is provable— that your product did not work as he expected, and that he had been injured in some way by that lack of proper performance. He may make that claim through proper procedures in an appropriate court.

You may be somewhat frightened in this situation, until you discover that one proper response to a claim may be to describe the product, the way it was designed, and the proper use and care for the product. Then, if you discover that the plaintiff's claims were based upon some incorrect assumptions on his part (or on the part of his attorney, possibly) you may point out those errors. By explaining the proper way the machine works, and by showing how the accident really happened, you may be able to refute the claims. A jury then, may find no fault in the design.

As a designer, you have a lot of publics to satisfy. You must design a product that will be successful for your employer. Your supervisor must be convinced that he can depend on you and your professional abilities. The product must meet the general plans and objectives of the business that pays your salary. You need to care for your family.

For that important reason, a designer will concern himself or herself that the work done is excellent. Salaries, promotions, and success depend on it. That is why I suggest there is seldom any malicious reason for a design not to be the best possible. Further, the product must meet the needs of the customer who will use it. Otherwise, neither you nor your company will be paid.

The product must do its job or perform as the buyer expects. An earthmoving machine that will not dig enough dirt in a day, or an electric range that will not roast meat in time for dinner, is not acceptable. If the machine or the product only works for a day and then breaks down, it won't be successful, either. And if your company can't provide parts or repairs, you are out of business.

Machines and products must also be safe. They are made for the use and benefit of society at large, although the machine is usually purchased and used by an individual or a single company. Consider what happens if the product leads to an injury or to some other property loss or economic loss. If the product is the cause of that injury or loss, the citizen who incurs the loss will look for someone to pay him for that loss.

The legal system gives that citizen the right to ask for redress or payment for that loss. This is where you may become involved.

If (and this "if" is the reason for lawsuits and litigation) the person claims that your design or your product is in some way responsible for his loss, he may ask the court to order you and your company to pay for his loss.

At this point, you may think the system is unfair and menacing, and you may even think it unreasonable to design anything again. The system is menacing at times, and in some situations, it may well be unfair. Consider, however, that you are the most knowledgeable person available to discuss the machine or product you have designed.

You have designed a product to serve a purpose or to do a good. You have made it reasonable in cost, so the public can afford it. You have made it to last a reasonable length of time, and to perform reliably. You have even made it possible for the product to be repaired if it should fail or break down. In short, you have designed and developed a successful product.

You have one more responsibility. That product should not offend, injure, or cause loss to the general public. If people are offended by the product, you can expect protests and boycotts. If they are injured by the product, or as a result of it and the work it does, you can expect to have a claim filed against you (your company) in the form of a lawsuit.

During the planning and development of a product, then, and during the production of that product, you need to consider the possible claims for injury or loss that may be made against your product.

I might be tempted to blame the plaintiff's bar and the "ambulance chasing" lawyers for causing this worry for us. Some people give them the direct and complete blame. However, I must tell you that our legal system, in the United States, is a critical and important part of our society that promises justice to all of us. Anyone who suffers hurt or loss, and who fully believes he knows the cause of that loss or hurt, has the right to apply to the court to have that loss made whole, insofar as it can be made whole. You and I also have that right, and so do our employers. I will defend that right. Maybe there are some abuses, but I believe it is important for the opportunity to be maintained for all of us.

The end goal of the legal process, then, is intended to be a just determination of who or what is at fault for the injury or loss, and what redress or payment (in money, usually) will make the plaintiff whole from his loss.

Although sometimes people think the result may not seem correct, the legal system must be praised for its thoroughness and its attention to detail. If the story of an incident or a dispute is told properly and effectively, the truth—or at least a just resolution—will be found. Most attorneys are diligent in their work. Most judges are compassionate, understanding, and even wise. Juries seem to perform exceptionally well, considering that they usually will be asked to choose between one side of the argument and the other.

This book, then, was not written with intent to criticize the legal system, nor to bemoan the fact that a company or a product may be sued for injury or loss. There will be no carping and raving at attorneys for "causing" this problem and the expense associated with it. (There are, of course, frivolous lawsuits, but there are ways to deal with them, too.)

This book will, however, tell the engineer (and others who may be interested) something about the legal system and how and why it works. It will also show the engineer how to conduct himself in the situation where he may be called into court to "answer for and explain" his product. This is not legal advice; you get that from your attorney. It is a view of the legal system as I see it from experience.

There is much that the engineer (and again, this can be expanded to others—professional or common citizen) can do to assure a proper and just disposal of claims and suits. We can do much, each of us, to make a good system even better. Good and true information in the technical specialties we represent will contribute to good resolutions to disputes. Factual information, presented in a highly credible form, will help even more.

Much of what is written in this book will deal with earthmoving and construction machinery. That has been my experience base for this book. Examples will deal with such machinery. However, the principles apply broadly to other equipment and to litigation involved with other matters. Use these examples as they fit your particular situation.

The discussion of various facets of litigation are sprinkled with examples from experience. The examples illustrate what really happens—or, at least, what really may happen and can happen. The examples, or "war stories" as attorneys call them, will serve to help you to transpose the subject to other scenes.

For example, in a discussion of a design defect alleged as the result of a bulldozer having backed over a worker, there may be a claim that a backup alarm might have avoided the accident. You may see a parallel in this incident to a claim that some attachment may be alleged to have been omitted from your product and that the omission had caused accidental injury or loss to someone using your product.

Perhaps someone didn't maintain a motor grader in proper condition and that lack of maintenance led to an accident. You might see similar requirements for periodic adjustment and maintenance in your product.

Don't lose sight of the purpose of this book—to make the engineer more comfortable and more effective in situations dealing with lawsuits, trials, depositions, and other facets of litigation. The law does not only apply to earthmoving and construction equipment or to manufacturers or to distributors. It applies to all of us.

A short story of the development of the law seems appropriate here. The complications and intricacies of the law are such that a short, comprehensive story of the development of the law is not possible. Still, an abridged and shortcut history may be useful. This is the brief story as it appears to me.

Ancient man must have had a mixture of needs and desires. He almost certainly did what he had to do in order to fill those needs. Sometimes, then, he certainly "walked on the other fellow," and maybe even killed him or took his property.

Such a system of dealing with one's fellow man could not last long without disaster. One form of that disaster is that one man would become dominant and completely control and subjugate the other men. This was tyranny, and it happened all too often. The other likely result was mass pandemonium and complete lack of control. Primitive life in the jungle was one such condition. Another was the common image of the Wild West, where everybody wore a gun.

As man began to see those two likely results, there developed the concepts of "rights" and "responsibilities." Mankind had needs to fill. In filling those needs, there developed an understanding than mankind had certain "rights" to go about the work of fulfilling those needs. But he also had responsibilities. He discovered that if he did not disturb his neighbor, the neighbor would probably not disturb him. Still further, he found he could make agreements and promises of cooperation between himself and others, providing himself a greater measure both of security and of ability to meet his own needs with less difficulty.

These discoveries—made probably over years and centuries, and maybe longer—led to tribes, clans, nations, and empires. People began to deal with each other in ways that served their needs. Nations did likewise. They began to deal with each other to the extent their mutual understanding would let them do so.

Early systems of laws were almost certainly religious in origin and nature. Present serious and practicing believers in religious faiths recognize those origins. About two to five thousand years before Christ, elemental systems of laws sprang up from those religious sources in general. The Hebrew "Ten Commandments" is one of the earliest systems, and it is still in use, with some modifications and extensions.

A system historically known as "The Code of Hammurabi" involved what may be summarized as the "eye for an eye and a tooth for a tooth" system. You take out my eye and I have a right to take out your eye in exchange. You knock out my tooth, and I get to knock out yours with no recriminations. You burn my barn and I am allowed to burn yours. The idea of equity or balance in personal dealings grew up out of this concept. The Old Testament of the Bible carries the same "eye for an eye" concept as a base.

The "eye for an eye" concept, however, didn't do any good until <u>after</u> a misdeed had been done. There were two problems:

- it didn't prevent misdeeds and,

- it punished a misdeed with another deed which turned out to be an identical misdeed.

This system of law and order in the Old West had people shooting each other. In short, all the system did was attempt to deter a misdeed by awarding a free misdeed to the victim.

As society developed, systems to prevent the misdeed (still, however, by threat of punishment) emerged. In ancient Greece and Rome, and in other emerging civilizations on the earth, there were laws and rules by which men were expected to govern their conduct. Mankind realized that with benefit and freedom comes responsibility. They discovered that when they exercised their rights, they had to do so in a way that recognized the rights of others on an equitable basis.

7

Since then, and probably beginning with the Magna Carta in England, constitutions and other bodies of law have been developed to express the general welfare of all and the personal freedoms of individuals to be irreversibly related.

The Constitution of the United States of America does that. It extracts from the individual certain responsibilities in order that it can provide those same individuals with other certain freedoms. Interpretations and agreements on those details, however, are difficult to attain in a single, concise statement that has universal application.

Therefore, a legal or court system is set up to resolve those situations in which two entities do not or cannot agree. If a person feels he has been injured by some feature of a machine, he may blame his injury or loss upon that feature he considers at fault. Thus, if a person feels injured or suffers loss as a result of your product, he can go into court and ask for correction of that alleged wrong. As an engineer, then, or as the designer of the product, you may be in court explaining or defending your design.

This is a reasonably fair system. You can use the system, too, if you feel wronged for some reason. It is that system, however, that frightens the individual who is attacked. It is that discomfort and fright that you will read about in the remainder of this book. I will not attack the system. I will show how to live with the system and to use it for resolutions to disputes.

Chapter 2

THE NATURE OF ACCIDENTS

Many of the lawsuits concerning products involve what are generally termed "accidents." In these incidents, someone has suffered injuries or losses, and they seek redress for those losses through litigation. This products liability litigation, or legal action, is the most frequent form of activity that gets an engineer involved in courtroom activity.

Of course, business matters, patent conflicts, family disputes, and other such problems may also involve the engineer. Sometimes, criminal matters get into the act, but not usually.

The discussions in this book deal mainly with the products liability actions. They are the ones which provide the experience and the ideas in this book. They are also the activities which are most likely to be the occasion of an engineer's involvement in litigation.

In this chapter, the focus is on "accidents." They are common elements in tort or products liability court activity. The word "accident" is in quotation marks thus far because agreement must be reached on a definition of the word if it is to be used.

The word "accident" has various meanings. To a philosopher, an accident is something that happens with no cause. The philosopher may go far enough to declare that the origin of life and existence as we know it may have been one big accident—that is, it may have been without cause. Most religious

9

philosophies do not agree that our life and our existence came about without cause.

As you study incidents in which injuries or damages result, you will see that seldom, if ever, does it happen that an "accident" has no cause.

To many people, an accident is something that cannot be avoided or prevented. A common concept is that an accident is an occurrence that is outside of the control of anyone. When one spills milk, it is an accident. When the rung on a ladder breaks, it is an accident. When you fall asleep in your car and hit a tree, it is an accident. When thousands of gallons of crude oil are spilled from a tanker, it is an accident. You can see that people have broad views on what makes up an accident. Those broad views come primarily from the tendency of the people involved in the incident to say, "It is not my fault."

To those involved in the safety business, an accident is anything that breaks the normal or expected activity and, generally, an accident is a happening that causes loss or injury. Things which break the normal pattern are not always "accidents" for the purpose of this book. If it costs nothing, or if no one is hurt, we tend to let the incident go by without calling it an accident.

I will define an accident as:

- an occurrence that is unexpected, <u>and</u>

- an occurrence that causes loss or injury, which can be expressed in some form of economic terms.

Those two conditions will be the character and substance of the "accident" as it is presented in this text.

From the definition of "accident" listed above, it is obvious that when an accident involves a product, the product and its manufacturer and seller are likely targets for claims for recovering damages or losses. If, in the process of assessing the cause and the cost of an incident which involves injury or loss, the injured party feels that someone outside his control caused the accident, he will seek candidates for the blame. Thus the engineer enters. As the creator of the design and the maker of decisions involving the product, he is in the position to defend the product and to explain the benefits of the design.

Litigation claims (if they are at all reasonably founded) usually offer a proposed feature or design detail which, if it were in place at the time of the accident, would have prevented the accident. These claims can best be formulated and expressed by an engineer. They also can be confronted best by the engineer who designed, developed, and applied the product.

For example, a worker is injured when he is hit by an earthmoving scraper moving in reverse. The expert for the plaintiff may claim that if the scraper had been equipped with certain mirrors and a reverse alarm, the incident would not have happened. The quarrel in the courtroom then tends to focus on the machine without those devices, as described by the defendant's engineer expert, and the machine with those devices, as described by the plaintiff's engineer expert.

The plaintiff's expert will explain (through his attorney) to the jury and the court why the device or feature was needed, how it would have prevented the accident, and why the design is defective without the feature. The defendant's expert will show (through his lawyer) why the machine is designed the way it is and why it is safe in the present design form, without the suggested attachments or features. Further, he may explain why the suggestions of the plaintiff's expert are not good or cannot be used. In some instances he may point out that the machine with the proposed feature is even less safe than the present design of the machine.

In another example, a maintenance man has been injured in a fall from the deck of a loader while he is fueling it. He may claim that the handholds were not proper or that a non-skid surface at the point from which he fell would have prevented his fall. The engineer-designer or expert for the defendant will explain why the machine is designed as it is, and why, perhaps, the changes suggested by the plaintiff's expert could not or should not be applied. Certainly there will be discussion as to whether the suggested changes would have prevented the accident.

Thus claims of "defects" in the design are alleged; those claims demand a response.

Keeping in mind the definition of accidents, and knowing that accidents frequently lead to litigation, it is worthwhile to look at the kinds of accidents that occur.

Accident Examples

To classify accidents in a rigorous manner is difficult and, usually, such classifications are not complete. Yet, there seems to be no better way to look at accidents and accident situations than to generally classify them.

Such a classification follows. It is not all-encompassing; you will find accidents which do not fit into any single classification except "Other Accidents." Further, many accidents will seem to fit more than one classification.

The classifications are based mainly on experience with earthmoving and construction machinery. They are, however, generalized to show broad application of the classes of accidents.

This list, and the explanations and descriptions of accident types, should be useful; it will show you most of the accidents types you will deal with in litigation activity.

1.0 Collision—Two Bodies Trying to Occupy the Same Space

1.1 *Two moving machines or vehicles.* The auto accident is typical of the collision type of accident. For whatever reason, the two vehicles involved try to occupy the same space or to pass through the same space at the same time. The obvious result is that the laws of physics and mechanics displace and deform the machines or vehicles and, sometimes, the people who are in those machines. This is a collision between two moving objects. The dispute develops as to which machine, if any, was moving improperly or in the wrong place in terms of location, time, or method of movement.

1.2 *A vehicle or machine hitting a fixed object.* Hitting a fixed object is similar to the matter of two vehicles colliding. However, when only one of the objects is moving, the case is changed. A fixed object cannot move, or, at least, has no opportunity to move in the specific accident considered. Results are similar in terms of deformation and possible injury. The dispute in such cases develops between the right of the stationary object to be in that location and the right of the moving object to be moving through that location at that specific time.

1.2.1 *A vehicle or machine hitting a parked or stopped machine.* This is a special case. On the first look, it may appear that the situation was entirely under the control of the operator of the moving vehicle. Yet, the location of the stationary or parked vehicle may be proper or improper. One may assume that the stationary vehicle could not move. That is true, if it is stalled or broken down. However, there still remains the possibility that the stationary vehicle could have been moved or should have been moved—at least prior to the collision. The other side of the dispute that may arise is whether the moving machine should have hit the stationary one. A specific kind of incident happens where an earthmoving or construction machine is parked and is hit by another machine or automobile.

1.2.2 *Airplane Crashes.* A separate grouping of aircraft accidents is made because of the three-dimensional characteristic of the movement of the vehicle involved. Sometimes two or more aircraft are involved, but more often, a single aircraft hits a fixed object in the accident. Although we include airplane crashes in this classification, there are many possible sub-classes of aircraft accidents.

1.3 *A vehicle hitting a person.* Pedestrian accidents are sufficiently frequent to justify a separate classification. This is true both in auto accidents and in factory and construction site on-the-job accidents. A characteristic of pedestrian accidents is the usual great differences between the pedestrian and the moving machine or vehicle in terms of weight, power, and energy involved. In pedestrian accidents, the pedestrian almost always loses, and his survivors will try to recover.

1.3.1 *A person running into a moving machine.* Some pedestrian accidents occur because the pedestrian moves quickly and unexpectedly into the path of a moving vehicle or machine or directly into the machine. The machine may be stationary or moving. These incidents have factors that differ from the basic pedestrian injury where a machine runs into a pedestrian. The typical dispute in this type of accident is whether the person ran into the machine or the machine ran into the person. Further, there may be a question about the ability of the machine operator to detect and avoid the pedestrian.

1.4 *A person running into another person.* Two people hitting each other can cause loss or injury, so this is a small but not uncommon type of accident. Contact sports are included in this classification, where the personal physical contact is intentional or at least part of the game. Also included in this class are intentional shoves and other types of contact that might be included under the legal definitions of battery or assault.

2.0 Slip and Fall Accidents This general classification of accident covers occurrences where the victim of the accident is not involved with anything else but the surface, location, or conditions upon which he is moving.

2.1 *Loss of traction between the foot and the surface.* This is a "slip." It may occur on a floor, on ice, in a bathtub, or on any other surface on which the person is standing or moving. In simple terms, sufficient friction (coefficient of friction) does not exist to hold the foot positively in the position it occupies or is passing through as it moves. Disputes will surround the question as to whether the surface is sufficiently "slip resistant" for its intended use. Handholds and other supports may also be involved. The requirement for the person to be in the position from which he slipped and fell may also be a matter of dispute.

2.2 *Tripping.* In a tripping accident, the person's foot does not move in an unrestricted manner to the next position it seeks in walking, running, etc. It hits an obstruction of some type, a bump, an unexpected step, a toy left in the road, or any of millions of other things.

2.2.1 *Scuffing.* This is a special class of incident in which the pedestrian's gait or step is interrupted when his foot no longer moves normally over a surface. (In the process of walking or normal movement, most people experience a small among of rubbing motion over the surface.)

2.3 *Physical malfunction of the person.* People may fall because a joint gives way and the person's gait is interrupted. Hampered vision because of seeing malfunction could be a factor. A sudden heart attack has been known to cause fatal motor vehicle accidents; it could also cause falls. People have had hips break under the normal stresses of walking, causing them to fall. These are examples of physical malfunctions leading to a fall.

2.3.1 *Dizziness.* A special type of physical malfunction is dizziness, loss of balance and/or direction control. A person so affected may well fall for reasons having little or nothing to do with the surface or the surroundings. A person may well become disoriented in one form or another; dizziness is a common form of disorientation. While in the disoriented condition, the person may make movement or balance decisions, consciously or otherwise, and fall out of control.

2.4 <u>*Unexpected change in surface level.*</u> Another cause of falls is the unexpected change in surface level. For example, a person who is descending stairs and believes he is at the bottom, and then falls when he "misses" the last step is involved with an unexpected change in level. Ramps, when not expected—even gradual ones—may also lead to falls. Changes of surface condition—from a carpet to a smooth floor, for example—may fit either into this class or into the classes involving loss of coefficient of friction or scuffing. If the person moves from a smooth floor to a carpet without realizing it, he may scuff and loose his gait. In reverse fashion, the person may move from a carpet to a smooth floor—perhaps wet and slippery—and suddenly experience a big change in condition between his foot and the floor. If he is not immediately aware of the change, he could possibly slip and fall because his gait had been based on the higher coefficient of friction between his foot and the carpet.

2.5 <u>*Loss of step support.*</u> When one places his weight on a step—a stair step, a floor, a ladder rung, or any other stepping place—and that stepping place gives way, he has lost support and may well fall. This is a particular type of accident. In classification 2.4, the surface may not be exactly where the person steps. In this class, the surface is there, but it moves or disappears.

2.6 <u>*Loss of balance and/or support of the body.*</u> This sounds like a secondary result of other types already listed, and it may be. In this type of fall, the person loses a handhold or other supporting contact that has been helping him to maintain his position or movement. He may lose that support because he lets go of it, or he may lose it because it moves or lets go of him. The breaking of a handhold may be a case in point. The failure of a railing around a raised platform is another.

2.7 *Fall from ladder or step*. Climbing ladders or getting on and off machinery are sufficiently frequent to justify a separate type classification of accident. In such incidents, the design of the ladder, hand supports, anti-slip surfaces, etc., may bear on the cause. So might the lack of care by the person. This type of accident happens with no apparent change in the physical makeup of the steps, handholds, etc. Friction between the foot and the step or other surface may or may not be involved. (You can see here that these classifications are now beginning to overlap and combine. The dispute over a slip and fall accident may be whether the surface is sufficiently slip-resistant and whether the steps and handholds are proper and safe. The dispute may also involve the care and concern of the person for his own safety.)

3.0 Loss of Control In "loss of control" a person is controlling a machine, activity, or process. This type of accident occurs when the person loses control over his machine or his responsibility. Steering failure, brake failure, and other kinds of control failures are included. The control system may malfunction, or the machine may not respond to the control, or the person may fail to use the control. The dispute in such a case may be whether the control worked or whether the operator failed to use it promptly.

3.1 *Inadvertent motion*. This type of accident situation involves the type of accident described as "jumping into gear." It does not include machines rolling downhill on a slope. It does include apparent unexpected movement while under power.

Two general types of accidents illustrate this classification. One is where the machine, left in what was supposed to be a neutral condition, suddenly begins to move under power. Design defect claims will be offered in such incidents. The other type is where a machine—a tractor, for instance—is started from the ground in a way that includes bypassing the normal (and safe) starting system. If the machine has been left in gear, it may well move and injure a person on the ground.

4.0 Hit by Falling Object This class of accidents includes all situations where the person or machine is hit by a falling object. The object may be big or small. It may have fallen a short distance or a long distance. The fall may be intentional and purposeful, or it may be unintentional or the secondary result of another action. More often than not, the falling object is unintentional. The criteria is that the object be moving, essentially unrestricted, under the force of gravity. If the object hits a person, injury may well result.

4.1 *Hit by rolling object.* A variation of the falling object accident is the rolling object accident. Such accidents happen when the person is hit by an object (or, in my experience with construction machinery, a tractor or other machine) which is rolling, under the force of gravity, down a hill or other incline. Vehicles which strike people or other objects while rolling downhill out of control and without power other than gravity are included.

The typical incident occurs when a machine that had reportedly been left secured—with the parking brake on and with the tools on the ground—suddenly begins to move downhill. Disputes over the adequacy of the brakes may be involved, as may arguments over whether the brake was adequately engaged.

5.0 Suffocation When a person is deprived of oxygen, he suffocates. The deprivation may come because the oxygen is replaced by a material that does not support life. It may come because the person is choked by external means or has a blocked windpipe. It occurs when a person's nose and mouth are covered by a material that blocks the normal flow of oxygen. It can even happen when a heavy weight is on the chest of the victim, preventing him or her from breathing in a normal way. (Although drowning is a form of suffocation from a physical point of view, it is not included in this class because drowning happens in a specific type of environment and during specific activities.)

A typical accident in this class is the little baby that suffocates when its face is covered by thin plastic of the kind used to cover clothing. Carbon monoxide suffocation in a closed area with a running engine exhaust is another example.

5.1 *Drowning.* This accident is suffocation in water—that is, water or other liquid that blocks out the required oxygen. (I know of at least one incident where the operator of an excavator drowned when his machine broke through the ice as he was taking a shortcut through a quarry. It can happen in construction work. Scandinavian regulations require hatches in the roofs of construction and forestry machines for just that condition.)

6.0 Electrocution Electric shock may interrupt normal body function such as breathing and heart action. It may also cause burns and other injuries to the body. These accidents are all included in this class. In general, if the accident is caused by contact with electric power, it is electrocution.

In construction, the typical incident resulting in injury happens when a part of a machine comes into contact with an electric power line. In some incidents, a second person is injured or killed trying to pull someone off such a contact.

7.0 Poisoning Poisoning includes the ingestion or contact with substances which injure or destroy any part of the body or its functions. Included are poisons taken through the stomach, breathed into the aspiration system (but blocking out or substituting for oxygen is not included), or contacting the outside of the body. In industrial accident circles, there are many subdivisions of this class, generally dealing with the many kinds and sources for such poisons. They are all included. So are poisons from botanical and animal sources.

8.0 Shock and Vibration The effect of sudden changes in forces acting upon the human body may cause injury. This class includes single force applications (shocks) and repeated force applications (including vibrations). Some injuries of this class occur suddenly, at a specific time. Others happen over longer periods. Repetitive function injuries are included in this class of accident. So are such things as Carpal Tunnel Syndrome.

A typical dispute in this type of incident is whether the shock or repeated vibration caused the injury.

Noise is a sub-type of the vibration type of incident. Repeated noise at levels beyond certain standards are known to cause loss of hearing. Limitations are placed on the length of time per day that a worker may safely be in the environment of high noise levels. Disputes of this type involve whether the noise was unreasonably high or whether the worker stayed in it too long without proper hearing protection equipment.

The physical shock to the person may happen in a collision. You now see that an accident may be classified by the outside cause or by the effect of the accident upon the person. A thorough consideration probably involves consideration of both classifications.

9.0 Entanglement The entanglement happens when a person gets some part of his body, clothing, or equipment too close to a moving part of a machine. Disputes about entanglement focus on available protective devices, shields, and other safety design steps, such as warnings.

10.0 Cuts and Abrasions Beyond entanglement, one may get cuts, abrasions, or other similar injuries from contact with a machine. The difference between this class of accident and entanglement is determined by the completeness of the involvement. Entanglement is usually total involvement, such as cutting off a digit or limb or completely winding up a piece of clothing. Cuts and abrasions result from partial involvement, touching a surface or an edge just briefly.

11.0 Fire Fire includes combustion of any sort. Fire may burn a person's clothing, equipment, and body. A fire accident may happen suddenly in a flash, or it may happen over several hours. Fire accidents include suffocation as a result of being enclosed in or by the fire. It also includes smoke inhalation. Fire accidents almost always involve property damage due to burning. They also may involve serious or fatal injuries.

11.1 *Chemical burns.* Fire, in fact, is a chemical activity. However, other chemical burns are listed separately to include those instances where visible flame and the usual character of combustion fires are not present. This class of accidents includes the effects of chemical contact to the exterior of the body, but excludes poisoning.

11.2 *Explosion.* Many fires have explosive characteristics. If the injury or damage is the result of a combustion burn, it is not included in this class of explosion accidents. If the injury or property damage is caused by a high energy shock from either sudden combustion or the sudden release of formation of high energy, then it is an explosion accident. An explosion is sudden and quick-acting. A fire may well be a slower, long-acting event. A flash fire offers some problems of choice as to classification. I prefer to classify them according to the injury or damage. If the damage or injury is a burn, the incident is a fire. If the damage is mechanical—perhaps the person is knocked down or off his position—the incident is an explosion.

11.3 *Radiation.* Another separate and special classification is radiation. Radiation damage may come from radioactive materials, other "radiating materials and situations," and may include electromagnetic radiation, should that prove to be a source of injury or damage. It is useful to note that radiation is usually not visible, and that the results of radiation may take substantial time to appear.

11.4 *Burns from contact with hot surfaces* are put into this class of accident. Injuries of this type are little different from fire injuries. The accidental contact with the heat source (a stove or an exhaust pipe, for example) may occur almost anyplace. Contact with a hot fluid also falls into this category.

12.0 Mechanical Failure In the man/machine relationship, it is possible for a machine to fail and lead to an accident with no expectation or participation of the people involved, either controlling the activity or affected by the failure. As a result of the mechanical failure, a person is injured. A broken rung on a ladder is an example, but is excluded from this class and included in another. A drive shaft which breaks and the broken piece, turning on the end of the machine, hits the machine operator, is an example. Another example is where a mechanical failure causes a piece of a machine to fly through the air, hitting and injuring someone.

13.0 Struck by Moving Projectile This includes being hit by almost anything flying through the air. Rocks, bottles, clubs, baseballs, and fruit are all included. Bullets are excluded, and so are arrows. They deserve a separate classification. Being hit by a rim from a tire from a passing car would be included. Being hit by a piece propelled from an explosion would not be included.

13.1 *Firearms and other such devices.* Guns and bows are included in this separate classification of accident. If a person was shot unintentionally, the accident probably belongs in this classification. Intentional shootings, to kill or maim, are not included because they are not unexpected, at least by the shooter.

13.2 *War.* Because war is a special situation, injuries and damage due to war are included in this separate class. Injuries of this type are expected, and they do not fit into our definition of accident.

14.0 Natural or Environmental Factors This broad classification of accident types includes earthquakes, tornadoes, cyclones, floods, and other natural and environmental events. The relationship of the damage to the natural disaster or cause is almost always obvious. Special cases are listed below.

14.1 *Heat.* Heat exhaustion and sun stroke are examples of accidents in this class. Burns from coming into contact with a hot surface do not belong in this grouping. Physical exhaustion from working in a hot situation does belong in this classification.

14.2 *Cold.* Any injury from cold exposure or contact belongs in this class of accident. Such accidents range from frostbite to numbness and death by freezing. Contact with dry ice or with other cryogenic materials or devices is included.

14.3 *Lack of water.* One may die from lack of water. Dehydration can temporarily or permanently injure the body. Failure to replace body water lost from sweating or from illness may be serious or even fatal. This special classification is placed generally with natural or environmental factors because water is as important to the body as oxygen.

14.4 *Animal attacks.* Being bitten, clawed, squeezed, or crushed by an animal belongs in this classification of accident. Accidental or unexpected sudden attacks by pets are included, also. Given the biological classification of "man" as animal, I also include biting, clawing, kicking, hitting, and choking attacks by one person on another. A fight between two people may be more properly classified as an assault, but I include it under this classification.

14.5 *Wind.* Tornado, cyclone, and hurricane storm damage are included under 14.0. Other damage from continuous, gusty or high winds is possible, and those accidents are included in this classification. Wind damage is more likely to be property damage, but injury can result in windy situations.

14.6 *Lightning.* Lightning damage and injury is another special class of natural accident. Lightning strikes may lead to fire. In that case you may call the accident either lightning or fire, as you choose in the specific circumstance. If an individual is injured in a lightning strike, the accident belongs in this category. If the person is injured by fire resulting from a lightning strike, it is a fire injury.

15.0 Homicide is the killing of a person. Homicide is included as a general accident type to cover those cases where the homicide or death is expected; obviously this does not fall within our definition of an accident, but this class is set up to include those activities where death is the objective and the expected result. Homicides may also be accidental—at least as defined by the law and as determined by juries.

15.1 *Suicide*. In this class of incident, one kills himself, with intent.

15.2 *Legal Intervention*. In this class of incident, the person is killed by some form of legal action generally termed "capital punishment."

(Obviously, 15.1, Suicide, and 15.2, Legal Intervention, are not purely unexpected incidents in our definition of accidents. Still, a proper pigeonhole for these incidents is made available.)

16.0 Other Accidents No list ever seems to be complete. This list of accidents is also probably not complete. Those which have no proper place in the scheme of things may be placed in this "Other Accident" classification. Pareto's Principle suggests that the above have provided classifications for the vast majority of what have been defined as accidents. Providing this "and so forth" classification keeps one from forcing an incident into an accident classification where it does not properly belong.

Of course, if this classification of "Other Accidents" becomes substantial, new classes may have to be created.

Examples of Accidents

Here are some examples of what can properly be called "accidents:"

1. A tire blows out and the driver loses control of the car and runs into a telephone pole.

2. A cook accidentally touches a hot stove surface and suffers burns.

3. A worker steps behind a backing earthmoving machine and is run over.

4. A worker pokes a stick into an auger that seems jammed. The auger catches the stick and causes it to hit the worker.

5. An earthmoving machine operator slips on the step of his machine as he gets off for a break, and he falls to the ground.

6. A scraper operator drives his machine into or through a hole and suffers from a back condition after the incident.

7. The boom on a crane touches an electric line. The operator leaves his seat and is electrocuted when his feet touch the ground while he still has hold of the handhold on the machine.

8. A hunter shoots at his target; the bullet ricochets off a tree limb and hits another hunter.

9. A book falls from a pile of books and lands on the librarian's foot, causing injuries.

10. A skier loses control while skiing downhill and falls, twisting her leg.

11. An accumulation of gas explodes, leveling a building and injuring the occupants.

12. A child falls into a swimming pool and drowns.

13. A group of workers in an office begin to feel ill because a foreign substance has gotten into the air through the ventilating system.

14. A chair leg breaks, and the user falls to the floor.

15. A bulldozer rolls over, pinning the operator underneath it.

16. A fire alarm rings and, in the rush to get out, several people fall and are trampled and injured.

17. A hose breaks, spraying oil onto a running engine. Fire breaks out.

18. An attorney slips on the wet floor of the courthouse while he is heading to the courtroom.

All of these are accidents. None of them are intended or expected. Yet, each of these incidents caused injury or other economic loss.

This list of classifications of accidents is not meant to be for all uses. Statisticians may well use others. Safety people have their own classifications. Medical people have still others.

What is intended is a classification of accidents that will be useful in further discussions in this book, dealing with how the engineer should perform before and during the time he might be in the court room, and even before the accident happens. I will refer later to some of the classes of accidents and to specific incidents.

Chapter 3

WHY GO TO COURT?

The sum and substance of the litigation process is the right of the citizen or other entity to seek redress for damages in a Court of Law.

The litigation system—filing suit, naming claims, and eventually arriving at a settlement or going to trial before a judge—is the process we use to settle disputes, and we must use that process properly. The attorney, of course, is supposed to do that. However, he will need engineering help to answer engineering questions and to explain the claims or rebuttals to the Court.

The matter for this chapter in the book, however, is the question, "Why go to court?" In a perfect society, there would be no disagreements. Everyone would be satisfied with the status quo, and no one would want to change. Two problems arise in our real world, however. First, our society is not perfect. The life of a society is grounded in its effort to get better. Sometimes that means growth. It certainly means there will be change. Sometimes, "to get better" means to arrive at better equality, or a better distribution of wealth, or total peace without violence. If you were to survey a thousand people to find what each of them considered to be a perfect society, you could get a thousand different responses—all differing from what we have now.

The second problem arises when we discover that the individuals who make up the organization of society are not perfect, either. Individuals respond in different ways to the differing environments and situations into which they are placed. Some consider the situation as a problem that needs to be solved. Others consider the situation to be an opportunity for improvement and advancement. Still others will look at what they do not like, and demand that someone (the government, usually) do something about the problem for them.

This mixture of people and viewpoints is not bad; rather, it may be good and even necessary. With no differences, there would be no effort to resolve the differences. There would also be no improvement, nor change of any kind. Worse, there would be no invention and creation of ideas.

The world would be boring. Still more bothersome, we wouldn't have the things that make our lives pleasant. Nor would our children and grandchildren have anything better than we now have. Without progress, our lives would be no better than those of our aboriginal or caveman ancestors. And, during that evolution, we wouldn't have learned a thing.

So we invent, and have new ideas, and we set about changing the world for many reasons. We try to understand pain and its causes. Learning those causes, we develop ways to relieve that pain. Eventually, we get good enough to prevent at least some of that pain.

We look at the discomfort of people. We seek ways to make them comfortable by inventing ways to protect them from the cold or heat, and to keep them out of the rain and snow. We look for better ways to move them from where they are to where they wish to be.

We devise means to protect the individual from wild animals. In the process we create weapons to do that job. However, the weapon soon seems to have two uses—to protect man from animals, and to allow man to frighten, injure, or kill another person.

The weapon has become both a good and a danger. Fire and common kitchen knives and hunting weapons and countless numbers of other ideas and inventions also have proven to be both useful and dangerous.

Whether an idea or invention turns out to be a good or an evil depends on the use to which it is placed. That is easy to see. However, whether a product or invention becomes good or evil depends to a great degree upon how society and individuals within society decide to use the product.

One person uses a knife to cut a roast or to slice bread. Some other person uses a knife to kill another person. Has the inventor, or the designer, or the manufacturer and distributor of the knife any liability for what happens with the knife? I think not. The knife has been accepted by society as a tool with proper and good uses and when that tool is improperly used, the responsibility lies with the one who improperly used the knife.

Some people use fire to keep themselves warm. Others may use fire to destroy an enemy's fort. Still others may use fire to destroy the property of someone they do not like. If we were able to find the first man who discovered fire and its capabilities, or if we were able to produce the first man who invented matches to start fires, would we hold him responsible for arson and other misuses of fires? Again, I think not. Rather, we look for the abuser of the fire or the matches.

Some people use automobiles to travel from one place to another. Others use automobiles to escape from a robbery, to joy-ride at twice the speed limit, or to conduct drive-by shootings. Again, we have a product both with utility and with possible improper and destructive uses. Should we, therefore, hold the inventor or manufacturer of the automobile responsible for the misuses of the product? Of course not—but here comes the substance of the litigation problem. When an incident happens with an automobile which causes injury or loss to someone, there may be—and frequently there is—disagreement as to the root cause, or the legally defined "proximate cause" of the injury or loss.

The auto designer and manufacturer says that the incident, and therefore the loss, is the responsibility of the driver or the pedestrian. The injured party sees the situation otherwise. He claims that if the auto had only had some device on it, the accident wouldn't have happened; thus he develops the idea of a defect in the product design.

If you think this is farfetched, consider this actual incident:

A driver of a pickup truck was traveling down the highway. He was under the influence of alcohol (0.38) according to the arresting officer who administered the blood alcohol test. As he traveled down the highway, he veered off the side of the road and struck and killed a 14-year-old farm boy who was walking along the shoulder of the road.

Seeking the cause of the death, one might find several possibilities, including:

- the driver was negligent,

- he violated the liquor law, and

- the person who sold him the liquor might have done so illegally.

However, the attorney for the family possibly found out that the driver had no insurance and no assets, and that no one could figure out who sold him the liquor (maybe he made his own). The attorney looked further for possibilities. He finally settled upon the manufacturer of the pickup truck, stating this theory:

- The truck did not have any of the devices on it that are supposed to prevent an intoxicated person from starting and operating the truck. The lack of breath analyzers and combinations of numbers which had to be memorized and repeated within a certain limited length of time were put forward as the "defect" of the pickup truck.

Consider another example of the development of a claim against the manufacturer of a crawler dozer. This, too, was a real case.

The plaintiff was operating the dozer inside a livestock feeder shed, cleaning out manure. He hit his head on a beam inside the building, suffering severe injuries.

The case theory against the manufacturer of the crawler dozer read like this:

- The manufacturer provided ROPS (roll over protection systems, or rollbars) on his standard machine. Those rollbars, if they had been in place, would have kept the plaintiff from being injured by hitting the

28

beam. The rollbars had been removed by the plaintiff in order to get into the shed to work. However, if the rollbars had been <u>welded</u> to the tractor frame, instead of being <u>bolted</u> onto the frame, the plaintiff could not have removed the rollbars and would not have been injured. Therefore, the defect (of being able to unbolt the rollbars) was cited as the proximate cause of the injury.

I'll not tell you the outcomes of these cases, but you can see the kinds of things that may be brought up.

Should we stop inventing because our inventions are used for evil? Of course not. I doubt that you can find many products or processes which can not be turned to improper or bad use. I have a clipping that describes the use of a motor grader to run through a customs check point between the Canadian and American borders. I have other clippings of other peculiar misuses of earthmoving and construction machinery. The machines were certainly not designed for those misuses.

Should we stop inventing automobiles, bulldozers, and motor graders because they can be improperly used in a way that might cause injury? Ask around the construction workplace and you will get a strong answer, "NO."

Because products can be turned to improper use, society has resorted to codes of conduct and systems of laws to guide our actions and to stop the misuse. Likewise, because two people may not agree on a claim or upon the cause of a loss, there are conflicts that need some form of resolution.

The legal system in the United States has been developed to urge and encourage the good and proper use of products and power. It also provides for deterrents against the misuse of products and power. Further, our legal system provides penalties for those who, in spite of the deterrents, break the rules and use products and power for the wrong purposes.

The legal system includes a body of laws that have been enacted by a legislature. Those laws are to be enforced by an administrative system, to catch people who may break or disregard those laws. A judicial system is established to determine whether an accused lawbreaker is guilty or innocent of the matter of which he is accused.

In matters of disagreement as to claims and causes, the legal system also sets up a series of procedures in which the disputes may be studied, presented, and resolved. This is the civil court system which most often becomes the site of dispute resolution in which the engineer may be involved.

Over time the judicial system has developed from absolute monarchs, who sat and acted as judges, to the present complex court system we now have. The present system tries to eliminate individual bias by providing for a hearing of the matter before a jury of peers.

A portion of that judicial system is established to hear disputes between parties who do not, cannot, or will not agree on some question. Courts of equity and civil courts have developed parallel to and separate from criminal courts. It is to these courts of civil dispute that I refer when asking, "Why go to court?"

The answer is simple. Someone believes that his relationship with someone else has been unbalanced. (Remember that the "someone" may be a single person, a partnership, a committee, a board, a governmental unit, or an agency.)

The complaint may also be simple, such as:

- Your cow is eating on my property.

- You stole apples from my tree.

- Your dog bit me.

- The mule you sold me died as soon as I got it home.

- Because of a will, this property belongs to me rather than to you.

- A bullet from your gun hit me in the leg while you were hunting.

- Your dynamite blast on the new road broke my dishes and cracked the plaster in my house.

- The wheel on the car you designed and manufactured broke, causing me to run into the ditch. In doing so, I and three passengers in the car were injured.

- The gas furnace you manufactured and installed blew up, damaging my house beyond repair.

- The tractor you designed and manufactured and sold to me suddenly jumped into gear and ran over my leg.

- I was hurt when my pant leg became tangled with the rotating power shaft on your machine.

- The rung in the ladder you loaned me broke, and I fell.

- I rented a bulldozer from you. I was working on a slope and the machine rolled over.

There are literally millions of possible incidents and claims. You can begin to see how the legal system may be the arena of argument between a purchaser, as user of your product, and you as the designer, manufacturer, seller, or maintainer of the product.

I'll not get into legal details and requirements. That is the job of the lawyer. I will tell you, however, that someone who uses your product may, through an accident, suffer some kind of injury or loss. He may well seek to have the value of that injury and associated economic loss paid to him so that he may return as nearly as possible to the condition he had before the accident.

Now, how does the product you invented get you called into court?

Over time, there have accumulated segments of a body of law—both legislated and judicial decisions—which spell out the requirements of a product. These requirements are couched in legal language and in court decisions, but they may be summarized as follows:

- The product must meet the expectations of the buyer and user.

- The product must not be unreasonably dangerous.

- The product must not be defective.

- The product must warn of hidden or unexpected dangers.

- The product must be manufactured according to specifications.

- The product must not be misrepresented.

- Proper instructions for safe use and operation must accompany the product.

These, in general, apply to the maker and seller of the product. Other conditions apply to the user, such as:

- He must use the product according to instructions and warnings.

- He must not misuse the product.

- He must maintain, repair, and inspect the product according to instructions.

All of these things are potentially the subjects of argument in a situation where an accident, injury, or loss has occurred. In fact, I do not recall a single matter in which I have consulted that did not include one or more of the above short list of requirements for either the manufacturer or the user. It seems reasonable that the one who incurred the loss should look to see if someone else should be blamed for the loss. It is this tendency to assign the blame, and thus the cost of the accident, to someone else that causes people to go to court.

Certainly the one to whom the blame is being directed has a right to respond and explain, if he can, why he is not responsible for the loss. The conflict of the claim and the response leads to law suits and the attendant activities.

A comment upon the development of tort law is appropriate here. At one time, one could not blame another unless he had "privity," or direct contact, with the other party. You could not sue for a defect in an automobile unless you had bought it directly from the designer and manufacturer.

Then practice and laws changed to eliminate privity as a requirement. Now, it is common for the plaintiff to sue the manufacturer, the distributor, the dealer, the renter (if one is involved), and anyone else who might have been responsible for placing the product into the stream of commerce, or who might have handled the product during its life cycle.

Another development came forward when "strict liability" was adopted broadly. Formerly, the plaintiff had to show negligence, carelessness, or even intent of some kind in order to recover. Decisions in the past 30 years or so have developed the doctrine of "strict liability" as sufficient to allow recovery, even if the defendants didn't know the so-called "defect" was there. The law generally assumes that if a defect was in the product at the time it left the hands of the defendant, and if that defect was the proximate cause of the accident and loss, then the plaintiff can recover.

A related legal doctrine said these two things, in defense of the strict liability theory:

- The cost of an accident should be assessed to those most likely to have prevented or avoided the accident. Those, the court seems to believe, are the designer and manufacturer.

- The cost of the accident should be assessed to those most able to pay those costs.

These doctrines led to what is known as the "deep pockets" concept. In short, sue those who can best afford to pay. If you are profitable or if you have large resources, you are high on the list.

Many attorneys, especially those who concentrate on plaintiff work, believe that this pressure on manufacturers to avoid litigation costs is what has driven manufacturers, designers, and inventors to make more safe products. Maybe so, but I believe the benefits of lawsuit pressure on safety is far overestimated.

At any rate, if you design, build, and sell a product or a service, you may expect to be the potential target for claims if someone believes he has been injured physically or economically as a result of your product or some characteristic of it. One might argue all day about the fairness of the system. If you are sued and you win, you will certainly feel that you have been unfairly attacked, even though you have won the lawsuit and have been declared "not liable" by the court. Maybe you have been treated unfairly and there are remedies at law for that, too. If you win, though, you are establishing your position and the position of your product.

If you lose, however, it may be for one of two reasons:

- 1. Under the guidelines of the law, your product is indeed defective—that is, you can do and should have done something more to prevent such accidents, or

- 2. You didn't tell your story well enough in court and you did not convince the jury.

That is what this book—and the process of litigation—is all about.

You may become involved, and you should know how to proceed beforehand.

Chapter 4

AVOIDING LITIGATION

The obvious way to stay out of court and to avoid litigation is not to have any accidents involving your product or machine, or with the service you provide. There are things an engineer can do to avoid accidents and litigation. In 1983, I wrote a paper titled "Engineering Considerations on Litigation Avoidance" (SAE Paper No. 831395). This chapter is a restatement of that paper, with some updating and expansion

If one sets out to avoid a particular accident or occurrence even while he is planning, designing, and building his product, he will have that objective in front of him throughout the design and development of the product. This gives him the greatest chance of doing something about a potential accident before it becomes a real accident.

It may seem a silly oversimplification to say "avoid the accident," but that is indeed the highest priority in defending against the effects of accidents. Sometimes, in the evaluation of a product at an early stage, it is indeed possible to eliminate some hazard completely by redesign or by even eliminating the part or function involved.

Avoiding or Reducing Litigation

In a philosophical sense, you can visualize a series of alternatives, or separate lines of defense, with regard to potential accidents with machinery:

1. Avoid the Accident.

If the accident doesn't occur, there can hardly be any claims of loss from it. For the engineer, this means to eliminate the hazard in the design. For the user, it means to avoid the accident condition, or to take steps to move safely through the potential accident situation.

The Chief Executive Officer of a large manufacturing company told his engineers that "to avoid the accident" was the first responsibility they had, as designers. This may seem altruistic, but it is an excellent starting place. If a hazard can be completely eliminated in the design without excessive compromise in the usefulness of the machine, or if the probability or possibility of the accident can be reduced without giving up the usefulness of the machine, that is good design.

2. Protect from the Accident.

If the accident cannot be eliminated for some reason, protect from it. Use shields, for example, or some other means to protect people from the potential accident. Users may do this by keeping people away from the work site. Designers do this by designing the hazard so that it can't be reached by the person during normal activities. Note that the design need not make it impossible for anyone to reach or touch the hazard. Good design, however, will make it difficult or impractical for the hazard to be reached. There is no such thing as a foolproof design, but you can approach that condition in some instances.

Watch out for the design "ad absurdum" in trying to protect from hazards. How many locks do you have to put on a door to prevent people from entering in an unwanted manner? How many shields do you have to put over a hazard? How many interlocks should you use, or how many backup systems do you need to prevent a hazard from being reached? In my experience, there is a practical number, usually one or two. Beyond that, the complication of the design far overbalances the safety shields or checks. Once you have put a check device or a shield in place on your design, think carefully before you put a check on the check or a shield on the shield.

3. Make the Accident Safe.

Next in order of preference is to <u>make the accident safe</u>. In other words, pull the teeth of the accident so no one will be hurt even if the accident should occur. Design the machine in such a way that even if the accident action happens, no injury results. Good roll-over protection systems do that, in case of a machine roll-over of a specific type. ROPS are designed to protect against crushing of the operator's space in conditions described as a normal roll-over. They will not work effectively during dynamic falls or hard roll-overs.

Here is a little piece of philosophy many designers and users of machinery miss. People tend to assume that a device, such as a roll-over bar, is placed on a machine or vehicle as a safety device. It is not really a safety device. A safety device is intended to allow one to operate safely. Almost never is it the aim of the operator of the machine to roll it over. Normal operation doesn't call for roll-overs. To roll the machine over safely is not a design goal of the engineer in this case.

Instead, the engineer looks for a way to <u>forgive</u> the machine and the operator, who for some reason or another, has gotten into a situation where the machine has rolled over. The roll-bar, together with a good seat belt, can provide that forgiveness. It is important to note, however, that the ROPS (roll-over protective system) does not invite the operator to roll the machine over.

There are data that show that people tend to drive faster when they have seat belts on. I suspect the same is true for air bags. I have experience and data from test groups that show there are more roll-overs of earthmoving machines equipped with ROPS than there are with machines not so equipped.

Keep in mind that if you can't eliminate the hazard or separate the person from the hazard, you can still look for ways to forgive the accident if it should happen. In automobiles, seat belts, air bags, door locks which do not spring open upon impact, collapsing front or rear compartments (engine or trunk), and shatter-proof glass are all good examples of forgiveness. They do not prevent the incident, but they offer a measure of forgiveness should the accident happen.

Take note that all of the so-called safety devices reduce the likelihood of injury, but if the incident is severe or the conditions extreme, the accident still may result in injury or death.

4. Warn of an Impending Accident.

A further method of protecting against accidents is to warn of an impending accident, if possible. A good example of such a warning device is the stall warning on an airplane. As the plane approaches the air speed and pressure conditions where it will stall, a horn, buzzer, or a voice warns the pilot that he is approaching a dangerous condition, or a condition where he must take some specific action.

In some autos, a voice gently reminds you that a door is open or a seat belt not fastened. In most cars, horns and bells and "information centers" do a similar job. In most earthmoving machines, gauges, red lights, and horns or buzzers warn of conditions which may lead to trouble.

Again I emphasize that too many warning devices or devices which give incomplete or erroneous information may be worse than no warning at all. Use warnings of impending accidents sparingly and carefully, lest you tire and confuse the operator with buzzers and lights.

Further, the warning of a condition which comes too late is also bad. It has been suggested that earthmoving machines should have an inclinometer or other tilting warning device on them to warn the operator that he is approaching a condition where a roll-over may happen. In a crane or a drill, or other machine which is operating in a fixed position, such devices are helpful. However, in a moving machine, such warning devices are not useful, for several reasons:

- Tilt conditions change so rapidly that the warning is not timely. That is, it doesn't allow the operator to do anything to prevent the roll-over.

- The warning devices read only static or stationary tilt conditions. Those are not the conditions that cause roll-overs; dynamic conditions do.

- The angle at which most earthmoving machines tip over approaches and even exceeds 45 degrees. No operator is comfortable at that position. His own gut feel will tell him far ahead of any warning device that he is tilted too far.

- The operator has other conditions and controls to watch, and should not be operating by instruments so far as tilt is concerned.

- The existence of a roll-over warning device or instrument will lead the operator to think he is safe from roll-over, and need not concern himself about the possibility. That is not true.

5. Warn of the Possibility of an Accident.

This is different from warning of an impending accident condition. In this level of defense against accidents, the operator or worker is informed that a hazardous condition can exist under certain circumstances. By instructions or warning decals, the person is made aware of the condition that may lead to an accident, and an attempt is made to precondition him to take the right action should those conditions occur.

Such warnings and instructions come in several forms:

- Warning decals on the machine,

- Instruction decals on the machine,

- Instructions in the Operator's Manual,

- Instructions in safety manuals and material, and

- Instructions given in training sessions.

Such warnings are limited, in some ways, as to what they can and will do.

Decals are not always read by operators on a machine. (It is my experience that they are seldom read.) Even a new operator is likely to ask someone to show him, rather than to read the warning decals. If there are too many decals—more than a half dozen or so—you can almost be assured that they won't be read.

39

Far too many operators never see the Operator's Manual, let alone read it. If they don't see it and read it, or understand it and heed the instructions, the instructions are worthless. The instructions in the Operator's Manual may show, when you are in court, that you tried to warn . However, this is merely covering your tracks in case you are accused of incomplete or improper warnings.

It should be noted that this warning is usually considered the last line of defense for accidents. It is logical to do so because, of all the methods of protecting a person from a hazard, warnings are less efficient than the others. This is a sort of no-win situation. If you warn, you may protect yourself to some degree in an accident lawsuit, but you have not eliminated the accident. Nor have you, probably, eliminated the lawsuit. Yet if you do not warn, you will almost certainly be in trouble and at fault in case of an accident. Today you should instruct or warn whenever and wherever it seems practical and appears to be useful.

One consultant, versed and experienced in the field of Human Factors, describes the sole purpose of warnings and instructions as: "to change the human behavior from unsafe acts to safe acts." The objective is a worthy one, but warnings and instructions fall far short of that objective. Many times, the lack of a warning is claimed to be the causal defect in an accident. Yet, evidence shows that the existence of the warning has little or no effect on the prevention of accidents. Opinions seem to be polarized on this matter—especially between plaintiffs and defendants.

6. Protect the Operator (or Other Personnel) from the Accident if it Should Happen.

A still deeper line of defense is to protect the operator if the accident should occur. Seat belts and hard hats do that in a roll-over. The philosophy here is that, if an accident cannot be avoided, then protect the operator. That is a legitimate objective of engineering effort.

In consideration of how to avoid litigation, the engineer should study this list (or a similar list of alternatives) and determine the level of engineering concentration at which he can be most effective. "Most effective" means most effective in preventing the loss and injury associated with accidents.

Other lists are available, and almost all of them follow the same philosophy—eliminate, protect, warn, and train—as a hierarchy of attack.

You might note an interesting thing here. If you can eliminate the accident, you leave nothing for the operator or bystander to do. If you protect from the hazard, you begin to offer the person involved something to do—some responsibility. The more responsibility passed on to the operator or the bystander, the more chance there is that he or she will err in some way. If you warn about the hazard, you place substantial responsibility on the person. The warning needs to be seen, read, understood, and acted upon in order to be effective.

Of course, the best thing to do is to eliminate the accident by eliminating the hazard, if that is possible. Frequently, that is not possible without serious sacrifice to the effectiveness or efficiency of the product.

Then, like an army general fighting a defensive battle, the engineer should back off to one of the other lines of defense. Usually, the one nearest the top of the list is best, if it is possible. Only when the higher items on the list have been exhausted should the designer retreat to a less forward line of defense.

As battle strategies are often stated, "The best defense is a good offense." Attacking hazards head on is often the best way to deal with them.

The Conflict Between "Efficiency" and "The Quality of Life"

To explain my views of safety and how safety fits into the other objectives of a product design, I must divert temporarily. I need to discuss a concept I learned from Dr. James O'Toole of the Center for Future Research of the University of Southern California. It applies in product design.

In everyday life, there seems to be an unresolvable conflict between two opposing forces. People tend to avoid discussion of this conflict of ideas, especially where safety is concerned. Man wants the right to do things he enjoys doing, regardless of the safety connotation. People refuse to use seat belts and motorcycle helmets because "they have rights."

41

However, Dr. O'Toole, in a 1979 paper, describes an anthropological approach for both societies and corporations in this matter (1). O'Toole discusses conflicting relationships between liberty and equality. We use these two words together in describing the kind of life we live and the kind of country we believe we have. However, Dr. O'Toole points out that to be completely free—in the direction of liberty—leads to a high likelihood of inequality between people. Looking in the opposite direction, if we create a society with absolute equality, we will do so only with the complete surrender of individual liberties. It appears, therefore, that a successful society may well be a delicate, careful balance of individual liberties and equalities—at least equality of opportunity.

In another direction, O'Toole describes a similar relationship between meritocracy and, opposed to that, security. In our democratic society, we are likely to believe that everyone has the opportunity and right to succeed and to be rewarded according to his success or merit. Success, however, carries with it the opportunity for failure and, therefore, some lack of security that one might wish. Again, it appears that society, in order to be successful, must walk a thin line of the balance between security and the freedom to succeed or fail.

Dr. O'Toole offers interesting discussions on the progress of a civilized society as a dynamic process dealing with the four concepts—liberty, freedom, merit rewards, and security. He shows how a balance must be maintained between all of those factors or desires. He leaves the strong impression that a successful society works to provide all of those factors, and doesn't simply trade off one for the other. Neither does it concentrate on one and ignore the others. When gains are made, they are made on all of the factors.

Corporations see that same conflict between desires for liberty and equality. Organizations and unions tend to emphasize equality—but they do so at the expense of some liberty for the individuals involved. Yet, looking in the opposite direction, no organization at all would mean total chaos; here liberty may be very high, but the results in terms of what each individual wants will be very poor.

In the same way, efficiency and quality of life appear to be characteristics that pull against each other. High efficiency tends to require some reduction in the quality of life. High efficiency tends to include monotonous work, for example. Yet, if the quality of life is pursued to the extreme, one can easily expect a complete deterioration of efficiency as each worker goes his own way and does his own thing.

Dr. O'Toole says that these conflicting pulls are common, everyday situations in societies and corporations. If that society or corporation is successful, it does not go to one extreme or the other in any of these conflicting pulls. Rather, it balances those conflicts. It succeeds when it operates at or near a balance of ideas that seem to conflict—that is, the ideas seem to say that if you have more of one, you must have less of the other.

At certain times or under certain conditions, it may be necessary to unbalance the pulls in one direction at the expense of the opposing pull. At a time of war, for example, a nation may give up some of its liberty and move toward the equality of a draft army in order to provide an efficient defense and security for the country. In a similar way, we see attention being raised on the quality of life of the worker in the workplace, because we have found that our present society needs some of that bias.

These unbalances, however, are and must be only temporary. This leads to great concern, for no one wants to give up gained territory. The worker wants a raise, and gets it when the business is highly successful. He does not, however, want to reduce his wage when the business falls into hard times.

Dr. O'Toole points out that a successful corporation or a successful society has found out how to balance the qualities that appear to be pulling in opposite directions. The societies that grow successfully do so by balanced growth, where all elements of the society remain in or near balance, and where they all grow together.

How about the fight between the conservationists and the forest products producers? Which is more important—our forests or 20,000 jobs? Or consider the need for fuel and the need for air pollution control. The answer in each case, and in hundreds of questions like them, is that we need both—not one or the other.

Surely none of these disputes is likely to be settled by a complete win for one side of the dispute or the other. If such a win should occur, it will certainly be at a great cost to some group, and to society in general.

We must develop a high level of understanding about both the long-term and the short-term effects of what we invent and build and do. We need to evaluate both the individual liberty involved and the rights of the community, and we need to balance them carefully. We surely must evaluate the rights of individuals and the cost (economically or otherwise) to the community to maintain those rights.

A Balanced Product

Using Dr. O'Toole's concepts, a similar portrayal may be made of a product or a machine, listing what are generally considered to be the objectives of the design:

- Specifications—the physical size, power, and other measurable details of the product,

- Performance—the work the product is to do and the rate at which it will do that work,

- Life—how long the machine will last or continue to work,

- Reliability—how dependable the machine will be or how often it will break down,

- Serviceability—how long it will take to do both the routine, scheduled service and maintenance and the unexpected repairs,

- Costs—the cost to produce the machine, an important and basic concern to the designer; and the operation and maintenance costs of importance to the user, and

- Safety—how safe is the product, and what hazards does it present?

These factors all compete for time and attention in the design and development of a product. All are important. The designer of a successful product must meet satisfactory levels of success with all seven. There is no way the designer can be perfect in all but one of the categories and ignore the remaining factor. If he does, he will lose.

It appears that Dr. O'Toole's concept of a balanced system applies to a successful product, too. If a product is successful, you can expect that all of the competing "pulls," including safety, will have reached a high level of achievement. No single factor will be very far from the desired level. No single factor will be the star characteristic of the product. Instead, all of the characteristics will be stars—or at least be acceptably high.

Furthermore, as Dr. O'Toole describes, the successful product will not have "traded off" to any real extent one factor for another. No successful product has traded away safety for lower cost, for example. Nor has a successful product traded higher performance for lower reliability or a much higher cost for just a comparatively small gain in performance.

I have stated in court that no requirement is higher than safety, but I also insist that safety is a top requirement—along with the other six factors. Safety cannot be above the other factors, or the product will not exist. (You see, a perfectly safe product is one that does not exist! If it did exist, it would do no work or function.)

Improvements in performance must be made with no sacrifice or compromise in other factors. Improvements in life and reliability must be made with no drop in safety or rise in cost, ideally. Herein lies the value and need for continuing research and improvement in technology. We need not only to make improvements to our products, but we need to do so without giving up anything significant.

The Idea of Cooperative Solutions

The designer and the manufacturer are not alone in dealing with machinery. The person who operates the machine, the one who services the machine, and many other people, including those who train people to work with and on the machine, are all participants in the struggle for safety.

Here I will introduce the idea of cooperative solutions to achieving safety. It is easy to see that only one person in the chain of those who are associated with a product needs to be careless, and an accident can happen. Likewise, all of the people and agencies involved, working together, can make the greatest inroad into reducing and preventing accidents.

I do not suggest that the engineer can rest while everyone else works on safety. He needs to include the best safety thought possible in his product. Moreover, he needs to help owners, operators, mechanics, and others in doing their jobs more safely too.

Neither can the user, serviceman, or mechanic work with little or no concern for safety, assuming that the designer has taken care of all of the potential accident hazards. Also, if the owner of the machine or the layout man for the work site is careless, he creates hazards that neither the machine designer not the operator can do anything about.

Avoiding Accidents Through Engineering Consideration

Now we are face to face with the question, "What can be done <u>through engineering and by engineers</u> to avoid accidents—and thus to avoid litigation?" Individual approaches follow:

Specifications and Objective Targets

An overworked but intelligent cliché is, "If you don't know where you are going, any road map will get you there." As a starting point for engineering activity to avoid accidents, this principle applies. The specifications for the product to be designed and the objectives for that product should include specific references to safety along with references to the other design objectives. Thus, when a designer works toward a specific performance, reliability, or cost goal, he also works toward specific safety objectives. A safety statement in the original plans for a product is a good way to keep the "safety" subject in front of the designer, and in front of everyone else working on the project.

Usually an employer or a company will have a written policy about safety. Even though this general policy exists, it is good to translate that policy into specific product goals.

For example, if the CEO says your first job in safety is to prevent the accident, the safety statement in the product objectives should refer to the elimination of hazards, if at all possible. Likewise, reference should be made in the plan for shields, warnings, instructions, and operator protection, right along with reliability and life objectives.

An important benefit from having well-stated goals for all factors—specifications, performance, life, reliability, serviceability, safety, and cost—is that the design for all of the seven factors is integrated into one activity and one product. Costs cannot be reduced easily and effectively after the design is completed. Safety cannot be added on to the design as an afterthought. Performance cannot suddenly be improved after the design is cast in solid form. These things do not and cannot happen.

Safety, if it is to be effective, must be integrated into the design just as the nervous system is integrated into the design of the body. A nervous system pulled from the human body is useless and worthless. So is safety considered separately from the other design elements of a product.

If you have no goals, you will probably meet them! And if you have no goals for safety regarding your product, someone may point out that omission in court.

Design to Those Objectives, Including Safety Goals

The obvious second step is to design the product to meet those objectives, as closely as you can. This may sound like an unnecessary instruction step. However, many sales are lost by the salesman simply because he doesn't ask for the order. Likewise, many speakers announce a topic and then proceed to ignore the original intent while they go on and on in their talks. That can happen in the design process, too. They may lay out a good specification plan for a product, and then proceed as if the spec plan didn't even exist.

During the design process, the designer should stop from time to time and examine his objectives. He should be satisfied that he is following those objectives sufficiently as to expect to meet the goals. If he appears to be off track, he needs to reevaluate his design and, perhaps, he needs to study the goals further. Realize that impossible goals may be set. You don't want to admit that the goal is impossible, but if it is technically out of reach, face the situation. Don't try to do the impossible. Remember, a foolproof design is not possible. Even the most severe critics of machinery admit that.

What does the designer do when a so-called "safety feature" will cause more risk and more new hazards than it eliminates? When that situation occurs, the designer needs to clearly explain—to someone in authority—why that condition is indeed a fact. Such an explanation will help explain why the design decision is made as it is. In addition, the explanation will be useful someday, perhaps, to explain to a jury. The explanation may not need to be recorded in hard form, but it needs to be remembered and understood.

Failure Mode-and-Effect Analysis

As the design is underway, and again when it is complete, a valuable step is to conduct a failure mode-and-effect analysis on the design, or to make some similar evaluation. This is an integral part of the design process and often is intertwined with the design process, so it isn't seen separately. Just as the nervous system is useful only when it is in the context of the body, so a formal failure mode-and-effect analysis is useful only in the context of the design considerations. A separate analysis, outside of the design realm, may well lack good input information.

Simply stated, the process involves listing the foreseeable failure modes of both the product and the person properly using it. Then follows a consideration of the effects that each of the failure modes will have on the machine, the operator, and the people around it. This analysis may well place before the designer one or more situations in which specific design changes will eliminate the possible failure mode or drastically reduce the effect that failure mode may have.

I do not get upset when a separate failure mode-and-effect analysis (FMEA) doesn't exist in a formal written form. I have already stated that safety must be integrated into the design. Likewise, such studies as FMEA are most useful and effective when those studies are integrated into the design as it progresses. If a person who is independent of the design team makes a FMEA or other analysis of the product after the design is complete, that person will be working with less than the information and knowledge of the designer. Any result from such an independent study will almost certainly recommend trading off something else to get what appears to be an increase in safety. That is not an acceptable result.

The after-the-fact safety analysis and the attempt to incorporate the suggestions from that study will lead to changes made for safety without considering other factors. Worse yet, such attempts to add safety later always add new safety issues which tend to go unnoticed.

Accident Probability/Effect/Severity Studies

This is another of the usual techniques that may be used in looking at the machine, its work environment, and the operator. In this process, the engineer asks three questions of each failure possibility.

First: What is the statistical probability of the incident happening? Minimum probability, of course, is desired. The second question is: What is the effect of the incident on the machine and operator, or the bystander, if the incident occurs? Again, the goal is to have that effect be as small as possible, with the ultimate being no effect at all. Finally, the engineer considers the severity of the injury should the incident occur. Taking steps to minimize the injury—or better yet, to prevent it—if the accident occurs is a proper design route to follow.

The second collision in auto accidents is a popular subject—that is, the collision between the person and the inside of the auto, after the accident happens. The engineer-designer needs to consider second collisions and other second and third effects of product failures in his design.

The result of a part failure or a control problem are, for example, considerations in the design of an earthmoving machine. The designer asks what happens if one part breaks or another part becomes unfastened. He then builds into his design such factors as:

- sufficient strength to resist the failure,

- conditions which make the failure occur in such a way as to eliminate or drastically reduce any potential injury,

- signs and indications of deterioration or impending failure to warn the operator or mechanic,

- any other means of lessening the possible injurious effect of the failure.

You see, I don't even think the designer can complete his design until he has considered possible failure and accident scenarios.

Let me warn further that this is a difficult task at any time, and for anyone. Having completed a design of a new product, a chief engineer once asked his team to list the top ten things that were likely to go wrong with the product once it was in the field. A study of that ten-item list led the team to two immediate changes on the product before it went into production. In addition, plans were made for three additional product changes just in case a suspected possible problem developed.

Even more eye-opening was the result two years after the product had gone into production. An additional problem developed in one of the areas changed before production. Of the remaining eight potential problems, only one developed to any extent, but four unexpected and unpredicted problems developed. Worse was that the product was sufficiently different from existing competitors so that it failed to obtain enough acceptance to make it a highly successful product, in spite of several major improvements and innovations it brought to the industry. The product was unique and interesting, and it performed well, but the marketplace never really embraced it.

A good designer will catch all of the potential problems and safety hazards he can. However, it is likely that some new ones will develop as the machine goes into the marketplace.

Audit the Design

A further step in the development process is for <u>test and evaluation people to independently repeat the design thinking</u> described already. Subsequent conversations between the design and test people will help lead to a consensus agreement that the best design steps have been taken to prevent the accident completely or to reduce the severity of the accident effects as far as possible. I look upon the test engineer's job as being to question the designer in much the same way as an auditor questions an accountant.

Maybe a designer can properly test his own product, but I think it is better done by another person in another part of the organization. Intellectual give and take between the two tends to give good results.

Simulate Failures Which Might Lead to Accidents

A second job for the test engineer may be to simulate or cause actual failures that might lead to accidents. For example, it is possible for an undesirable condition to exist when two or more independent actions occur at the same time. One might dismiss that situation as not likely to happen. However, it may be useful to create these simultaneous occurrences during the test program, to see what really happens. For example, one might test the operator's reaction if the brakes and steering should both fail at the same time, or if a tires blows and the steering becomes erratic at the same time.

In the development of a new, automatically controlled transmission in a scraper, the test engineers decided to test for what the effects might be if certain "worst case" failures happened in the transmission control system. The testers rigged up the controls to make the machine shift suddenly from full speed forward to full speed reverse. There were some interesting results. The worst case, for the operator, was in second gear, at about five mile per hour. In first gear, the effect was slower and less violent. At higher speeds— 3rd, 4th, and 5th gear—the shift modulation of the transmission and the spinning of the wheels actually lessened the effect on the operator. This information has been useful to me many times since. If your test engineer is accumulating such experience, he will find it useful, both as to the product at hand and as future experience information.

In field testing construction machines, it is a practice to roll a machine sideways downhill to evaluate the effect of a roll-over on the machine that has had several thousand hours of use. This roll-over test is done just before the machine is scrapped. A drop test, as part of an evaluation to see if a product may be "air dropped," may yield good accident information. Simulated accidents and failures are valuable parts of a development program.

51

Life and Reliability Predictions

After having done all of this, the designer and test engineer may consider methods of predicting when failures are likely to occur and to provide the users with instructions for periodic inspection and maintenance. Included may be signs of impending failure.

In my experience, seldom does a failure occur with no prior indication or warning sign. For example, I have twice driven automobiles down the road and heard distinctive and peculiar thumping sound and vibrations for some time and many miles before a wheel came off. (Yes, I did drive the cars until a wheel fell off, in each case. I have learned to watch for signs now.)

Part of the engineering activity to prevent accidents, then, may well lie in identifying warning indicators and signals, and by making operators aware of those signs so he may stop safely before the failure. Signals may even be created, like the sound of a brake lining as it wears to the level where it should be changed.

I have seen earthmoving machines in operation when they were screaming to be repaired or stopped. One operator drove a machine back to a repair location with an obvious hydraulic leak; it burst into flames before he arrived, causing severe injuries.

In another incident, a machine went over a high wall when it was being returned to the shop because "something appeared to be wrong with the steering."

We need to emphasize signs of impending failure—obvious and obscure— and we need to teach operators to heed those signs.

Share Your Information and Data

The engineer can help prevent accidents by sharing his data and experience through his sales and service people with the customer and user. Technical input to customer information is important. Eventually, the operator, the owner, the serviceman, the mechanic, and others will need to know some of the things you can tell them. Engineering input to manuals, training materials, and sales materials is important

An engineer tossed his hard hat to a test supervisor just before the test supervisor tried to remove a crawler from a precarious tipping condition. The machine did tip over, but the test supervisor was unhurt. The hard hat was scratched in the incident.

A consultant, examining a machine that had been involved in an accident, found a highly dangerous condition in the machine's controls. He was told by his attorney-client not to disclose the information, since it would prove to be critical in the defense of the lawsuit. At the same time, the consulting engineer, knowing the machine was still being used on a regular and daily basis, realized he had an obligation to warn the present user of the machine that there was indeed a problem and that the problem could well cause an accident not unlike the subject of the litigation.

This conflict was resolved when the consultant made the decision to warn the present user about the problem. The warning probably kept the present user from a serious accident. It may have removed some of the "surprise" in the defense of the case, but that was a small price to pay.

In cross-examination, at trial, the questioning went something like this:

Q: "Did you testify that you examined the subject machine?"

A: "Yes, sir, I did."

Q: "You said you found a problem in the adjustment of the controls which you believed caused the accident to the plaintiff. Is that true?"

A: "I did find such a problem in the adjustment of the control linkage, and I do believe strongly that the misadjustment was the cause of the plaintiff's accident and injuries."

Q: "In your earlier publications, didn't you say that an engineer who finds a problem on a machine ought to notify or tell the owner or operator of the problem, so that an accident might be avoided?"

A: "Yes, I did say essentially that."

Q: "In this instance, when you inspected the machine, you didn't tell anyone at the site about the bad adjustment, did you? You didn't think it important to warn the operator of the problem, did you?"

A: "That is not an accurate statement of what I did, sir."

Q: "What did you do?"

A: "I considered it of top importance that I tell the operator of the problem, and I told him, so he could get it fixed and avoid any new troubles. I even offered to assist him in readjusting the control."

Q: "No further questions."

Play "What If" Games

As a further approach, the engineer might consider playing "what if" games. What if A, B, and C happen all at the same time? Sometimes a second opinion from an outside viewpoint is helpful. The transmission test just described is a case in point.

I once asked a group of librarians how they would get out of the library if they were suddenly faced by a wall of fire at the front of the library area. (A major street, with lots of trucks, ran only a few feet away from the front glass wall.) No one knew what to do. However, with a little bit of coaching and thinking, they soon decided they could break through the thin rear wall of the library using the heels on their shoes to break the relatively weak wallboard.

Another time, I heard a speaker at a large safety meeting demand that the chains and locks be removed from four doors out of the auditorium before he would continue his talk. He said, "What if a fire or a gunman appeared at the front end of the auditorium?" The other doors were locked. Incidentally, it took over 20 minutes for the janitor to cut the chains; he couldn't find the keys to the locks.

If you get caught with nothing to do, such as in an airplane circling and waiting to land, or waiting for your boss to show up for a meeting, play some "what if" games.

The Product Safety Review Team

Apart from the direct engineering involvement in the product, there is still another useful step that may be taken with regard to the review of products from a safety viewpoint.

A Product Safety Review Team (some companies call them "boards"), made up of a broad spectrum of technologies and viewpoints, could evaluate the product. This type of team would include design and test engineers, manufacturing specialists, inspection people, materials experts, professional safety people, etc., and would provide a multi-focused, wide variety of inputs and observations. The differing viewpoints, when brought to a consensus, will provide an excellent screen for safety items.

The operation of such a team would be separate from the day-to-day engineering, manufacturing, and sales activity of the business. Yet, it would include the expertise of all of those activities. The results of considerations of such a team or review board, then, would be a high level and practical consensus resulting in what we believe is the most effective and consistent method of reviewing a product for safety.

The operation of such a board would come into play as part of the routine review of a new product at several stages during the design and development of the product. (Other similar groups may indeed be reviewing the performance, the specs, or the costs of the product in a similar manner.) In addition, when there are incidents or failures reported which may be of safety consequence, the board would review and consider those incidents in light of the design. If a problem developed in the field, the safety board could determine whether that problem related to a safety matter. Having considered the matter, the team would then suggest appropriate changes to the management of the business.

The activity of a safety review board or team would begin and continue throughout the life of the product, from the original specification plan to the orderly removal of the product from use as it is replaced by even better products.

Summary

In short, the engineer can make his first contribution to the business of litigation by doing the engineering-related things to avoid accidents and, therefore, to avoid litigation.

The engineer/designer should do these things during his product design activities:

- Include a consideration of adverse effects and specifically consider safety.

- Consider options—designs, features, materials, processes, etc.

- Foresee the uses and environments through which the machine will go.

- Foresee, to the extent possible, the <u>misuses</u> to which the machine may be subjected.

- Make <u>reasonable</u> choices. Perfection is not required or even possible, but good professional judgment on the part of the designer is required.

- Document the choices and decisions, and the reasons for them.

- Provide good instructions for the proper use and maintenance of the product. It is not unreasonable for you to expect such proper use and care.

- Warn of hazards that are hidden and that cannot be eliminated.

- Provide a way for the user of the product to provide feedback.

Perhaps you should record your product philosophy somewhere where you can review it and improve it with experience. Include safety.

Note:
(1) Dr. James O'Toole; "What's Ahead for the Business-Government Relationship," <u>Harvard Business Review</u>, March-April 1979.

Chapter 5

THE LITIGATION PROCESS

In this chapter, I intend to describe the process of litigation. Doing so will define the "playing field" in general terms so the engineer has some understanding of the game of litigation and where and how it is played.

I do not mean to derogate or downplay litigation or those involved in it. It is an important part of the liberties and rights we enjoy as citizens in this democratic society. However, by treating litigation as a game and by describing the "playing field" of litigation, some of the systematic processes are better described and understood.

Activity in litigation is different from activity in designing, testing, and other engineering work. The objectives are different and the rules of procedure are different. You do not argue successfully in the courtroom the same as you might argue in the engineering conference room. In fact, you should not argue at all in the courtroom. Leave the arguing for the attorneys.

The Basic Idea of Suing Someone

It is worthwhile to repeat, briefly, the reasons for lawsuits.

When a person has reason to believe that an injury or other damage has been incurred for some reason, that person may seek to determine if others may be responsible for the loss. If one determines that such responsibility actually

57

exists and that the responsibility can be sufficiently demonstrated to persuade a court to find the other party responsible, the plaintiff may sue for those damages. (The plaintiff should have reasonable claims, because if he doesn't, he may be subject to frivolous lawsuit charges.)

During the total orderly process of law, the plaintiff's claims and the defendant's responses are heard in a court. At the end of the process, a judgment or verdict is handed down by the court, assessing damages or denying the liability. (It is more complicated than that, but let the lawyers take care of the details.)

The Steps of the Litigation Process

The litigation process can be divided into several steps. These steps do not necessarily go in order or sequence, but they do represent the basic and elemental parts of a legal process of litigation. Some claims may be made with no intent of entering the full process of litigation, but every claim that seeks payment or redress is a potential lawsuit—especially if the claimant doesn't like or accept your response.

There are estimates made that indicate that at least 85%, and as much as 95%, of all lawsuits filed do not get to trial. They are settled or otherwise disposed during the preliminaries to trial. Further, many claims are never filed as lawsuits. They are settled between the parties or with insurance adjusters before the matter gets to the filing of a lawsuit.

As an engineer, you may be involved in any of these matters. Regardless of the status of litigation, you should act and react the same way. For purposes of your conduct, a possible lawsuit is the same as an actual lawsuit.

The segments of the litigation process are as follows:

- The claim (Summons and Complaint),

- The response and defense (Answer),

- The discovery process, including:

- Interrogatories,

- Requests for Production,

- Requests for Admissions,

- Inspections, and

- Depositions

- The trial.

There are also post-trial activities and settlements to be considered.

I shall deal with each in a general way. I will not write from a legal stand-point, but I will seek only to make the process understood. The discussion will obviously be from the view and experience of an engineer who has been involved in litigation activities to a major extent, both as a representative of the party being sued and as a consultant or expert for others involved in lawsuits.

Claim

The start of a lawsuit is the filing of the claims in a "Complaint" along with the plaintiff's request to the court for trial and redress for the damages. The initial filing should give some specific reasons why the defendant is felt to be responsible for the claims and, therefore, is a legitimate defendant. Some-times the claims are not specific. They may be so for tactical reasons—the plaintiff does not want to tip his hand as to his full case. Sometimes the claims are vague because the real causes and involvement of the accident are not known or clearly understood by the plaintiff; the lawsuit is being filed in expectation of the development of real and arguable claims. In either case, one may expect the claims to become more specific and focused as the pro-cess continues. Certainly before trial, the claims should be clear to both sides and to the court.

A word of caution here: it would seem that the incident which may involve claims would be well known to all parties, including the defendants, before the lawsuit action was formally filed. Sometimes that is true, and the oppor-tunity for working out an equitable resolution is present before the lawsuit is filed. Sometimes, however, the first knowledge of the defendant that an incident has happened and that a claim is being made is the serving of the notice that the lawsuit has been filed. In such case, a close and careful look at the claim is important. I confess I don't know how it happens, but the claims are frequently changed as the litigation process develops. One good explanation is that as discovery proceeds, new information and understanding, previously unknown to the attorney and his client, reveal new or modified claims.

The claim has to be clear enough and logical enough to justify the court to continue the process. At any time the judge thinks the case has no merit, he may dismiss it. If the claims are too fuzzy or distant, the case may well be dismissed without any other activity. If either party to the suit reaches a point where his contention is considered to be untenable by the judge, that judge may dismiss the suit or grant certain judgments and impose sanctions. That possibility always stands before the claimant—and sometimes also stands before the defendant who makes unclear and incomplete responses to claims.

For that reason, claims are made to express, at least in general terms, what the accident was, and why the plaintiff believes the defendant is liable for the losses incurred.

(Note that there are many different jurisdictions, levels, and types of courts. Each has its own rules, forms, and time schedules. The attorneys are to take care of those details. As an engineer—the plaintiff or the defendant—you need mainly be concerned with the claims and the reasons for seeking redress.)

Response

The next general step in the process is the response, or "Answer." The defendant is given a reasonable time to study the claims and allegations and to make a response to those claims. If the defendant agrees with the claims and allegations, he merely says "yes" and settles the claims and dispute. In fact, a dispute doesn't happen.

More commonly, the defendant responds by denying the claims or at least most of them. Sometimes and in some jurisdictions, he will also offer his own defenses. At least, he may give some reasons why he denies the claims.

This claim and denial process leads to a full-blown litigation process—unless one side or the other gives in enough to effect a settlement.

Defenses

At the time of the response, or shortly after, the defendant will list his defenses, or the reasons why he denies the allegations and disputes the claims.

Defenses frequently involve legal matters, such as the lack of jurisdiction of the court in the subject matter, the expiration of some statute of limitations, or some other legal reasons. These are the business of the lawyer. They may be valid and important, and even critical, but they do not generally involve you as an engineer.

A common claim that the product was defective in design, however, does involve the engineer. So do claims of foreseeability and allegations of negligence or of failure to meet standards and codes. You can easily see that the engineer may well be needed early in the process. The good attorney will seek engineering information and answers to questions raised in the claims of the suit.

Such engineering responses may well be a part of the early responses and defenses raised in the matter. They must be well-thought-out and well-stated. You will be stuck with the response, once it is made.

Discovery

At this point, it becomes apparent that the ideas and beliefs of the plaintiff and the defendant are sufficiently different that the matter is not likely to be settled quickly or easily. In such a situation, the two parties will likely hold contradictory views and positions.

"You caused the accident and I got injured."

"I did not, and you aren't even injured."

"I am hurt, and now that I think of it, I am getting worse, and your defective design caused it."

"My design is not defective!"

"How so? If you had a gadget on it or had designed it like ABC machines, I wouldn't have been hurt, or at least I wouldn't have been hurt so badly."

You can see the process in this brief argument type of confrontation. At this point of obvious differences, the "discovery" process begins.

Under the rules of litigation, each side is allowed to "discover" relevant information, what the other side contends, and the basis for those contentions. Typically the plaintiff will want to know (and he has a legal right to know) how the product was designed and why it was so designed and built. He may look into details as long and as deeply as the court believes his requests are relevant.

The defendant will want to learn all he can about the plaintiff, the incident of the accident, the surrounding circumstances, and the other people involved. In addition, the defendant will want to understand in detail what the alleged defect is and how the plaintiff (perhaps through his expert engineering consultant) believes the product should have been designed, modified, or equipped.

It is for these and hundreds of other related reasons that the various methods of discovery will proceed—seeking to discover and understand all of the claims, all of the responses, and all of the reasons and proofs involved.

Note that "discovery" includes interrogatories, inspections, investigation, requests for production of documents and other materials, and depositions. In fact, everything that might be properly and legitimately done to prepare for a lawsuit trial—that is, to discover all possible and proper information relating to the incident and the trial—might be generally included under the single heading of "discovery."

Some types of discovery are sufficiently common and important in the scheme of things legal that they deserve separate discussion. If there is a dispute, the court will determine what is proper and what is improper discovery. If the court rules or the judge says the discovery is proper, you are obligated to respond. Responses to discovery requests must be truthful. If the responses are not truthful, the results can be disastrous, both for the lawsuit and for you personally.

Interrogatories

The first discovery method used is usually the "interrogatory." This is simply a set of questions that each side serves upon the other in a formal way, with the powers of the court demanding appropriate answers within some time limit. (You will find that lawyers use their own words. An interrogatory is simply a question presented in written form and requesting a written answer in a given time frame. In litigation, you will gain a whole new vocabulary of words like this. Don't let them scare you. Most of the lawyer's words can be translated into more common language. In fact, that may become part of your job.)

To illustrate, assume that a plaintiff believes his injury or loss is blamable to a claimed defect in the machine being used and involved in the accident. Dozens of questions may be asked of the defendant-manufacturer similar to these:

- Who designed the product?

- Who made the decision to use a hydraulic control instead of a mechanical control?

- List all of the standards, codes, and laws considered and complied with in the design of the product.

- Is part number "000000" used in other models? If so, which models?

- Describe the testing procedures used to evaluate the model or part involved in the claim.

- When did you begin to produce the model, and when did you cease to produce it?

- Why did you stop producing it?

- What replaced the model?

- What model preceded the subject model?

- Why was the subject model placed into production? Was something wrong with the predecessor model?

- Did the subject model solve some problem experienced on the old model?

- Did the successor model solve some problem experienced on the subject model? What problem? How did it solve the problem?

- Name all of the people who had anything to do with the design, development, testing, and analysis of the model.

- Name all of the competitors to the model.

- Name all accidents on the subject model of machine of which the defendant has information or is aware.

- Did the manufacturer or its employees consider the possibility of such an accident as happened to Mr. Plaintiff? If so, what was that consideration and what was the final decision?

- What trade associations and technical organizations do the manufacturer and his people belong to and deal with?

...and on and on. You see, the plaintiff wants to find out all he can so he has a better basis for making his arguments to the court.

I haven't even attempted any complete listing of questions. Attorneys have their own sources and lists of interrogatory questions. Law books and other sources of references used by attorneys give sample or typical lists. Some of the questions, from example lists, won't even apply, but they will be asked anyway. Other lawyers and firms, specializing in certain kinds of litigation, may have developed their own lists.

To control the amount and size of questions, some jurisdictions now have limits as to the number of interrogatories that may be asked, or other means of attempting to keep the questioning within a reasonable limit.

The defendant does the same. Typical interrogatory questions to the plaintiff are:

- Tell in detail what happened at the time of the accident.

- What do you claim specifically was wrong with the product? How did that cause the accident?

- What was your job? Your experience? Your education?

- Are you married? Family?

- Who else saw the accident, or knows about it? What do they say?

- Describe your injuries or losses. Are they permanent?

- Describe the medical treatment you had. Where? Who were the doctors?

- Did the doctor tell you not to return to work? When do you expect to go back to work?

- Had you consumed any alcoholic beverages in the 24-hour period before the accident? Any other drugs?

- How did you learn to run the machine (if the plaintiff is the operator)?

- Did you read the operator's manual?

- Who else runs the subject machine?

- Have you operated other machines?

- Who gave you instructions to do the work you were doing when the accident happened?

- Why didn't you ....? It would have avoided the accident.

And more. The defendant, you can see, is trying to learn as much as possible about the accident and the causes and circumstances. He may be seeking other causes of the accident.

Requests for Production

Another form of written discovery is the request for production. Each side will ask for the other to produce written and physical evidence and information by this process. The plaintiff may request prints of the machine and its parts, service records and warranty records of the model, or records of other accidents and lawsuits involving the model. Operator's manuals and advertising literature are common requests. There are many other items.

The defendant may request photographs, accident reports, medical records, machine history information, broken parts, and so on, if he believes they may help him understand the accident and the circumstances.

Response to RFPs (Requests for Production) is usually paper—sometimes a lot of it. If it is engineering paper, the engineer will certainly be involved in finding and producing the paper.

Examples of requests for production of documents and other material things:

- Please provide a complete set of the prints and specifications involved in the manufacture of the product.

- Provide copies of all manuals delivered with the product.

- Provide copies of all standards and codes adhered to in the design and manufacture of the product.

- Provide a list of names of all the engineers and designers who worked on the subject product. Include present addresses and phone numbers.

- Produce a list of all accidents and claims for damages made with regard to the subject product model. Provide information on all accidents of which the defendant is aware which are similar in nature to the subject of this lawsuit.

- Provide production samples of part numbers 0000, 1111, and 2222.

The defendant may ask the plaintiff to:

- Provide all medical records relating to the claims and injury.

- Provide his IRS tax returns, showing his earnings for a certain period of time.

- Provide all photos, statements, and other evidence which describe the incident.

- Provide copies of his personnel file or other records of his employment or training.

Again, this is only a sample list of Requests for Production. If there are objections, the Court will rule on what is a proper request and what is not proper.

Requests for Admission

Another form of discovery that needs separate mention is the "Request for Admission." The attorney, following the rules of law and of the court, must "make his case" in a certain form and following certain steps. That means he must show and prove certain things in order to have properly presented his case.

To do this, the plaintiff's lawyer may serve the defendant with Requests for Admission. (The defendant's attorney may do this also, but it is not common practice.)

Requests for Admission (RFAs) look like this:

- Admit that you are the designer and manufacturer of the model or product.

- Admit that you sold the subject machine without certain attachments or suggested features.

- Admit that you changed from the subject machine model to the replacement model because of certain difficulties or complaints you had from customers.

- Admit that you had notice of several prior accidents of the type that occurred to plaintiff in this case.

- Admit that you have been cited by OSHA for certain product deficiencies in the past.

- Admit that you considered other design features and intentionally decided not to use them.

- And so on....

Admissions are responded to by saying "admit" or "deny." Sometimes further discussion is added.

The impact of admitting such a request item is that it now becomes evidence that needs no longer be proven in your opponent's case. Further, if you deny and the opponent later proves the contrary, you are in bad light with the jury and possibly with the judge. Obviously, truth is always important.

Objections to the Request for Admission—or to a Request for Production or to Interrogatories—are made through the attorney, who has the understanding to make appropriate objections and to argue the question before the judge if necessary. Still, the engineer may well possess and best understand the technical information and material that is the basis for the responses. The engineer will help the attorney make the proper truthful responses.

Inspections

Inspections of the machine or parts involved, the accident site, the injured person, and other relevant things may be necessary or desirable in the discovery process. In such matter, the inspection may be made by agreement of the parties to the litigation. When such agreements are disputed, a court order may be necessary in order to make the inspection. Also, the court order is sometimes necessary when the machine, product, or other property involved has changed ownership.

Technical inspections, by consultants or experts, are frequently made under the watch of the opposing side, though that is not always done. The results and findings of the inspection are discoverable by interrogatory or through deposition of those involved. That is, the side with the information should properly disclose that information to the opposition by some time limit before the trial. Otherwise it may become inadmissible evidence—that is, regardless of the importance of the information, it may be excluded from the trial.

<u>Note:</u> At this point, I should insert an explanation. I will, from time to time, remind you that information and material you have and develop may be discoverable. However, you need not disclose it unless you are asked by the opposing side to do so. In doing inspections, for example, you should do them knowing that the opposing side may well have the opportunity to ask you about the inspection. If they do, you will probably have to disclose the information. That is what I mean by the phrase "may be discoverable."

That is the game of discovery. Each side attempts to learn as much as it can about the matter and the case. At the same time, a side will try to limit what it gives up as much as is proper under the rules. Theoretically there should be no surprises—to either side or to the judge—at trial. Sometimes that works, but more often there are surprises. Then the trial gets exciting.

Depositions

The most intense and interesting discovery process is the deposition.

In a deposition, a witness or potential witness, or someone believed to have information or knowledge relating to the matter at hand, is asked questions in a special circumstance. Depositions are given before a court reporter and under oath, just as they would be at trial. However, the atmosphere is more informal—though no less important.

Only the witness, or deponent, and the attorneys representing parties in the case are generally in the room, along with the court reporter. Some depositions are videotaped. Sometimes other people attend. I have seen engineering consultants for the questioner at the deposition. Also, I have seen plaintiffs, family members, and others on certain occasions. I once heard arguments to the effect that the deposition was a public court proceeding, and that the public could attend if they were inclined to do so.

Suffice it to say at this point that the deposition gets those involved into what seems, at times, to be almost a practice trial. Attorneys are asking questions and witnesses are answering them; this gets exciting and important. When the case gets as far as depositions, all parties to the litigation seem to be getting serious. (Yet, over half of the cases in which I have given depositions never went on to the trial stage.)

I will discuss the deposition, as the engineer might be involved in it, in more detail later in this book.

Trial

At trial, each party to the lawsuit has the opportunity to present his case, his evidence, his witnesses, and his arguments before the judge and, if he elects to do so, in front of a jury.

At trial, the process follows long-established and well-developed procedures. This is the point in the litigation process where the participants essentially agree to disagree and to allow the court, the judge, and the jury to settle the matter for them.

Trials are awesome because of the seriousness of the matter to be decided. They are awesome because of the responsibilities of the jury, the judge, the attorneys, and the witnesses. But they are especially awesome when one realizes that this is the way to settle disputes in a developed and intelligent society. You will have feelings when you enter a courtroom similar to the feelings you have when you enter a church. Those feelings come in both places for some of the same reasons.

Typically, the trial will consist of the choosing of a jury, opening statements by each attorney, the presentation of evidence and witnesses for the plaintiff, the presentation of the case for the defense, final arguments by each participating party, the jury charge, the jury deliberation, and the verdict.

This brief description of a trial will be expanded later, not in terms of legal technicalities, but in terms of the plaintiff, the defendant, and the engineering witness who may be involved.

Post-Trial Activities

When the trial has been completed and a decision handed down by the jury and judge, there may be post-trial activities. There may be handshakes all around and agreement that the court has led the participants to a reasonable and proper decision. I have seen that happen and I have taken part in the handshakes. It does happen, and when it does, it is a delightful experience.

At other times, there is strong disagreement and resentment toward the decision of the court—usually by the loser, of course. I have seen losers jump over tables and go after the winner, but that doesn't happen very often. More often, there are cool, formal acknowledgments around and among the attorneys and a quiet strolling away from the court.

Then there are motions for retrial, judgment notwithstanding the verdict, reductions in judgment, and a variety of other legal steps that are entirely the province of the attorneys. Sometimes there are appeals to higher courts. These are seldom, if ever, on the basis of anything but legal technicalities, although some of them sound as if they are on the facts and the evidence. These are also the province of the attorneys.

As an engineer you probably won't be involved, although I have been involved in appeals in several cases. The legal technicalities, however, and not the facts or the evidence were under discussion.

Settlement

The objective of all of this litigation is the resolution of the dispute or a settlement of the matter. A resolution certainly comes—after the trial and all of the appeals have been exhausted. If your company or client loses, the judge enters a judgment against the loser requiring him to pay such awards as the jury determined proper in the case. When you pay that judgment and the plaintiff accepts the payment, you have resolved the case.

The case may be resolved by settlement anytime during the process of litigation. All that is required is an agreement between the parties that spells out the terms on which the matter will be settled, and the execution of those terms. I saw a case settled in the dining room of an injured party, in a manner that left good feelings among both the parties. That matter was settled even before a lawsuit was filed.

I saw another case settled between the parties after the jury had announced it had reached a verdict and before the verdict was read. (The settlement agreement wasn't the same as the jury verdict, either.) I have seen other cases drag on for years as the attorneys and parties haggled on and on.

This, then, is the litigation process. It is a short description, and it is by no means complete. I don't even know some of the legal thinking, and I don't understand some of what I have heard or experienced. Yet I still do proclaim that it is a good system.

Chapter 6

ENGINEERS AND ENGINEERING INFORMATION

Engineers understand how a design was made and how the machine design was developed. They know test programs. They know why one connecting design (four bolts, for example) was chosen rather than another design (seven bolts, or a single large thread or welding). They know engineering data and what it means. They are familiar with standards and common practices. They know what their competitors are doing.

The engineering process and the engineer's understanding of machines, designs, materials, applications, failure modes, etc., are not usually known by the attorney. Yet such information and judgment are frequently critical to the successful conduct of the case and the arrival at a proper equitable resolution.

More important, engineering information is not reasonably known nor understood by the juror or the judge in a products liability matter in a court of law. This gives the engineer his authority for testifying in such an action—to assist the court in understanding the facts and information in the case.

An engineer may testify as either a fact witness or as an expert witness. As a fact witness, he testifies to what he knows to be fact. As an expert witness, he is allowed to testify as to his opinion, where that opinion will assist the judge and/or the jury in understanding some technical information, or details that are not common knowledge.

I'll discuss the importance of good engineering information and the reasons why attorneys ask for that information. In Chapter VIII, I will discuss interrogatories and other legal questions to a party in a lawsuit. I will not cover the legal art of answering those questions, but I will show where the engineer gets involved in the answers.

Why is Engineering Information Important?

Engineering information is that data and discussion about a design that is recorded. The blueprints obviously represent the final form and detail of the design. The blueprint contains the information needed to make the part or machine <u>just as the designer intended it to be made</u>. Blueprints are engineering information. So is the same information in a computer program. More and more designs are being made by computer instead of the conventional drawing and blueprint method.

So are notices or papers releasing the design, or subsequently changing it. Good backup or record paper explains the change and reasons for the change; that is true also for the original release. The information allows the engineer to retrace his steps and to reconstruct previous versions of the design. This information keeps the engineer from reinventing the previous version. It can also keep the engineer from moving back and forth between two design choices because the reasons haven't been kept carefully. Sometimes even the reason for the first change doesn't keep other changes from happening. I once saw a part which had been changed six times from the original design. Changes 1, 3, and 5 were identical. Changes 2, 4, and 6 were also identical. Worse yet, each time the change was made, the designer who initiated the change claimed significant cost reduction. Now, in a world of changing material and process prices, this may be possible, but it is unlikely, to say the least.

Likewise, any letters, memos, policy statements, procedures, and similar paper may well be important to the successful design of a product. Such paper is also engineering information.

All of this information is important because it leads to a successful design. Therefore it is also important to litigators who may be critically examining the design and comparing it to some proposed alternate.

This means that any of this paper or information may possibly be "discovered" by opposing litigants. "Paper," I should point out, includes computer records, tape records, recordings, microfilm, and other such methods and forms of storage. It may also include what is in your memory; you may be asked to tell what you remember.

Information and the Plaintiff

The plaintiff in a case will be interested in the engineering information as a basis for evidence that there was a defect in the design or that there was negligence in the process. (There are other forms of expressing the claims, but I will let the attorneys worry about those.) If the plaintiff is going to be successful in his claims, he may well need to look at your drawings and your records, and under the present rules of procedure, you may as well assume that he may be allowed to see them.

The plaintiff will probably hire an expert who will express an opinion that if a certain design feature or device had been on the machine in question, his plaintiff-client would not have been hurt. Alternately, he may single out a particular feature or design detail as the culprit in the case. That expert may not know what he is talking about without your engineering information. He will almost certainly need your engineering information to prove his contention.

That is why the rules of discovery allow your opponent to discover anything he believes, and of which he can convince the judge, is relevant to his case.

I don't mean to frighten you unnecessarily, but plaintiffs, under the rules of litigation, can discover almost anything you have in your place of business. From the viewpoint of the plaintiff, he needs it. In fact, he almost certainly cannot prepare a good case against your product unless he has that kind of information.

One plaintiff's expert constructed his case on a runaway machine on the basis that it had a torque converter in the drive train of the machine. His theory was that if a "straight stick" transmission had been in the machine, the accident scenario couldn't have possibly happened. He was embarrassed when, at trial, he discovered the machine in question did indeed have no torque converter; instead, it had a straight stick transmission. In essence, he disproved his own case—just because he either didn't ask for the correct information or he didn't pay attention to it.

Another plaintiff's expert based his case on detailed knowledge of the hydraulic system of the subject machine. As he developed his accident scenario, he asked interrogatories, through his client-attorney, which produced precisely the information he had theorized would exist—that the problem had occurred several times before, and that it had not been corrected.

Information and the Defendant

The defendant in a lawsuit needs good engineering information to show that his design is proper, that it is safe, and that it did not cause the incident for which the suit was filed. I am not being facetious or sarcastic. That is what you will have to show to the court if you are successful in defending your product.

You will need to talk about how and why the product was created. You will need to show how the product works and to discuss the benefits of the product. You will need to describe the testing, evaluation, analysis, and development of the product. That is in your engineering information.

Further, you may be asked about options and choices you made:

Why did you do one thing instead of another?

Why did you not do something differently?

A thousand questions of this type have been framed for use with company engineers in deposition and on the witness stand. They exist and are listed in legal textbooks and references, and in the minds of attorneys.

An engineering expert witness had worked for one manufacturer who did not use a component product made by a competing company because of corporate policies against purchasing components from competitors. When that witness testified that the competing company indeed made the best component product of that type in the world, he was asked in 15 or 20 different cases, "If the competitor's product is so good, why didn't you use it at your company?" You can expect such questions. There are answers, of course— patents, market availability, internal corporate policies (although that may not be a good reason), and the fact the component simply may not fit your machine. However, you will almost certainly need an answer. When you need an answer, you need it in a timely fashion and with confidence. Without good engineering information at you fingertips, you may not answer well.

Still further, you will need to respond to suggestions and proposals made by the plaintiff (probably through his engineering expert) for things that he believes would have prevented the accident and his injuries:

Would they have prevented the injuries?

Would they have worked?

Would they have made the machine more safe, or would they have created new and possibly worse safety problems?

Did you even consider the plaintiff's expert's idea when you designed the machine? If not, why not?

If you considered it, did you use it? Why or why not?

At the end, you may have to explain why you didn't use the device or feature. Keep in mind, the court and the jury will have to understand, believe, and trust your explanation. They must understand you—and if they do not understand the technical details, they must believe and trust you.

You will need engineering information to respond to such questioning. At the very least, you will need a memory and understanding of the design and development process that went into the design.

Where is the Information?

Simply, engineering information is in any of the sources of information that you use in designing and developing a product and in maintaining the design.

Your attorney will tell you how to deal with questions about the sources.

The information may be any of the various places that such data are created, used, processed, stored, or translated into something else.

Obviously, there are reasonable data retention policies. These will be examined. If the information no longer exists, so be it. However, you can expect at least a raised eyebrow from your opponent, whichever side he is on, if you say the information no longer exists.

Experience has convinced me that the existence of good, rational, believable information is far better than the loss of the information in some far away warehouse or retention policy. Experience also has shown that information may be found in unexpected places.

An engineer, for example, who keeps a copy of every piece of paper that crosses his desk may well be the source of information that had long since been discarded by the corporate retention policies. One marketing specialist kept copies of each draft of all of the letters he wrote. Such files give a clear guide to the thinking used in arriving at a conclusion. And those drafts and modifications are all discoverable under most court procedural rules. Personal files should conform to corporate retention policies.

If the information is in the minds and memories of employees involved in the development and production of the product, that memory may be searched (by way of deposition) to get information and leads on information. Keep in mind that in answering interrogatory or deposition questions, people are under oath to tell the truth.

Who Can Explain the Information?

In my experience, the best one to discuss and explain engineering information is the one who had responsibility for it. That may be just a single person or one of the group responsible for the product or design. Such a person would understand the information and the design from the standpoint of active participation or line of responsibility involved in the creation and development of the machine or product. These are the people who are deposed by the plaintiff's attorney, and who are asked to assist in the defense by the defense's attorney.

Second best would be someone familiar with that type of product, either by experience (with a competitive product, for example) or by use and application of the product. That person may have engineered similar or competing products. He or she would know the reasons for making design choices and would understand and be able to explain the processes to a jury. Both plaintiffs and defendants seek outside experts who can present such testimony and opinions with authority and confidence.

Next would be the engineer with the basic training and ability to understand the principles of engineering and those processes involved in design and testing products. He will explain, using his basic training and technical skill, how the design was done and why it was so fashioned.

It would seem obvious that the hands-on designer would be most knowledgeable concerning the product, and would be most authoritative and believable. As one follows the spectrum through competitive engineers, general practitioners, professors or teachers, or somebody in completely different industry or field of work, that knowledge appears to lessen with distance from the facts. In general, this is correct. Obviously, the designer can testify best in regards to facts about the design.

Note, however, that courts are liberal in determining the qualifications of an expert to testify on a given subject. We can argue effectively that the one who designed the product should know more about it than either the competitor or the general practitioner. I believe that is a true contention. However, that is for the attorneys to argue and the court to decide. If the witness is admitted and allowed to testify, it is up to the jury to decide if they believe him or not.

You can see where you would fit in this picture, regarding certain products. You may have firsthand experience or information on the product. Or you may have knowledge of the product by having been in the same industry and having dealt with similar competing products. Or you may be a person technically educated in the basic fundamentals of the engineering skills and specialties in the design and the development of the product. Further, you may

79

be teaching engineering subjects or doing research in certain engineering fields at a university.

How Does that Engineering Information Fit into the Litigation Process?

Information is evidence or, at least, potential evidence. It may be offered as proof of a contention that a product is defective, or it may be offered as rebuttal to claims that the product is defective in terms of safety. In either position, it is potentially important evidence.

The plaintiff will typically say the product should have been different in some way, giving it the characteristic that would have avoided the accident and thus, avoided the plaintiff's injury. He will probably offer specific design suggestions. If he does, he stands a better chance of convincing a jury of his cause than he does if he makes only claims with no offer of alternatives. He will use engineering information—some of it yours—to do this convincing.

The defendant will have to use his own engineering information to demonstrate the propriety and benefits of his design in order to counteract the claims of the plaintiff. He will also have to respond to the plaintiff's suggestion. He can't say merely, "My design is better." Well, he can say that, but it probably won't sell to a jury. He will have to prove his position—explain why his design is best and why the plaintiff's suggestion is not best.

Juries are not necessarily expected to understand all of the intricacies of a design or a process. That is why an engineer is allowed and even asked to explain the machine or the process to the jury. That explanation partially discharges his responsibility to assist the jury and the court in understanding the technical and scientific details of a matter. His ability and right to offer opinions on the matter is the remainder of his responsibility.

Note, also, that in addition to being an expert in the case, you may also be called as a fact witness. If you did the work or took part in it or know about it, you may be called to answer such fact questions.

What if There is No Information?

Sometimes, there is no information, or the information is so sketchy or buried in the past that to find it would be unreasonable. What do you do then? People do die, and take their knowledge with them. Everything is not written down; records are not made of each conversation or each exchange of ideas or each line that is tried out on a drawing. Retention programs provide for orderly disposal of information and data subject to legal limitations of varying kinds.

I do not suggest in any way that information should be intentionally destroyed to prevent someone from seeing it. That is criminal. But information is sometimes lost in the normal processes of life and business.

If you don't have the information, you don't have it. If someone remembers it, fine. But if someone thinks he remembers the information and is not sure, that is not alright. Sizable cases have been won and lost on the basis of someone who "thinks" he remembers; it is easy to make errors that way.

If, however, there is no information available, that does not go well with a jury.

My Advice on Information

My advice, in brief, is to make good engineering information recording decisions and have good reasons for those choices. It supports your good processes and intentions. Keep that information according to a reasonable retention schedule—preferably set out in a policy statement. Don't store all of your extraneous material and data. If it didn't help you, you probably don't need to keep it.

I have seen bad things happen in the courtroom as the result of paper found by chance in the file of a witness who had the habit of keeping everything. And the paper he kept had nothing to do with the accident at hand, either. Don't become a pack rat who keeps everything, regardless of the source or the information. Jurors will understand that there aren't enough warehouses or microfilms or time to do the processing for everything to be kept, and they know that too much paper will be a fire hazard.

Chapter 7

HOW THE ENGINEER CAN HELP THE ATTORNEY

Engineers and attorneys do not always agree on all matters. But here is one key to success. I have seen that when attorneys and engineers who are working on the same matter of litigation try to understand each other and to cooperate, they become significantly more successful. The work of understanding each other's views, thought they may vary widely, seems to lead to positions that make good sense to a jury.

One attorney expressed it this way in a letter, after a particularly difficult case: "I am convinced that when good attorneys and good experts and engineers get together and talk out the details of each day's happenings until they arrive at some point of consensus, success will follow."

The engineer, because he has a different background, can help the attorney in a large number of ways. He does a different kind of work, day in and day out, than the attorney does. The engineer deals with physical things and numbers with a reasonable degree of consistency and repeatability. The attorney deals more in concepts and relationships, all of which have a significant rate of change.

You will find that the attorney thinks and reasons in what appears to be a different way than you do as an engineer. The attorney looks at the engineer in the same way. Between the two of you, you can bridge that natural gap in language and understanding. Listen carefully, and explain carefully. Be patient. The attorney has the same difficulty you do. You have what appears to him to be a different way of thinking and reasoning.

The engineer deals with a body of knowledge that might be roughly classified as scientific. The methods of study, the so-called "scientific methods" are quite clearly spelled out. The attorney deals with the law, which is a constantly developing and changing subject filled with philosophy and other less physical topics. Some elements of the lawyer's methods of thinking are less well defined than are those of the scientific engineering methods. (This is not a precise comparison, but it is typical of the reactions that attorneys and engineers have to each other. If you realize and believe this, then you are on your way to help bridge the gap between the two.)

Attorneys tend to need broad information and knowledge in doing their work—knowledge such as medicine, engineering, physics, mathematics, accounting, psychology, and a host of other bodies of information, depending on the case at hand. Because the attorney has to concentrate on the law, with its many nooks and crannies, rules, and constantly changing directions, he seldom has time to become sufficiently expert at these other areas of knowledge to do his work in litigation and in court as he would wish.

Therefore, the attorney often uses experts from other fields of learning as consultants. He will use a medical doctor to explain the nature and cause of an injury. He may use an economist to discuss and propose appropriate economic estimates. He will use a bus driver to describe the job of driving a bus, or a crane operator to describe the proper way to operate a crane. He will use an engineer to discuss the suitability of a product or machine, and to explain why the design is or is not satisfactory. The same engineer will describe the processes of successful design and product development. In this chapter, I will list most of the many ways an engineer can be of assistance to the attorney.

Let me point out here that although the attorney needs an engineer, that doesn't mean the case is an engineering argument. Not at all! It is still a legal dispute—and will probably remain so—dealing in engineering claims, information, and understanding. The engineer can help, but he must realize that he is dealing in a legal matter and that he is the helper, not the leader, of the effort.

It is important that the engineer understands that he is assisting, and that he conducts himself in that way. As the helper, he can and should give the best information, advice, and judgment he can to his attorney-client. But final decisions as to whether and how that information and understanding is to be presented is the job of the attorney.

He may ignore your ideas and advice. If so, it is his call. He understands the intricacies of legal procedure, and will usually have good reason to act as he does. Help him, don't fight him. If you, as the engineer on the case, feel you do not or cannot agree with the path he is taking, get out of the case. You are sworn to tell the truth and you are expected to do so. If you cannot agree with the course the matter is taking, or if you disagree with the claims or responses of the attorney, say so—privately and sincerely. Your honest position should be made known to the attorney you are assisting. In fact, it must be made known.

Obviously, your help, advice, and information must be the truth, to the best of your ability. If you "think so," say so. If you "guess so," say so. If you know as a fact, fine. If you don't know, say so. The attorney will then make the best use of your remarks.

Keep in mind that the attorney is an advocate for his client. As such, he has certain responsibilities as a member of the court, and he is obligated to do so properly and ethically, and to represent his client in the best way he can.

Now, assume that you have talked to the attorney with whom you are asked to work, and that you are in agreement and in synchronization with what he is representing in the case. (You may be an engineering employee of a company being sued, or you may have been contacted to act as a consultant in the matter—for either the plaintiff or a defendant.)

My purpose in this chapter is to examine in considerable detail how you can assist the attorney. Some ideas may be obvious. Others are not obvious and are frequently missed entirely. Once in a while, even the obvious ways are missed.

The suggestions will be numbered to separate them. I believe many apply to both plaintiff and defense matters. I have no trouble treating both together because the engineer's objective should be to provide valid, truthful, and helpful information and advice.

1. As a designer and engineer, he knows the <u>design and development process</u>. He knows exactly how designs are made and developed. (This is why engineers with specific experience are usually sought for a specific accident case and litigation.) He can describe the technical processes and methods used in designing and in making design choices between two or more possibilities. More important, he knows <u>why</u> designs are made the way they are. It is common for machinery and product litigation to turn upon claims that the product should have been designed and built in some other way. If he works for the plaintiff, the engineer has to propose and explain that "other design." If the engineer works for the defense, he will explain why the design is as it is, and why that design is proper, and perhaps why it was even the best or the only way to make it.

Thus the case may turn upon which of two or more conflicting engineers is most convincing to the jury or to the judge.

I will note here that I am well aware that reasonable people may not agree. Reasonable engineers also may not agree. That does not disturb me. If the engineers on opposing sides do not agree, they may present their views before a jury and those views will be resolved, at least for the subject case, by the decision.

Note further that the stated legal reason for using an <u>expert witness</u> (and that differs from the consultant) is to "help the court and the jury to understand information and matters not generally understood by an average lay juror." In court, you will not be an advocate; your testimony will and should be to explain the engineering complications to the jury so they can discharge their duties. Your job is not to argue; rather, it is to answer the questions put to you by the attorney. He may ask you to explain in detail, or he may not. Your are the explainer of the engineering process to the jury, if that explanation is called for.

Your job as a consultant to the attorney will be much less restricted and more far reaching—that is, you have not been designated an expert witness in the case. You will need to understand and discuss reasons, choices, and options, as well as design details of the product under study. Your relationship to him in terms of technical matters will be the same—to describe and explain, in whatever detail the attorney may wish. As a consultant, you may suggest and even argue on occasion (but only with your attorney, and only in private.) However, in the end, the attorney is the final decision maker as to what should be used and how it should be used.

2. By virtue of his training and experience, the engineer can <u>explain products, systems, parts, and operation of the machine</u>. Such explanations are different from and in addition to the explanations of the <u>processes and methods of engineering</u>. He will understand and explain the details and specifics of a particular machine, product, or model. That will be a big job for him—he will need to explain to the attorney everything he can about the product. He will need to show him why the machine was made as it was. He may have to talk about alternative designs and show why the present design was chosen.

    Then, the engineer should listen as the attorney plays back his understanding. If he has it, good. If not, maybe the engineer didn't explain it well enough or maybe the listener doesn't have the basic understanding to comprehend the explanation. He may be tempted to throw up his hands and blame it all on the attorney, but he shouldn't do that. He may eventually have to explain the same thing to a jury of housewives, corn flake salesmen, store clerks, and retired railroad men. These good citizens may not have the ability to comprehend his explanation, either, and if not, he loses the case.

    By getting the attorney to understand the product and any peculiarities the product might have, the engineer is part way to doing what may eventually bring the case to a successful close. The good engineer is a good explainer.

3. Likewise, the engineer can talk about <u>how the product is developed, evaluated, and tested</u>, as well as how and why it is designed. A good description of the way a machine was tested can go far in assuring the jury that

it is a good machine and suitable for the uses in industry. The same tests and test results that impress businessmen and accountants in the corporate offices will likely impress attorneys and juries.

The engineer will know that product development and evaluation are done three ways. Knowing what the product is supposed to be and do, he can use any one or combinations of all three methods.

First, he will describe the test program. He can talk about the many hours of operating in the lab, on the proving grounds, and in the field. He can talk about overloading and intentional misuse, and he can describe the continuous improvement of the machine through the process of testing, redesigning, retesting, and redesigning.

Second, the engineer will describe the use of analytical methods, even up to full computer simulations. A large and growing body of understanding of the physical and mechanical relationships in parts, systems, and machines allows the designer, together with the analytic specialist, to get the design very nearly right the first time, and almost always the second time. (You need to avoid reams of computer paper in court, however. No lay juror can ever be expected to learn and understand the material on them and further, they will suspect you of trying to overwhelm them or talk down to them.)

Third, expert information can be used. The expertise may be your own experience or it may be the experience and judgment of someone outside who can look at your idea or your design and say whether it is good.

An important point is that designs are seldom completely new products. As time passes, we use and reuse those things which work and are successful. We do not have to reinvent the wheel every time we make a new design. Neither do we have to reinvent the bulldozer nor the loader nor the excavator. We do, however, keep making improvements to make the machines more useful and effective. The engineer can talk about the continuous evolution of an idea, a product, or a design. Often the reasons for the evolutionary development are the same reasons that explain why the present design is the best choice today, given what we know and can do.

Note, too, that some engineers lacking experience with a particular product or machine may have ideas, too. Engineering educators may have important different points of view. So, also, may engineers in another discipline or with other product experience. A good product has probably been exposed to others with different viewpoints.

4. The designer or engineer can tell the attorney about the successful product, and why it is successful; he can help the attorney tell that story to the court. He can talk about the features that sold it, the work done by it, and the value created by the product.

He can also describe products that were not so successful, and products that failed. I know there are economic and other reasons for product failures, but I remember marketing people telling me that the economic failure was sometimes directly related to the machine design features, too.

Understanding the reasons for product success and/or failure becomes important when you are defending a good product or when you are attacking a product by suggesting that it would be more safe (and would have prevented our client's accident) if it had some proposed device, design feature, or characteristic.

Frequently I wonder how a highly successful product can operate and dominate an industry for years and then, suddenly, become defective in a single situation. I have seen many such situations. I am convinced that a product cannot be so successful as to dominate an industry and still be "defective" in a safety sense. It is likely that such a defect would show up early on. Likewise, I do not believe the engineer who says his product is as good as it can be, and that it can't possibly be improved.

It may be that the proposed change might make the product more safe and might have prevented the subject accident. It may also be that the proposed change would make the product less useful and attractive, or it might even make it dangerous. These are things the jury will have to understand and believe if you are to succeed.

Juries tend to look at such positions as listed in the above two paragraphs with suspicion, too. Any tendency to deal in superlatives, perfection, or totality will certainly not sound realistic.

There are cases on record where the claim of defect was pointed out by the plaintiff's expert only to have the idea completely blown apart. If you are working for a plaintiff and criticizing a design, you need to be sure about your proposal. You need to be certain that the idea will work. If a jury catches you suggesting something that is later shown to be unreasonable, you will look bad and your plaintiff-client will lose.

Likewise, if you are defending a design and make statements that are later shown to be unreasonable or incorrect, you will probably lose. I'll discuss that further in later chapters.

5. Where needed, the engineer can <u>test or analyze</u> (or assist and guide the test and analysis) to provide demonstrations and evidence for resolving technical questions. Some of these tests and analyses may be useful for courtroom proof and demonstration.

    Frequently the attorney asks, "What would happen if ...?" The engineer may already know, or he may know how to find out. I have seen many calculations used in the courtroom and in the study of a case. On several occasions, I have even seen proof that the accident could not have possibly have happened the way it was claimed.

    I once drove an earthmoving machine through a ground bump hole the size of which was claimed to have injured the operator. It didn't hurt me, but the video tape was so rough looking that the client decided not to use it.

    Sometimes a test will tell you that you are right in your position. Sometimes it won't. But if you decide to run a test, have the engineer do it, or at least have him plan and direct the test.

6. The engineer is familiar with the <u>uses and applications</u> of the product. He can tell you if driving through a hole is even reasonable. The claimant may say a certain thing happened by accident. The engineer can evaluate the conditions under which the accident might possibly happen.

He can identify misuses of the machine easily. He can describe the conditions of proper and foreseen uses of the machine. An engineer familiar with a product or the product history will spot potential problems in the story of the accident. These may be starting points for rebuttal or disproof. He will recognize any areas in the story of the accident that are not consistent with normal and proper use of the product. (I am not suggesting claims are untrue, but it is not unusual, in the heat of an accident, for a witness or one involved in the accident to react and perceive incorrectly. Recollections of what happened may not always be accurate.)

The engineer can describe the use and work of a product or machine to show the court the benefits of the machine. He can describe long, successful experience with the product, if that long experience exists. The engineer's knowledge of the product and its use will help to build confidence among the jurors.

In one situation, the plaintiff claimed to have been injured when he was operating a wheeled, front-end loader, loading material out of a virgin bank. He claimed to have hit a rock, hidden in the material in the bank. He hit that rock, he said, while moving ahead at about four miles per hour, the top speed in the loading gear of the machine.

A potential witness in the matter, having designed loaders and watched them in test and at work, and even having operated them for a few hours, spotted a problem at once. A good operator will slow down as he enters a bank to load his bucket. He uses the forward motion of the loader (or crowd), the curling (or breakout) action of the bucket, and lift action of the loader boom arms in coordinated concert to break the material loose and fill his bucket. An overemphasis on any one of the three actions would drastically hurt the performance of the machine and its money-making ability.

It was obvious to the knowing observer that no reasonable operator of such a machine would go into the bank at four miles per hour without slowing down, unless he were a "cowboy" unconcerned with good performance. Since the plaintiff was an experienced operator, it was easy to suspect the original story, for good reason. This information, given to the defense attorney, sent him on the way to settling the case quickly and easily.

In a different matter, an engineering consultant noted that the plaintiff had been pinned under the roll bars of a machine which had rolled over on its side. The claim of the plaintiff's attorney was that the operator had been thrown from the seat as the machine rolled over. Two immediate points came to light. The consultant pointed out that if the man had been thrown from the machine, he had not properly worn his seat belt. The plaintiff changed his theory. Next he said that the man had tried to jump when he sensed the impending roll-over. Still not so. The consultant pointed out that the man was facing the machine when he was pinned. If he had been jumping, he would not be doing so. The final conclusion was that the operator had been either getting on the machine or off of it, sitting on a precarious slant in a wet field, when the machine moved enough to roll over. This action was perhaps aided by the weight of the man getting on or off the machine, and by the muddy, constantly changing condition under the tires of the machine.

The case was dropped.

7. There is a specific and important <u>relationship between a machine and its operator</u>.

Machines are essentially extensions of the operator, allowing them to do work that they could not do without the machine. The operator could pick up a handful of dirt and throw it a few feet, scattering it all over. He could choose to lay the handful down in a pile or even to carry it a few feet before he dropped it. With a modern front-end loader, he might pick up as much as 15 to 20 cubic yards of dirt weighing up to 30 tons and more, lift that dirt, and dump it onto a truck with a side 20 feet off the ground. If he wishes, he can carry the dirt several hundred yards and dump it into a hopper.

The machine allows the man to do work of a kind and at a rate not possible without the machine. Thus appears the economic benefit of the machine, an important factor in product liability cases.

In the design of the machine, the designer keeps the operator in the center of his thinking. No matter how good the machine is, it is useless unless the operator can easily and comfortably operate it.

That relationship between the machine and the operator is often considered to be a factor in accidents. Sometimes it is, and sometimes it is not. Nevertheless, the attorney will need to know how the man and the machine "fit together." Controls will be a factor to be considered. How the man and the machine work together will be an even bigger factor.

Visibility in all directions, noise levels, shock and vibrations, ability to get on and off, placement of controls, power, speed, reaction to external stimuli—all of these and more play an important part in the successful man/machine combination. Many major developments in earthmoving and construction machinery are aimed at exactly that area.

These relationships can be understood and explained by the engineer. In most accident scenarios, these relationships are very important. Note that there are three factors the designer must consider: (1) the machine, with its abilities and potentials, in terms of performance, specifications, cost, safety, life, reliability, serviceability, and repairability; and (2) the human being, with all of his characteristics—physical, psychological, and mental; and, (3) the interface between the two, the machine and the human. These should all be known and understood by the engineer.

8.   The engineer is technically equipped to conduct accident reconstruction.

An accident reconstruction is a rebuilding of the accident scenario from evidence provided by the final position and result of the accident, by witness descriptions, and by other evidence. A reconstruction of an incident is important when there are no witnesses or when witness information conflicts or is unclear.

In a typical case, several witnesses may differ in their descriptions. This is not unusual, and there are often emotional reasons for it. I don't suggest falsehood, necessarily, but that can happen, too. The job of reconstructing the incident as accurately as possible, then, becomes a way of resolving conflicts in witness testimony and even in the claims of the lawsuit.

The reconstruction of accidents is an art all by itself. I use the term "art" because it is, in my view, a combination of science, engineering, good judgment, and thinking.

To reconstruct an accident, the reconstruction expert uses good physics, mechanics, engineering, and mathematics, along with a good understanding of people and their reactions to situations, to develop a list of possible scenarios of the incident. Some scenarios will be eliminated because of physical impossibilities or time constraints. Other scenarios will be eliminated by physical evidence at the accident scene. Still other scenarios may be eliminated by agreement between the testimony of witnesses or even by agreement between adversaries.

Finally, the reconstructor ends with only a small number, usually one to three, possible scenarios for the incident. If there is only one possible scenario, he has rather well arrived at his answer. If more than one scenario remains, he may study the probabilities that each could have of happening. Frequently, one or two scenarios stand out far above the others in likelihood. That one scenario, in the lack of strong contradiction or counter-proposal, may be accepted as "the most likely" reconstruction of the incident.

The engineering practitioner is the person likely to be able to reconstruct the accident scenario on a time scale and on a three dimensional space scale. I have seen claims blown completely apart by competent preliminary reconstructions. I have used them successfully in court cases. The only problem I have had is with the scenario that I can prove did not happen (because of flaws in the original claims), but in which I have no proof as to the correct scenario. It is useful to prove it didn't happen in a way that is being claimed, but that may not be enough. The court and the jury will want to know how the accident did happen. If you can't tell them, they may be less inclined to take your reconstruction seriously.

We will consider accident reconstruction in a little more detail in another chapter.

9. The engineer should be the best spokesman available to discuss "state of the art." Technology is continually changing, and the engineer is in the best position to describe the state of the art situation at any legally important point.

"State of the art" is frequently a misused term. It has been widely defined as anything from "what might be conceived as possible" to "what is commonly done in everyday life." Several writers dealing with "state of the art" in legal terms have properly described this misuse and have suggested a proper use definition. I agree, and adopt and use the definition(s) discussed below.

When it considers state of the art, the court usually is trying to evaluate the feasibility (another often misused word) of doing what the claimant suggests would have prevented his accident. The court is really trying to determine if the suggested feature, design, or process is reasonable, and would have been used by reasonable designers and manufacturers at the time the subject machine was designed and produced.

I refuse to accept a single state of the art. There are several possible levels, and they ought to be spelled out.

First is what I call a "conception state of the art." If a scientist thinks that a feature, a design, or a process may be possible, it may be in this category. No one has tried it or seen it, and we are not sure it is going to work at all. These are hardly usable features or devices, but sometimes they are proposed anyway. The legal loophole for this is "or should have known."

Next is "state of the scientific art." The device or process may work in a laboratory situation, and it may even have been proven to some extent, but it is not embodied in a useful form or in a working design yet.

Following this is a "state of the design art" in which the idea has been embodied in a mechanical or working form. It may even be offered for sale. One may make an argument that the invention ought to have been on the defendant's machine. There may be reasons why the proposal is limited or why it wouldn't work on this situation or on the defendant's machine. It becomes potent, however, because in this form it can be seen and pictured. It may have jury appeal.

Last is what I call "state of the industry art." The idea is designed, manufactured, sold, and used commonly on machinery in the industry involved.

I have seen aerospace technology offered as being "usable on construction machines" by opposing experts who had no good understanding of the state of either industry. I do not suggest that the state of the industry art is fixed. Far from it. The state of the industry art is always changing, and it should be. The question in most matters of litigation is, "What is the appropriate state of the art for the subject kind of machinery at the time it was designed and manufactured?"

The engineer involved in an industry and with an eye toward the future as well as a history of the past should be in a good position to testify about and explain the state of the art.

Sometimes state of the art claims or defenses are offered in cases where they are no more than "red herrings," that is, they really have nothing to do with the case. I don't mean to suggest that you ignore red herrings. Not at all. You need to expose them or defuse them, but you must avoid getting caught up in red herrings to the exclusion of the important issues.

10. Engineering literature is growing very rapidly. The engineer can summarize that literature as it concerns his technical expertise, or as it might relate to the case or some technical subject at hand.

The engineer is also able to sort the important technical and engineering information from the unimportant information. Lawyers refer to these diversions and argue at length about relevance. The engineer can pick out the things about a machine that are important as concerns a specific accident. The possible use of literature as what attorneys call "learned treatises" makes one who knows the relevant literature of a field useful in dealing with such approaches.

Engineers can also help the attorney find useful information, data, demonstrations, examples, and references in literature sources. The attorney does the same thing with legal information in his books. The two work together in cases involving machinery.

To do that job effectively, engineers should be avid readers of any material that deals with their design, products, and technologies. Note, I didn't say "any good material" or "any material that happens to agree with you or please you." Contradictory opposing material should also be read. Unless you know what the other side may believe or say, you cannot react clearly to it.

11. The engineer can assist the attorney in the examinations, interviews, and depositions of those involved in a matter. Often, at the side of the attorney asking the questions, the engineer can interpret answers, suggest new questions, and spot fallacies that might escape the attorney.

I have worked on both sides of this situation. I have helped the attorney and I have been badgered by questions handed to an attorney in notes from an attending consultant. In favor of the engineer, in either case, he may well understand things that the attorney doesn't comprehend. Likewise, the engineer can catch discrepancies in responses that disclose weakness in the opponent's case. I view a competent attorney and a competent engineer as a formidable team at a deposition or at an inspection.

I have, on occasion, written suggested lists of questions for the attorney to ask, representing things I wanted to know specifically and suggesting general lines of questioning to follow. In one case, I saw an opposing expert's testimony go all to pieces with a couple of questions that I had suggested. In other cases, my ideas never touched him. In any case, questions suggested by the engineering consultant may well help the attorney do a thorough job of questioning.

It is not your job, as an engineer, to ask the questions. That is the attorney's job. However, you can suggest and give him ideas until either of you have exhausted the possibilities.

12. As with questions or with reconstruction, the engineer can list possibilities, practical scenarios, and likely conditions and results, thus limiting the blind alleys that might be searched and getting into the alleys where the real value is. In the game of litigation, some time is spent trying to figure out what the opponent is likely to say or do. A list of the possibilities is generally of good use.

Sometimes you feel so good about your own position that you say, "What can the opponent possibly do now?" That is a good question, and you ought to try to make a list of the possibilities. You may find exactly where you are about to be hit and tripped up. If you are consulting for a plaintiff, and have suggested the presence of certain devices or design features that might have prevented the accident, think about what reactions the manufacturer will have to your suggestion or claim. If you are consulting for a defendant, think about how your responses to the claims are likely to be accepted by your opponent. His probable responses may well be critical to you and your case.

There are many things to attend to in the process of litigation. Some are unimportant and should be left alone. Some are unimportant but have to be taken care of because of rules or procedures. Some are critical and demand continuous immediate attention. The engineer may well help his attorney by tending to some of the things dealing with the product or machine or technology.

13. A good engineer will be able to translate technical information into common language, to assist both the attorney and others. I take certain risks when I say this, but the most successful engineers I know have been able to talk to draftsmen, mechanics, machinists, welders, salesmen, neighbors, children, and school teachers about engineering things in both technical terms and in more general terms. This is important and even critical for several reasons:

- The engineer, the attorney, and others involved in the litigation must understand each other in order to work well together. If they do not— if, for example, the engineer cannot express his opinions and design reasoning in lay language—the team will not win.

- Most trials are before a jury, typically made up of a cross section of society. I have seen janitors, retired housewives, social workers, postmen, retired railroad men, jewelry salesmen, real estate saleswomen, college students, factory workers, an unemployed man with a Ph.D. in physics, a taxi driver, a home economics teacher, mothers, grandmothers, and so on. These are the people who I believe try very hard to do a good job as jurors. But they need to understand you before they can give you good consideration. If you talk technical jargon to them, or worse yet, if you talk down to them, you lose.

- Most attorneys and judges are not as well versed in engineering matters as you should be. You can reach them by explaining things in terms they do understand. I once had a manager who had a background in accounting. I quit talking about <u>design reviews</u> and talked instead about <u>design audits</u>. He understood the meaning and objective of that process, while he wondered if design reviews were really doing anything. Maybe you can pick up a few phrases that the attorney uses and use them in some of your translations. I like to know the backgrounds of jurors, so I might be able to speak a more understandable language.

- Most of the work product of the litigation process and the court trial is in the form of words. If you can contribute lay or general words and explanations which are better understood, you have helped your team.

14. Part of the arsenal of the engineer is the mathematical science of probabilities. The engineer will be able to evaluate probabilities and risks. (If he can't, he falls short as a good engineer.) He can distinguish significant risks from insignificant risks as expressed in numbers. Expert testimony generally has to be "within usual and reasonable engineering probabilities." No one has ever told me in numbers what that means, but several times I have put solid probability numbers on a factor, giving my attorney-coworker a feeling of confidence, or, at least, a more proper understanding of the probabilities involved in the matter of discussion.

I learned to communicate with the attorney who gave me my basic training in litigation for engineers by a method that allowed both of us to understand and agree upon the chances with which we were dealing. We talked about chances of winning the case or losing it. We talked about the probabilities of successfully defending the case in court and the comparisons of the costs and risks involved.

Our common system of communication was based on a combination of probability statements and common sense talk. We almost always agreed on our positions and decisions. We were right more than we were wrong.

If the attorney needs to deal with risk and probability, chances are the engineer can help him.

15. The engineer can explain <u>complex technical processes</u>. Again, if he is good, he can translate that explanation into the kind of language that the attorney, the judge, and the jury will all understand.

People tend to suspect things they do not understand. In fact, they sometimes downright fear them. If an attorney doesn't understand a process or a complex item in engineering, he will certainly not make good use of it. If a juror doesn't understand a process or a complexity, she will not consider it favorably in her deliberations. At the very least, she has to believe you, and believe that you understand the process or thing you are explaining. If she doesn't, you don't get her vote.

Explanations of complex things need to be pruned and timed and nursed along. Try them out. If your attorney merely shrugs his shoulders, go back and rework it. If your wife or a neighbor understands what you are saying, chances are that you are making headway.

The important point here is that the engineer or scientist may be the only one who understands the complexity in the first place. That situation is no different from the medical doctor who understands the injury and chances for recovery, or the psychologist who can describe a person's state of mind, or an electrician who can tell you how your phone or VCR works. He must learn how to explain it in lay language if he is going to help the jury understand the matter.

A detent on the shifting mechanism of a transmission on a bulldozer has the same feel or "click" as one feels when he turns the knob on the stove. An optical illusion may be just like the vision of water you see across the road when you are traveling down a long highway on a sunny, hot day. It isn't water, but it sure looks like it.

A transmission is like a multiplier of forces. It changes high forces and low speed to lower forces and higher speeds.

Friction is the rubbing resistance between the foot or a tire and the ground. A high coefficient of friction (say .95) means that it takes a force equal to just less than the weight of the object, or .95 times the weight of the object, to make it slide on the surface. If the coefficient of friction is low (say .15), that means it only takes .15 times the weight of the object to make it slip on the surface.

These are the kinds of explanations I mean.

16. The engineer can <u>listen and react</u> both as a technical person and as a layman. This is important. To often, we forget that engineers are people, too, and the important thing is to have them listen both as laymen and as engineering experts. Anyone who is listening to an attorney may be listening to the attorney as a layman.

The best attorneys I have seen turn to a nearby secretary or another attorney after a technical discussion and ask, "How did that sound to you?" One of the best attorneys I worked with turned to me after an hour of medical talk with a doctor and asked me the same question. He wanted to know if I, as a layman concerning medical matters, understood what the doctor was explaining.

After explaining for a half hour why we didn't put a certain device on a tractor, a clerk in one office asked me, "But why didn't you just put the device on?" I went back to the writing pad.

To the attorney I suggest, ask the engineer, whether or not it is an engineering question. He is a layman for non-engineering things and his reaction may be helpful.

17. The engineer can <u>testify,</u> both in deposition and at trial. Moreover, it may be necessary for him to do so. He needs to be taught the intricacies of the processes by the attorney, but he may well have the position and the background that makes him the obvious choice for the assignment. I will discuss later in the book both deposition and trial testimony, and take look at the matter and meaning of questions, too.

Further, remember that if an engineer has or understands some information or evidence concerning the matter, he may be required to testify. Begin training the engineer to do so early.

18. Reports and other written materials are sometimes requested and required in the litigation process. The engineer can provide such reports and written materials to explain his beliefs and opinions. As with spoken material, the engineer needs to make sure he writes in a language that the court and the layman can understand.

I am a believer that reports ought to look like anything but reports. I try to make my reports look like letters. I also try to make the reports deal strictly with the matters and questions of the case. Too much formality leads to boredom, which leads to uncertainty, which may lead to "you lose."

19. I keep repeating, and I will do so throughout this book, that engineers should not ask questions; that is the job of the attorney. However, his participation is not limited to answering questions. The engineer can suggest questions for deposition and cross-examination of opponents, perhaps because he has been asked those questions himself. He can even suggest questions for his own direct examination in court. Some attorneys like to have help in preparing questions. If you help, you are more likely to be comfortable with the questions. You will look and be more confident.

At the right time, the engineer can ask questions that lead to useful ideas. I don't mean for the engineer to quiz or second-guess everything. He may try to do that, but he isn't good at it. Yet, normal curiosity works in him and some questions may be valuable. Beyond that, if the engineer asks, he may learn, and so might the attorney at the same time.

Chapter 8

THE DISCOVERY PROCESS

The discovery process is a legitimate process for an opponent in a lawsuit to discover information that is permitted by law to be found and possibly used in the matter being litigated. Typically, any information about the product, the philosophy, the design, the process, testing, analyses, etc., can be discovered. Questions, called "Interrogatories," need to be answered, and the engineer can help prepare the answers to be written under the guidance of the attorney. (The litigation process frequently includes bitter arguments between attorneys as to what is proper discovery and what is not proper. Many times, a judge has to make such decisions.)

It is important that the attorney direct and guide the handling of matters involved in discovery. This is legal territory. My comments are from experience, and are directed toward the engineer who will become involved in the discovery process of a matter of litigation.

I have already mentioned discovery and forms or methods of discovery. Interrogatories, Requests for Production, and Requests for Admissions are the most common formal forms of discovery, along with the deposition.

In short, the other side wants and, more accurately, needs information about you and the product you made or designed. Information—that is the name of the discovery game. No matter which side you are on, you need to know about the other side as much as you can and the law allows you to "discover" any information that is relevant to the matter under litigation.

Further, the law spells out the rules and procedures for the discovery activity. Among the rules are those saying what is and what is not proper discovery. Also, sequences and patterns of discovery may be stated by the specific courts and jurisdictions. The attorney will deal with those.

At this point, though, understand that getting information following appropriate steps is the objective. I will discuss the formal methods of discovery, at least in terms of how they might involve and affect the engineer.

There are other less formal methods. Inspection is one. Inspection of the site of the accident, of the equipment involved, and of similar or related items may give important information. Attorneys generally do these types of inspections and have their consultants do them, too. Still, simple inspection is sometimes forgotten as a source of information.

Many times, I have visited a dealer's yard or stopped at a construction site to look at a machine and to check it for precisely the claim or condition stated in the complaint of the lawsuit. I have also inspected and photographed accident sites, and inspected accident machines. On a few occasions I have been asked by my attorney-client to talk with certain other people. It is not unusual for a consultant to a plaintiff's attorney to be asked to have such conversations. Those conversations have been with the plaintiff, witnesses to the incident, other experts, and assorted other people who had information or understanding of the accident or of the product.

Other obvious but less used methods are the library, trade journals, competitors, or talking to machine users (contractors and operators, in the case of earthmoving and construction machinery) and asking questions.

One prominent teaching attorney points out that talking to attorneys, and even your opponent over lunch or a drink, can often divulge useful information. The rule is: Don't miss any opportunity to get good information that is properly available to you.

The same rule applies to the engineer. If you are involved in litigation, get all of the information you can. If you see a gap of understanding, try to fill it. Of course, you must follow the guidance and limitations stated by your attorney, to avoid improper contacts, but there are still a lot of opportunities.

Keep in mind that any information you have or get may well be subject to discovery. If you have conversations regarding the matter, you may well have to disclose what you talked about—what questions were asked and how they were answered. The information you get you may have to disclose if the proper interrogatories or deposition questions are asked.

Interrogatories

As a starting place, consider what information the plaintiff may want to know in a matter involving an injury to an operator running an earthmoving machine:

- When was the machine designed?

- How many of them were made? During what production period?

- What is the history of accidents on the model in question?

- What is the history on similar models?

- What is the history of complaints on the model in question?

- What is the field and service history of the subject machine?

- Starting with the specific complaint of defect, what is the design history of that part or system?

- What alternate designs were considered?

- Why was the present design chosen? What was wrong with the other choices?

- Who made those choices? (You may start getting names, or you may be asked to give names.)

- What kind of testing was done on the model?

- Is that testing done on every machine made?

- Was it done on the subject machine in this incident? If not, why not?

- What testing <u>was</u> done on the subject machine?

- How were alternate designs evaluated?

- How do others do the same thing or design the same part or system?

- What standards, codes, laws, and industry practices are considered and followed in designing and developing the machine?

- ...and on and on.

However, the formal Interrogatory doesn't look like the list above. More likely it will look something like this:

INTERROGATORIES

In the matter of Plaintiff v Defendant Corporation,

Comes now, the Plaintiff, who, through his attorneys and Councilors propounds the following Interrogatories to the Defendant Corporation. These questions, under the appropriate rules of the court, are to be answered clearly and completely and correctly. Said answers are to be submitted through proper communications channels no later than 45 days after receipt of the Interrogatories.

Where information is requested, <u>all</u> information is meant. The proponent of the Interrogatories expects and demands the defendant make energetic and thorough effort to provide correct and complete answers. Information and information sources and depositories are to be thoroughly examined for information and answers requested.

(The preface to the Interrogatories may go on for several pages and include definitions and broad statements meant to make the questions as inclusive and complete as possible, and yet make the questions so they will obtain the desired information.)

INTERROGATORY I

Give full name and address of the person answering these Interrogatories. State that person's background and experience with the Defendant Corporation, and state his or her present position and responsibilities with the Corporation. Describe the answering person's knowledge and basis of knowledge regarding the machine and design involved. Certify that the answers given are based upon full and proper search for the information requested, and that the person is properly qualified and authorized to give such answers for the company.

INTERROGATORY II

State when and by whom the ABC machine, Model 234 was designed. Give the names and present addresses of all employees of the Defendant Corporation who were involved on or worked with the design of the ABC Machine, Model 234. Identify, from this list of persons, the ones who are most knowledgeable with the ABC Machine, Model 234. Further, identify system or component specialties of each person identified.

INTERROGATORY III

State when the ABC Machine, Model 234 was first put into production, how long it was in production, and how many were made and distributed. Further, describe in detail the distribution method of the product, listing the various stages and giving names and business addresses of the agencies or entities who are involved in the distribution process. These answers should be given both generally for the model and specifically for the subject machine in this matter of litigation—ABC Machine, Model 234, Serial Number 000567.

INTERROGATORY IV

List all complaints and accidents and other incidents in which the ABC Machine, Model 234 was involved. Indicate the nature of the complaint and the disposal or handling of the complaint. If the matter involved a lawsuit or other legal action, list the names and addresses of the courts involved and the names and addresses of the attorneys involved in the matters.

INTERROGATORY V

The plaintiff in this matter contends that a defect in the hydraulic system was a proximate cause of the injuries to him. Provide a complete schematic drawing and description of the hydraulic system of the ABC Machine, Model 234. Provide blueprints or other suitable plan information on all of the parts used in or affecting hydraulic system or the design and operation of that system. Certify that ABC Machine, Model 234, Serial Number 000567 is correctly described by the schematic drawing and the description of the hydraulic system.

INTERROGATORY VI

List alternate hydraulic system design features and details which were considered but not used on the ABC Machine, Model 234. State why the system or design feature was not used in the final design. Also state the rationale and logic for making the design of the hydraulic system in the subject machine as it was.

INTERROGATORY VII

List all of the complaints received concerning the ABC Machine, Model 234, including and especially separating out those complaints involving the hydraulic system of the subject machine. Complaints should include test reports, field reports, letters, service and warranty claims, and lawsuits filed involving the Model 234.

INTERROGATORY VIII

List those parts and components of the hydraulic system which are made by someone other than the manufacturer of the Model 234. Include a description of the part and the name and address of the supplier of each part so procured.

INTERROGATORY IX

Name the person or persons who are deemed to be most knowledgeable about the ABC Machine, Model 234. Also name the person or persons most knowledgeable about the hydraulic system of the subject machine. List the names of those considered most knowledgeable about the major components of the hydraulic system.

...and so forth.

And onto Requests for Production, a similar sample list:

REQUEST FOR PRODUCTION OF MATERIALS

made to the Defendant Corporation by the Plaintiff.

REQUEST TO PRODUCE NO. 1

Produce clear, readable copies of the drawings referred to in Interrogatory V. Further, provide specification sheets, advertising brochures, and other sales and distribution materials used in the distribution of ABC Machine, Model 234. Further, provide copies of specification sheets and sales brochures and literature for other models of similar machine made and distributed by the Defendant Corporation.

REQUEST TO PRODUCE NO 2.

Provide Counsel for the Plaintiff copies of Operator's Manuals, Owner's Manuals, Parts Books, Service and Technical Manuals, Maintenance Manuals, and any other similar publications that exist for the ABC Machine, Model 234.

REQUEST TO PRODUCE NO. 3

Produce copies of all complaints made to the Corporation concerning the hydraulic system of the ABC Machine, Model 234. Include customer letters, formal complaints, lawsuits, and claims for warranty.

REQUEST TO PRODUCE NO. 3

Produce any and all records dealing with the manufacture, inspection, test, and distribution and sales of the subject machine, ABC Machine, Model 234, Serial Number 000567.

REQUEST TO PRODUCE NO. 4

Produce copies of the complaints of any other lawsuits filed in the past 10 years involving the Model 234. Include claims and a complete listing of the venues of such lawsuits and give the names and addresses of the attorneys involved, both for the plaintiff and for the defendant in such cases.

REQUEST TO PRODUCE NO 5.

Please produce one sample each of the following part numbers representing parts used in the hydraulic system of the ABC Machine, Model 234.

...and so forth.

(The above Interrogatories and Requests for Production have been written as from the plaintiff, to illustrate the discoverable—or at least, the requested—information sought.)

Why does the plaintiff need all of this information? Simply, if he is to be successful in getting the plaintiff a recovery, he has to show these things:

- The plaintiff has incurred injuries or other economic loss.

- A feature or component or action of the machine caused the loss.

- That feature, in one of the legal theories allowed, was a proximate cause of the accident or the incident that resulted in the loss; that is, the accident wouldn't and couldn't have happened without that feature or characteristic of the machine.

- That feature amounts to a defect in the design or the manufacture of the machine as it existed at the time of the incident.

- The "defect" was in the machine at the time it left the hands of the manufacturer.

- There were alternate designs or features that would not have caused the accident or that would have prevented the accident.

- Those alternate designs would not have hurt the operation or usefulness of the machine.

- The alternate design was not prohibited by cost.

- The alternate design made a significant improvement in the overall safety of the machine.

And in short, the defendant is thus responsible for the injuries or loss to the plaintiff.

This is for starters, along with many lesser rules and requirements. Chain of ownership or chain of physical possession may be important. Service, maintenance, and prior use and applications may be relevant. Local law will certainly be a factor.

The attorney will know which of these is needed for him to present a strong case in support of his claims for the plaintiff. In effect, he begins to build up a little outline of these pieces of information and to fill them in. His outline of the case will usually change as information develops and as his opponent, the defendant, responds to discovery information.

The defendant attorney, likewise, will develop a response outline to the claims, He, too, will have an outline or list of pieces of information that he will want to fill in order to make what he expects will be a strong response and rebuttal to the plaintiff's claims. To successfully defend his defendant client, he will have to show one or more of the following things:

- the claims of the plaintiff are not valid,

- that the injury or loss did not happen,

- that the fault or "proximate cause" of the accident was not as the plaintiff claimed,

- that the fault for the accident lies elsewhere; that no defect existed on the subject machine or in the design,

- and, probably, that other claims of the plaintiff were not valid.

He will need to respond to the suggestions that another design or feature would have prevented the accident.

To do this successfully, he will need to know answers to questions such as:

- Exactly how did the accident happen?

- When and under what conditions did the accident happen?

- Who saw the incident?

- What did they say or report about the incident?

- What were the position and condition of the person before the accident?

- What were the position and condition of the person after the accident?

- What were the physical positions of machines and other people involved in the matter?

- Did the injured person or the operator have any physical or mental limitations?

- What was his education and training?

- What was his work experience?

- Had he previous illness or accidents? How? When? What was the result?

- Have there been any other problems or complaints concerning the machine?

- Who services the machine? How is it serviced?

- What is the work history of the machine?

- Who trained the operator?

- Who supervised the operator?

- Have there been any OSHA or other violations on the work site?

The question list on the Interrogatory will not be so simple, however, as you see from the earlier examples. As each set of questions or requests is made, there are responses. Depending upon the responses, other questions and requests may be made.

And, as the exchange of discovery paper continues between the plaintiff and the defendant, the questions and requests may get even more complex, but more focused on the real issues of the matter.

Three cautions are worth spelling out at this point:

First, watch out for words that are inflexible or infinite, such as:

- always

- never

- all

- none

- impossible

- absolute

- certainly.

Such words, when used in Interrogatories or Requests for Production, usually carry a hidden danger. For example, if you are asked if it is possible to do a certain thing, you probably should answer that "anything is possible, I suppose, but this is not likely," or "it is impractical." Such kinds of absolute words with precise meanings may need hedges built around them. They may need to be further defined and modified. In answering, watch that you do not use such infinite words, also. You may well hedge yourself in and find yourself trapped in later trial or deposition answers.

Second, don't be misled from the real and base issues of the matter.

An example:

An operator jumped off a machine that had burst into flames, leaving the machine in motion under power. After getting off, he observed the machine was heading for a group of fuel tanks. He tried to remount the machine, and in doing so, fell and was fatally run over by the tires of the machine. Claims were subsequently made that the machine was defective because it had caught fire. The defendant's response denied any defect involving the machine design so far as the fire was concerned. The defendant then countered by saying the operator had been killed not because of the fire, but because he tried to remount the machine, which is a dangerous thing to do and which is clearly warned against both by the manufacturer and by other industry and trade union materials and training. In defending the machine, the attorney and consulting expert concentrated upon the fire causes, when they should have more properly concentrated upon the attempt to remount the moving machine.

Third, watch out for the careless use of generic, vernacular, or idiomatic terms.

An example:

I once sent four people to examine a failed engine and report back to me what had happened. A person who just happened to be passing by at the time of the engine failure said it had "blown up." A technical secretary looked at the engine and said that the block had failed; there was a hole in the side. A young engineer looked more carefully and reported that it was obvious that a connecting rod had broken, and had punched a hole in the side of the engine. An experienced mechanic waited until he was able to inspect the connecting rod and the bearing, and he reported that a bearing failure had caused the lower end of the connecting rod to seize, and this caused the engine failure.

It is obvious, I believe, that incomplete answers can be wrong and misleading, and even dangerous. The earlier reports might have started work on the block, or the rod, or even toward looking for the cause of an explosion.

Now as you examine the development of the discovery process, you can see that things are beginning to overlap; both sides of the dispute need to know many of the same things. That is not a surprise. Nor is it a surprise to the court. The final result of the discovery process should be (according to the intent of the process) that each side will know what the other is going to say and present at trial. Ideally, there will be no surprises.

It is almost inevitable that there will be some surprises, however. To the extent that the attorney has not completely pursued his discovery activity, the other side may not have "given up" all of the information. They have not intentionally withheld it, mind you, but if no one asks, no one has to answer. Attorneys have developed the answering of interrogatories into an art form. The art form is limited only by the rules of the court and the decisions made by the judge.

For that reason, discovery activity on both sides will be intense and as complete as the attorneys can make it. Neither wants his client to lose the case because of careless or incomplete discovery information

How do surprises happen? First, as I have already suggested, some attorneys do not do a complete job of discovery, for one reason or another. Sometimes he may not ask a discovery question because he fears the answer will not be favorable to him. It seems illogical to prefer not knowing any answer to knowing a bad answer.

Further, in some instances, the late arrival of a witness or information may harbor surprises. Such late arrivals may have been legitimately lost, or they may have been unknown by anyone involved in the matter until late. (Note that if information is withheld until late, there may be claims of improper procedure and conduct.)

At trial, surprises may happen when a witness on the stand gives a surprise answer—surprising to either or both attorneys, and to the judge. If the surprise is too great, there may be a mistrial or other result, and there may be sanctions imposed on the one providing the surprise. Of course, if the opposing attorney merely forgot to ask, the surprise may be legitimate.

I have also seen a surprise followed by another surprise. An expert testified that he had done certain work on a similar machine and that the result was to prevent the accident under consideration. The testimony was a surprise, both to the opposing attorney and to his own client-attorney. A quick check by an investigator disclosed that the expert hadn't even been near the machine he testified about, and that he had done no work or testing on it at all. The second surprise blew the first one out of the water and destroyed the expert's testimony and credibility.

If you have to prepare answers to interrogatories, you can be sure that the questions will be penetrating, broad, deep, and seeking specific responses.

The responding party, through its attorney, may well make objections to some questions on a number of bases. They will try to respond truthfully and fully, if possible, without necessarily tipping off the other side to their own strategy.

This process then leads to (or at least toward) the point where both sides know the same things. In total, that should be what will be presented in court. Rules of various courts differ, but the process is generally the same.

A well-conducted discovery process will find all that is known about the case. It will do that in a logical process. Answers to Interrogatories will disclose names of people as well as information. Responses to Requests to Produce will provide information and perhaps more names. Depositions will provide information, possibly more names, and will also tend to show the plan and tactics of the opposition.

Each of these steps is followed and may be repeated until the attorney has filled in all the blanks he needs for his case, or until a judge-imposed time limit is reached.

A word about "fishing" is appropriate. Some defendant attorneys feel that the plaintiff may be "fishing," that is, he may not be sure of his case and is looking for ideas or information on which he can base a case. This is a matter of judicial discretion, generally. If the judge thinks the plaintiff is going too far, he will stop what is called "a fishing expedition."

On the other side, many plaintiffs' attorneys feel that defendants are holding out or refusing to give up information that is relevant to the case. In such a case, a judge may, at his discretion, order rather wide and sweeping disclosures by the defendant.

These situations, and the resolutions to objections of both sides, usually make the discovery process a tense and serious activity.

The Smoking Gun

A word or two should be said about the "smoking gun" concept. An attorney may feel that he has the absolute information or proof he needs, either to prosecute or to defend a case, when he comes upon a certain piece of information. He calls that information or evidence a "smoking gun."

The term came from criminal actions with such strong evidence as a gun still smoking in the defendant's hand at the scene of the murder. That seems to be strong proof, and it usually is.

Some examples of "smoking guns" in products liability litigation are these:

- A letter from a field serviceman says, "Fix this problem before we kill someone with it!"

- A letter in a marketing manager's file says, "Why should we spend $4,000,000 on this field upgrade when we have only one record of an accident involving this part?"

- A report in an engineer's file says, "We have two design choices, A and B. A is a little safer, but B costs much less. We will use B."

- A letter from a vice president to his chief engineer says, "I agree that your proposal would increase safety, perhaps by a significant amount, but the time schedule we are working on won't let us put the idea into production. Save it for two years from now, when we make the next update."

- An engineering memo reads, "I am not sure that adding this warning decal will do any good, but the attorneys say we should add it because it may help us avoid some lawsuits."

- One file in a group of files had a cover tag saying, "Don't look in here. You will probably not like what you see."

- A letter from an engineer in Germany says, "This is how we do this in Germany. You should make the basic design that way." The American engineer responds, "We don't like the German way here, so we are not going to change it."

- A report from the Cost Reduction Committee says, "Forget everything else for the next four months. Concentrate on cost reduction. If we don't, we won't make a profit."

- A note from the shipping floor says, "Ship it anyway; we need to get all of these off the floor and out the door by Friday."

All of these are smoking guns in the hands of an attorney who is trying to show your company is not as careful about safety as it should be. You need to make good record paper. Don't allow smoking gun kinds of comments to occur.

Sometimes what appears to be a smoking gun is not really one. When this happens, the explanation must be careful and open, so it doesn't appear that you are only making excuses.

For example:

A plaintiff is suing because he claims injuries which occurred when the axle on his earthmoving machine broke and the machine rolled over. During discovery, the attorney finds a change in the axle design changing the heat treatment in the area of the bearing race on the axle. He thinks he has his smoking gun, proving you had an axle problem that you had to fix, and that smoking gun was the specific problem that caused his client's injury.

The engineer for the manufacturer of the earthmover may show that the change in the axle was to lengthen the life of the bearing race. Further, the failure in the subject machine was not near the heat treated race, nor did it fail in a manner that related to the hardness or to any transition area around the hardened area. He has not, by doing this, proven that the failure was not the fault of the manufacturer, but he has wiped out the smoking gun as a potent piece of evidence.

It may be useful to play "what if" games with records. "What if this information were in the hands of an attorney suing us?" It just might be.

Review of General Discovery

Discovery is a proper part of the litigation process. The presentation of a case—plaintiff or defendant—requires information, and the law provides for the proper and orderly discovery of that information. Each side will want to know about the other side, and the final result intended is that both sides will know what is to be presented at the trial. In effect, then, each side will know the same things—their side and the other's side, too.

I have already discussed the general matter of Interrogatories. That is simply asking a question and expecting an answer. The opposition will respond in some fashion to the question. If the two parties do not agree that the question has been properly asked or properly answered, a judge settles the matter by a ruling, ordering one side or the other to ask or respond properly.

The legal details of Interrogatories and other discovery forms are the job of the attorney. You, as the engineer, may have to provide the information.

There are three other common forms of discovery: Requests for Production, Requests for Admissions, and Depositions. The last I will treat separately in a later chapter in this book.

Request for Production

Rather than ask thousands of questions, an attorney may file a Request for Production of Documents, and sometimes, may file requests for other physical things. By doing so, he may discover a mass of data and information, rather than the simple limited answer to one question. Usually the request asks for documents that have known groupings of information.

Typical documents requested are these:

For the plaintiff:

- operator's manuals,
- parts books,
- service and technical manuals,

119

- drawings, blueprints, and layouts,
- notices of memos with the drawings,
- letters,
- product information records,
- employee lists,
- organization charts,
- test information and data,
- warranty data,
- field complaints,
- information on other similar accidents,
- historical information of the company and the product,
- advertising brochures,
- specification sheets,
- policy statements and letters,
- design manuals,
- publications dealing with the subject or the product.

And for the defendant:

- medical histories,
- police or other accident reports,
- OSHA reports,
- maintenance records of the machine,
- bills of sale or lease papers,
- etc.

Both sides will ask for:

- witness statements,

- information about witnesses and potential witnesses,

- information about experts expected to testify,

- etc.

This list and the other discovery lists may be so long as to look unmanageable. However, I need to emphasize that the attorney may do all of this discovery. As a matter of practicality, he will actually do only that which serves his needs. Not every question is asked and not every request is made. We are discussing those things that may be discovered or are subject to discovery. The attorney may ask for answers, materials, and documents that are not really a part of his case; he may do so to conceal his real thrust in the matter. Likewise, the attorney may omit asking for information and documents when he already has the information by other means or from other sources.

Again, there may be arguments between attorneys about Requests for Production, but these arguments are settled by the judge.

Request for Admission

A request for admission, according to some authorities, is seldom used in products liability cases. I have experienced otherwise.

Several times I have seen Requests for Admission used to streamline the case presentation. If the one to whom the request is directed agrees or admits the statement, he has stipulated that the statement is true and it may be used without further proof. The information becomes evidence. If he denies the question, the opposing side then may not assume it to be true without showing further evidence or proof. If the one to whom the request is directed denies falsely, severe sanctions may be placed upon him; responses to formal requests are given under oath.

Examples of the Request to Admit, when they are used, look like these:

- Admit that your company designed and manufactured the subject machine.

- Admit that you were aware of other similar accidents prior to the date of this accident.

- Admit that Mr. (NAME) was the designer of the machine and that he still is employed by the corporation.

- Admit that you have a document retention policy that disposes of all engineering drawings and data not current each two years.

- Admit that you know operators do not read the operator's manual or pay attention to the warnings.

This is just a sample of the requests I have seen.

The proper response to such requests is either "Admit" or "Deny."

If one admits to a request for admission, he has totally and completely agreed to the statement propounded by the opposition as being true. If it is, fine. If any part of the statement is incorrect, deny the admission. Sometimes an explanation of the denial is appropriate.

An admission then becomes evidence that no longer needs to be proven or demonstrated by the opponent.

Depositions will be studied in the next chapter.

Chapter 9

THE DEPOSITION

The discovery process usually includes depositions, wherein the attorney for the opponent is allowed to question a witness under oath and before a court reporter, but outside the courtroom. The questioning is less formal than in the courtroom at trial, but the process of deposition is extremely important. A deposition may be rather accurately described as half-way between an informal conversation and a formal trial. The purposes of the deposition may be any or all of a number of reasons.

The engineer may be officially representing his employer, or he may have been brought into the case as a witness who may know something about the matter at hand, or he may be appearing as an expert witness, to offer opinions. All of these situations have differing requirements. It is imperative that the witness understand accurately what his role in the matter will be, and that he or she works closely with the attorney in any deposition.

General Comments on Depositions

Although I have pointed out that the deposition is a part of the discovery process in litigation, it is time to show that the deposition, along with other discovery activities formal and informal, also has other purposes. All of these purposes are directed at a successful end of the litigation activity. Ideally, that end is a just and equitable result for all parties involved. Cynics

123

may deny that this ever happens, but my experience indicates that it usually happens.

The deposition usually is conducted when the matter is getting closer to trial; at least chronologically, the deposition may tend to trail other forms of discovery. Because it is closer to trial, it tends to have more to do with trial strategy than the other forms of discovery. The chronological position of a deposition, however, is not fixed. A deposition may be taken very early in the litigation process if it serves the purposes of the attorney taking the deposition.

All of the discovery has a relationship to the trial, but because the deposition is a face-to-face contact between attorneys and witnesses—some of them for the first time—that direct contact takes on additional importance. Depositions have been referred to as mini-trials, and trial practices. They are, to some limited extent.

The deposition presents your first chance, as a witness, to deal directly with the opposing attorney. It will also be his first opportunity to deal directly with you, most likely. He will ask you questions and you will answer them, not unlike what you may do eventually in the courtroom. In that view, a deposition is good practice. Unlike most "practice" sessions, however, the deposition is deadly serious. Cases have been lost or irreparably damaged by things said and done in deposition. What you say in deposition is just as important as what you say in the courtroom.

It is important that you understand what your part is in the scheme of things your attorney is developing for his presentation in the case at hand. When you understand just how you are to be used, and what information you are to present, you can concentrate on those assignments, and be better prepared for your participation.

You need not concern yourself with the legal technicalities of the matter. If you are responding to fact questions, you need to be as certain as possible about those facts. If you are weak or unsure, you will be a good prospect for tough cross-examination. If you are dealing in opinions or other matters an expert deals with, you need to be sure of your opinions and of the bases for those opinions.

If you have no idea why you are called to be deposed, you need only to answer questions about which you have knowledge. You can say, "I don't know." That is a good answer if it is the truth.

Usually you will have been well prepared by your attorney and by having involvement in the litigation process and with the specific incident being litigated.

The Place of the Deposition in the Discovery Process

Consider the deposition as part of the discovery process. As discovery goes on, it becomes apparent to the opposing attorney that you, if you are going to be a witness or if you have had a part in the history of the machine at question, may have information that the opponent hasn't yet gotten. Assume, for this discussion, that such information is properly a subject for discovery— that is, the opponent has a proper right to discover that information because it has something to do with the case.

The opposing attorney then has an opportunity to depose you, or ask questions of you, face to face. As a matter of tactics, he may or may not choose to depose you. There are risks and downsides to depositions that he must consider.

One potential downside is that by talking to you, he may not only learn about you, but you may and should learn about him. You and your attorney may also learn about his plan of attack or presentation from the questions he asks you or the things he seems to be most interested in or concerned about. (There have been depositions that reaped no information for the attorney asking the questions, but which practically gave away the case for the questioner.)

Consider, for example, the plaintiff's attorney who believes the lack of an alarm on a machine is the cause of the accident under dispute. The initial claims in the case have stated clearly that the lack of that alarm is believed and claimed to have caused the accident, injuries, and losses. Further, the plaintiff claims that such an alarm should have and could have been easily provided by the defendant/manufacturer.

If the plaintiff's attorney suddenly asks questions dealing with the visibility from the operator's position in the machine, or if he begins to ask questions about brakes and steering of the machine, it becomes probable that he is changing his approach to the whole case. Now he seems to be dealing in possible visibility problems or in the controls and operation of the machine.

Usually, the attorney will have learned of names of people from the Answers to Interrogatories or from other disclosures. He needs to evaluate whether each named person can fill in blank spaces in his case with needed information or whether he might be the source of other names of as yet unknown information. Most depositions deal with other names.

Within the rules applicable to the court in which the litigation is pending, the attorney may discover any and all information that is relevant to the matter or which might lead to relevant information. A witness may not know the information, but he may know who does have the information or knowledge being sought. When the proper questions are asked, the witness at a deposition may need to disclose the names as he remembers or has knowledge of them.

I have, by order of these discussions, suggested that first comes the Interrogatories, then the Requests for Production of Documents, then the Requests for Admissions, and then the Deposition. This is a good order of these activities for explaining purposes, but in practice, the order may be mixed and intertwined in almost any way.

It is not unusual for the notice or subpoena for a deposition to require the deponent to bring documents with him. Sometimes a deposition is followed by interrogatories asking for answers to questions that have been newly raised as a result of the deposition. The order, the time, and the amount of these discovery activities are under the control of the local rules and the judge handling the case.

If your subpoena is a "Subpoena Duces Tecum," it instructs you what to bring to the Deposition with you, and requires that those items be produced. Requirements include such things as a resume or "Curriculum Vitae," a record of your writings, copies of items in your possession and bearing on the matter under litigation, copies of reference materials, and, of course, your file, notes, calculations, inspection reports, and other paper you may have pro-duced in the course of your work on the specific matter being tried.

General Rules for Deposition

Regardless of the reason for your deposition, there are some general rules that will help you. (This discussion does not replace specific instructions from your attorney. The general rules are from those repeated in most prepa-ration sessions with witnesses about to be deposed, and from some lawyer sources. They are common, with only a few specific and special exceptions.)

The general rules are these:

1. Listen to the question.

Make sure you hear it and understand it. If you do not listen to the question carefully, you cannot answer it properly. If you don't understand the ques-tion, say so. Ask for it to be repeated, or tell the attorney questioning you that you do not understand his question. He should offer to repeat or re-phrase the question.

Most attorneys start depositions by listing the rules. That listing may sound something like this:

"Mr. Witness, I am Mr. Attorney, representing Mr. Plaintiff in the lawsuit titled <u>Plaintiff v. Defendant Manufacturing Company</u>. The purpose of our meeting today is so that I can ask you certain questions about your involve-ment with the machine that is connected to the injuries my client has sus-tained. I have a legal right to do so. Your attorney will advise you when he feels that any of my questions are not appropriately asked.

"I will assume you have never been deposed before, and for our mutual help, I will briefly list some of the rules and guidelines we will follow.

"First, listen carefully to the question. If you do not understand the question or did not hear it clearly, or if the question confuses you in any way, ask me to restate the question. I will try very hard to state the question in a way that we both understand it. If you do not understand the question clearly, of course, you cannot answer it properly. Then we shall both be missing the real purpose of this deposition.

"Second, give me you best and most honest answer to the question. The court reporter is taking down what we say here, and this deposition record can be used later in court for certain purposes. For example, if you change your answer between now and the time of trial, I could use your answer in this deposition to show the jury that you changed your answer, or that you have given conflicting answers.

"Further, if you give me an answer, I will assume you properly heard and understood the question. You see, I want to make certain that you clearly heard and understood the question. Otherwise, I can not guarantee I have gotten the proper answer.

"Now, Mr. Witness, this court reporter is taking down everything we say. When we are finished, she will transcribe this deposition conversation. We will ask you to read it over, make any corrections on a special sheet, and sign the deposition, indicating that it is properly and correctly your testimony.

"You should not interrupt me when I am asking a question. In return, I will not interrupt you during your answer. You see, if we are not careful, the court reporter will have difficulty taking down our conversation correctly. If we both talk at the same time, her job becomes almost impossible. And we need a good and accurate record of this deposition.

"I want you to be comfortable during the deposition. If you need a break, just ask. I will gladly agree to one. If you need to discuss something outside with your attorney, ask for a break. If you need to refer to your notes, or to anything else, let me know, and we will take time for you to do that.

"We may come upon other matters as we proceed, but I think I have covered the main rules. Do you have any questions before we begin?"

Such a start to a deposition should assist you in understanding the process. If there are any special rules dealing with the matter at hand, or if there are special rules or procedures stated by the local court authority, these may also be explained.

That is a typical and courteous start to a deposition. You should listen to that start, as well as you listen carefully to questions.

If, during the deposition, you hear the deposing attorney say, "Thank you, Mr. Witness, for the information you have so kindly given me, but I would like to have you answer my question, which was...," you may have made two errors. One, you may not have listened to the question, and two, you may have given information and answers not asked for.

Listen to the question, and give a truthful and accurate answer—and no more. That is all you are asked to do.

2. Pause before you answer the question.

You should pause for three reasons:

First, you should make sure you are about to give the proper and true answer to the specific question asked. This need not take a long time, but a second or two will help you to frame better answers.

Second, if any one of the attorneys at the deposition has any objection to the question, he needs time to express that objection. If you answer too quickly, he cannot give timely objections. In addition, the court reporter is taking down both the question and the answer, and exchanges between the attorney and the witness that come too quickly can confuse the reporting of the deposition.

In addition, you will feel more like you are controlling the pace of the deposition. That may be important. Do not allow yourself to be hurried.

3. Answer only the question asked.

The deposition and discovery process are based on the assumption that the questioning attorney will ask questions for which he wishes answers. You are under no obligation to give him more information than he asks for. If he fails to ask some question, that is his problem.

To illustrate this to new deposition witnesses, one attorney plays this game:

He says, "Let's practice a little. I'll ask questions and you'll answer them."

Q: "Can you tell me what time it is?"

A: "Sure, it is 2:10 p.m."

The questioner responds, "Wrong, you didn't answer the question! I asked you a question that can be answered 'yes' or 'no' and you told me what time it is. Try it again, and listen to the question."

Q: "Can you tell me what time it is?"

A: "No."

Q: "Why not?"

A: "Because I do not know what time it is."

Q: "Well, you have a watch don't you?"

A: "Yes."

Q: "Well, if you looked at your watch you could tell me the time, couldn't you?"

A: "I believe I could."

Q: "Will you look at your watch and tell me what time it is?"

A: "Sure. According to my watch, it is 2:10 p.m."

This game gets a little extreme, but it illustrates the idea.

Answer the question and no more.

Q: "Do you have an opinion as to the cause of this accident?"

The correct answer is "Yes" or "No," and not the opinion. If the attorney wants the opinion, he will ask for it.

4. Answer truthfully and completely, to the best of your ability.

From time to time, I will repeat, "Be truthful." That is the most important rule of all. Regardless of whether you think the answer will help or hurt your effort or is good or bad, give a truthful answer. Any falsehood will damage your attorney's case and may well destroy your usefulness as a witness. Further, you will be in danger of criminal action and punishment for perjury.

You may be tempted to shade you answer, or slant it by distorting it a little, in order to help your client. Don't! You will hurt both of you. To say, "The glass is half full" may well be the identical answer as, "The glass is half empty." However, don't venture into shading the answer by claiming that a glass with a little in it is "partially full" or that a glass that is 98% full is "not full" or, worse yet, "partially empty." Such shaded answers do not look good to a judge or to a jury member to whom it may be later read.

5. Don't volunteer.

Often, there is a deafening and oppressive silence between your answer and the next question. Don't fill in the silence by adding information, or explaining your answer, or by any of the other things you think might help. They might help, but your job is not to make this determination. It is to answer questions.

Some questioners use the tactic of long pauses. Don't fall for it. They may even sit there and appear to be waiting for you. Let them wait. You are there to answer questions and if no question is pending, you don't have to speak. Suppress your urge to help educate the non-engineers in the room. I know you know, and they know you know, also. You do not have to educate them unless they ask the proper questions.

Sometimes open-ended questions will be asked, giving you the opportunity to answer at length. Answer only what is needed to answer the question truthfully and properly. Do not elaborate. (In certain special conditions, your attorney may instruct you to explain in detail. If so, follow his instructions. In my consulting experience, I once had an attorney tell me to lay my entire position and list of opinions on the table, complete with bases and explanations, even if I had to volunteer them. The reasons for this performance had to do with the fact that one side of the dispute knew that the case would never go to trial, and that my deposition was solely for purposes of providing material for the settlement conference scheduled two weeks later.)

Most depositions will be generally courteous if not openly friendly. Be careful not to get into general, apparently lighthearted conversations beyond the normal social courtesies. Be polite and businesslike. You don't have to be buddies with everyone in the room.

6. Don't argue or advocate.

In the legal system, the attorneys are advocates; each represents the interest of some client who has retained him. That is the nature of their work. You should not go beyond responding to questions with true answers. If there is any arguing to be done, leave it for the attorneys.

When you start to argue, or to represent some point too strongly, you lose your perspective and fall into saying things not required of you. The questioning attorney may even try to get you to do that. Don't get trapped.

You may, of course, have to advocate and argue your technical position with certain boundaries.

Example:

Q: "When driving, when do you believe is the proper time to put on headlights on your automobile?"

A: "From a half hour before sundown until a half hour after sunup, and at any other time the weather or other conditions hamper visibility."

Q: "That sounds like too much light time. Why do you need to put the lights on <u>before</u> it gets dark, or after the sun rises?"

A: "There are two good reasons. First, to make sure you have them on <u>when</u> the sun is down. Second, the terrain may not be level, and the sun may seem to have gone down at one point in the road and to still be up on top of the next hill. By putting the lights on a half hour before sundown, any terrain variations are likely to be covered. Also, people seem to forget that lights will make them more visible to the other driver in marginal visibility situations. You have seen signs ahead of tunnels and before industrial foggy areas warning the driver to put on his lights."

The opposing attorney may thrive on the situation where you do not have, or seem not to have, a good reason or explanation for your position or answer.

Above all of these general rules, follow the instructions and the lead of the attorney for whom you are working. Do what he says, and if you or your attorney do not agree with my suggestions in this book, still do what he says. If you don't, you will certainly be blamed for some troubles.

The Reasons for Depositions

At the start of this chapter, I claimed there were several different reasons for a deposition to be taken. Sometimes the reasons overlap and interlock.

I have experienced only two depositions which I believe were single scope depositions. One involved a major fire. I had taken to the fire a roll of film with a new camera and a new zoom lens to try out the camera. The pictures proved to be good, and some were useful for information. I gave prints to the facility director of the buildings that had burnt. My deposition was taken only to determine, as far as I could tell, why I had taken those pictures. In the attempt to place blame for the fire, the litigants were seeking to know whether I had any reason—other than curiosity—for taking the photos.

The other single purpose deposition was to ask one question. "How do you think the subject accident happened?" At the end of my description of the accident scenario, the matter was settled.

Seldom is a deposition so simple that it deals with only one reason. Although they may intertwine, I will discuss the reasons separately for easier explanation. You will see, in your deposition, that the reasons intertwine, but that they are specific and for single specific purposes.

First is the purpose of Discovery.

I have already discussed this purpose and objective—simply for the purpose of gaining information. Facts and data that you have may well be proper targets for the deposing attorney. He has the right to ask you such questions, and he has the right to truthful answers.

Throughout the deposition you will hear questions that are aimed primarily or entirely for the purpose of discovering or obtaining information.

Second, depositions are taken to establish facts and to determine the origins of and bases for those facts.

Part of this reason deals with the process of discovery uncovering other discovery avenues. Those avenues may be names of other people or the existence of records and information banks of which you may know.

Information is the substance from which good cases and good case presentations are made. The attorney must have all of the information relevant to his case both good and bad. Without all of it, he may have holes in his argument and blank spots in his logic.

Further, the attorney needs to know the sources of information and the bases for opinions. He may, in rebuttal to your testimony, want to use the source or the basis of the information to refute your testimony, if he can.

If you have truthful information and sound opinions, based on sound sources and good reasoning, the testimony is more likely to be effective and to withstand any cross-examination attacks. Therefore, he uses the deposition to gain information and to seek sources of additional information.

Third, the attorney uses the deposition to determine the opinions an expert witness may offer at trial, and to explore the bases for those opinions.

Here, I will distinguish the "expert witness." Such a witness is considered expert by education, training and experience, and his ability and qualifications to offer testimony in some area (usually technical) not normally understood by a lay person. (Engineering, designing, testing, developing, and applying earthmoving and construction machinery is one of many such broad fields.) By law, and under the rules of most courts, an expert is allowed to offer opinions when such testimony will help the court and the jury understand the technical matters in the case.

This matter of offering opinions is unique and important. Generally, a lay person may testify only about what he has seen or otherwise sensed first-hand. He may not usually give his opinion. Because expert witnesses are allowed to give opinions, it is important for the deposing attorney to learn of those opinions and to explore the bases of those opinions.

Courts are quite liberal in allowing the qualification of an expert. If he simply knows more about the technical subject than the common citizen, he may possibly be qualified as an expert. This leads to comparisons between two opposing experts. The jury is allowed to consider the background and the credibility of the expert in deciding whether to accept all, or part, or none of his testimony. The deposing attorney will, therefore, explore the background and professional competence of the expert at depth, as well as his or her opinions and the origins and sources off those opinions.

A judge once ruled that I would not be allowed to testify as an expert in a lawsuit between a garage builder and the operator of a small trencher. The entire dispute centered around whether the operator should have shut down the machine before the two of them worked on some obstruction near it or the garage builder should have known not to work around the machine while it was still running. The court ruled that an expert was not needed to explain that matter to a jury; the lay juror supposedly could understand that question without the help of an engineer. That was probably a good ruling.

Fourth, the attorney will be seeking information and bases to impeach the witness, if such opportunity exists.

Assume the information and opinions the witness offers are damaging to the case of the questioner. He will want to use the allowed and appropriate steps to discredit or "impeach" the witness. This will be discussed at more length when I discuss cross-examination. There are proper ways to discredit a witness. One is by showing conflict between what he says in court and what he has said in the deposition. Another is to show obvious errors and discrepancies in the testimony of the witness. Still another is to show bias by the witness, in favor of his client.

In the case of the expert witness, the opposing attorney may show discrepancies between the testimony of the witness and of prior writings or statements of the witness or with "learned treatises" on the subject. Any and all of these things may be examined in the deposition. Any bias or vested interest of the witness in the matter at hand may also be a subject of examination for the possible use in impeaching the witness at trial.

If your deposition or trial testimony hurts your opponent, you can expect him to try to hit you back.

Fifth, the deposition may be used to pin down testimony, so it may not be changed at trial.

The trial is a search for the truth. The deposition is a part of that search. In a situation where uncertainty exists, it is important to limit that uncertainty as much as possible. By "pinning down" the witness at deposition, the attorney has pinned down the testimony so it is unlikely or less likely to change at trial.

For example, a witness may say that he has never seen or known of an operator being killed in a roll-over when the machine he was on was properly equipped with roll over protection equipment and a seat belt, and those devices were properly used. When he so testifies at deposition, he will certainly be questioned further:

Q: "How many rollovers have you seen?"

A: "Perhaps a dozen or so."

Q: "Can you tell me when you saw them, and the circumstances under which you saw them?"

A: "Yes, sir, I can."

Q: "Will you please do so?"

A: "Well first, I rolled over a scraper at our proving ground in Texas and burned it up. I was essentially unscratched. Second, I experienced some six or seven intentional roll-overs during test procedures. Third, I saw a crawler tractor operating at the side of a highway roll into a ditch while it was moving laterally on the side of the ditch. I also recall seeing a motor grader on a side hill roll onto its side while trimming the hill. I also saw at least three machine accidents involving roll-overs shortly after they happened."

Q: "Now, Mr. Witness, did you actually see all of these roll-overs?"

A: "Yes, except for the three accident site situations I mentioned."

Q: "Did you actually see your own machine roll over—the one you were driving? How did you see that one?"

A: "Yes, I did see it—from the inside of the machine. Later, I had a good look at the machine from the outside." (This is obviously not a piece of information to attack in cross-examination.)

Q: "Did you actually see the six or seven test roll-overs you talked about?"

A: "Yes I did, and maybe more that I have forgotten about."

Q: "Did those machines have live operators in them?" (A good question! Most test people do not crash or roll machines over with live operators in them.)

A: "No, they did not. Some of them had dummies in the operator's seat, however." (Caught, and with only a weak response. This is the kind of cross-examination fodder the attorney seeks. Now he has at least six or seven roll-overs where no operator was involved. He can argue with some effect that these are not good proof.)

Q: "So these six or seven roll-overs didn't have operators, did they?"

A: "No, sir."

Q: "Therefore, you don't know whether the operators would have been killed, do you?"

A: "I do not know, but I have a good idea." (The questioner has to ask about that idea. It may bite him later on if he doesn't.)

Q: "What is your idea, and on what do you base it?"

A: "My idea is that the operator, if he had been in the machine when it rolled, would not have been killed, providing he had his seat belt properly fastened. I base that statement on three things. First, all but one of the machines was driven away after the test roll-over. The engine and the transmission were not rendered inoperable in the test. Second, slow motion video pictures of the action of the dummy in the operator's seat gives evidence that the operator would not have been killed or even seriously injured. And third, I am right back to my original statement: I know of no fatalities that happened when a machine rolled over and when that machine was equipped with proper ROPS and seat belts."

Q: "OK, that gets us to the next question area. What do you know about roll-overs in the field, on construction and road jobs? How many roll-overs do you know of that had no fatalities, and how did you gain that knowledge?"

A: "I have reports of over 450 roll-overs made during the past year involving machinery manufactured by my own employer. None of them involved a fatality. Further, I have surveyed industry sources and safety statistics and found no record nor knowledge of a roll-over where the ROPS was properly installed and the seat belt used and the operator was fatally injured. Further, I assume that many other roll-overs were not reported because no injury or damage was done."

Q: "I don't have any interest in what you assume, Mr. Witness. Let's go on to something else."

You see, it is important to have good sources and bases for your information and opinions. The opposing attorney will certainly dig into them—especially if the information or opinion hurts his client's case.

Where a witness has testified to something in deposition that is detrimental to his own side of the case, the questioning attorney will want to freeze that testimony as much as he can, so the witness cannot change it or squirm out of it or explain it away. The witness in the above example will probably not stress the six or seven test roll-overs, even though he might explain them and his reason for depending on them to a jury.

The need to pin down testimony so it cannot be changed should be of little concern to the engineer. He should be always telling the truth. If he is mistaken, he should admit it. If something changes, he should say so, and describe the change and explain it. Juries dislike apparent dishonesty; they generally approve of forthrightness.

Sixth (and related to number five), the deposition is used to preserve testimony for trial.

In the event the witness cannot, for some reason, appear at trial and testify live, the deposition will preserve the testimony and it usually can be used at trial just as if the witness were there. Reading a deposition to a jury is boring for everyone involved, and especially for the jury. It is not a good idea, but there are situations in which it is the only way to enter evidence and testimony that may be important to the case.

On occasion, the deposition is videotaped for exactly that reason. Business schedules, the health of the witness, and other reasons may lead the attorney to videotape the deposition for use at trial, thus relieving the witness from the requirement to be there in person. In such instances, the videotaped testimony is presented at trial just as if the witness were there.

There is a growing trend toward videotaping depositions, both for purpose of preserving testimony and for assisting or replacing the court reporter. The same idea is being tested in some courts for the purpose of reducing the work the court reporter needs to do. There are those who feel that a videotaped trial retains more of the real feeling and character of the trial for possible use in appeal than does the reading of mere words. What you see and what you hear together are thought to give a better and more accurate record than just what is heard.

As technology progresses, you may see new methods of recording depositions and trials.

Last, the attorney may use the deposition as a means of learning the plans or strategy of his or her opponent.

This is a double-edged sword—you may learn about the opponent and, at the same time, he may learn your strategy, too. Attorneys are keenly aware of this purpose, and may choose to depose or not to depose, depending on how they view this possible exchange of strategies. They will almost certainly ask or not ask certain questions of the deponent, depending on whether they feel the are gaining more or less information from the answer than the opponent will gain from the question.

You need not be concerned about this purpose except to recognize that there may be strategic reasons why the attorney asks or does not ask you certain questions. You may have even discussed or expected certain questions. Don't worry if they aren't asked.

For this specific reason, your own attorney will seldom ask you any questions at your deposition. Unless something is in dire need of clearing up, to prevent some misunderstanding or misuse of the deposition, your own attorney will probably say, "No further questions."

The Corporate Representative

If you work for a corporation that is a defendant in a lawsuit, and if you are deposed, it may be that you are appearing as a corporate representative as what attorneys call a 30(b)(6) witness. The Federal Rules of Civil Procedure, and many state rules, allow the plaintiff to ask for someone to be designated by the corporation to speak for the corporation, someone who is knowledgeable about the subjects at issue. The court may not let the plaintiff depose every corporate officer, but it will demand of the corporation that it provide someone knowledgeable and qualified to give answers that speak officially for the corporation and that bind the corporation.

If you are in such a position, you will be carefully prepared by your counsel for this deposition. A notice of such deposition usually lists in some detail the subjects that will be covered in the questioning. As a 30(b)(6) witness, the rules are not different from any other deposition—listen, understand, answer only the question, don't volunteer, and be truthful. The rules allow for these depositions, and if you fudge or are hesitant or refuse to give information, the result can be bad. On the other side of the coin, if you talk too much, that is also bad.

You may also be subpoenaed on a follow-up deposition to give further information. An earlier 30(b)(6) witness may have answered a question by saying that you are the one most closely connected to a certain type of information or to a certain technology. Perhaps your name showed up on a drawing or in a test document that was produced in response to a request. In such a case, your deposition will probably be limited to that subject, although it need not necessarily be so limited. Again, the rules continue to be the same, with truthful answers being the most important factor.

In any and all of these situations, keep in mind that the opponent has certain defined rights to the information he is seeking. Your attorney-counselor will guide you.

The Fact Witness

If you are called and are being deposed as a fact witness, the questioning will concentrate on the areas of those facts—what the facts are, how you know those facts, and whatever background material the questioner might ask.

An engineer may be called as a fact witness. One engineer was called several years after he had inspected a machine and a site of an accident. He no longer had any connection with the parties in the case, but he did have "fact evidence" from his inspection. He was required, on his own time and effort and at his own expense, to respond to a subpoena and to be deposed concerning his knowledge of the case.

You may have seen an accident. Your involvement, then, is obvious. You are an eyewitness, at least to that part of the accident which you saw or heard. You are probably only a fact witness, and that may be important to one or both parties involved. Depending on your expertise, you may be an expert witness, also.

141

You may have firsthand knowledge or involvement with a part, a design, or a test involving the product. As such, you may be called as a fact witness. If you are the designer, you may be asked to explain the design, and how you arrived at it. You may be asked what else you considered, and why you chose this particular design. Such questions seem to get into both fact and opinion testimony. In any of these situations, your attorney will guide and prepare you for the deposition.

The rule is still truth.

The Expert Witness

As a technical person with certain expertise, you may have involvement as an expert witness—that is, you may be asked to offer opinions based on your expertise. The deposition of an expert is somewhat different from the deposition of a fact witness or a party to the matter. Remember, the expert witness may offer opinions, while the lay witness generally cannot. In the position of an expert witness, you will probably have been retained or hired by the attorney for one side or the other.

The expert's opinions and the bases of those opinions will be the major interest of the deposing attorney. He will ask for the opinions and may question in detail the reasons for those opinions and the technical basis of each opinion.

Also, whether you are the plaintiff's expert or the defendant's expert will make some differences. I will treat the two separately, although most basic rules and advice are the same for both.

The Plaintiff's Expert

If you are an expert for the plaintiff, you will be aware of the claims made by the plaintiff. You will also be aware of the scenario of the incident as described by the plaintiff. You will probably have inspected the accident site and the machinery involved, so you have knowledge as complete as possible about the incident and the people and equipment involved.

Specifically, you will be expected to offer opinions concerning defects or other inadequacies, and their relationships to the accident. You may have helped the plaintiff and his attorney develop the theory of the incident, and the specific claims put forward in the Complaint. You would have done that early in your involvement, perhaps as a consultant, even before you were designated to be an expert witness in the case.

Further, you will probably have proposed alternate designs or features that would have prevented the accident or reduced the injury. These are the subjects that will be explored at your deposition.

You will be asked to state your opinions, and the questioning attorney will ask you to be specific and definite. You may be asked to list your opinions in summary. Make sure they are your opinions and that the deposing attorney has not misstated them or distorted them in any way.

Even more intensive will be the questions about the basis of your opinion. You will hear the single word question, "Why?" often in such depositions. The questioner will be seeking to understand why you believe what you do, and he will seek to find whether your opinions are well-founded and solid. If the opinion is contrary to his client, of course, he will look for ways to lessen the impact of your opinion at trial, or to destroy or discredit the opinion.

He will want to know what you were told, what you read, what you inspected, what you already knew, what you found out, and where you found it. He is likely to ask when you did all of these things and when you acquired the information on which you base your opinions. He will certainly ask when you arrived at your conclusions. Your opinions need to be sure, and the bases of those opinions need to be solid if you are to be effective and successful. Further, the deposing attorney will look into other things. (I will later discuss cross-examination at trial, but he is looking for ways to discredit you.)

He will look in detail at your education and work history. Sometimes an attorney will spend hours on your resume alone. He will determine whether you indeed have the expertise you claim. At the least, he will want to compare your experience, education, and expertise with those of his own expert. He will look at your work assignments and your job movements. He will look at your continuing education and at your involvement with technical and industry societies.

He will be particularly interested in your publications. Most engineers have excerpts from their publications read back to them at one time or another.

The deposing attorney may even be interested in your hobbies and pastimes. I have seen attorneys accuse experts, at trial, of having so many hobbies and pastimes that they could not possibly have time to do the professional work they claim to do.

The Defendant's Expert

The same general rules and conditions apply, whether the expert is consulting for the plaintiff or for the defendant. The two, however, have differing objectives. The plaintiff's consulting expert is going to testify about defects and how those defects caused the accident or loss to the plaintiff. Further, he will suggest what alternate designs or features would have prevented the accident.

The defendant's consultant, on the other hand, will be trying to show that his client's machine is not defective or that his client was in no way responsible for the accident or loss. Further, he will have to deal with the alternate designs or ideas suggested by the plaintiff's expert as a prevention to the subject accident.

Each, the plaintiff's expert and the defendant's expert, will be offering technical and factual information to support their individual opinions and testimony. In deposing the defendant's expert, the plaintiff's attorney will probably dig deeply into the reasons why the expert disagrees or differs in opinion from his own expert. He will ask questions as if he thought you were sandbagging him.

To complete the defense story, the defending expert will probably have to give his opinion as to who or what caused the accident, if the defendant did not cause it. In a way, each side is trying to show what caused the accident. The plaintiff blames the defendant, and the defendant will counter with his own belief as to the cause and the responsible party. To prove one cause was not possible or did not occur in the subject case, and to not offer what you really believe caused the incident, is to leave the work partially complete. Juries do not react well to that.

It seems to me, using engineering logic, that if you have proven that the accident could not possibly have happened as the plaintiff claimed, then you have proven the defendant is not responsible for the incident. However, the credibility of that defense is not highly effective with juries. They would like to know what was the cause of the incident. Then they will decide who is responsible. If you cannot show a cause or an accident scenario with a good degree of certainty, you probably do not have a good story for the jury.

The questioner will, of course, seek information with which to discredit your testimony. A retired employee will be asked about his pension, his stock in the company, and any other income from the company. A full-time consultant will be asked how may cases he has done for the company or for the law firm, and he will be asked about his charges, his earnings, and other things that may attempt to brand him as a "hired gun."

Again you see the importance of credibility before a jury. If an attorney cannot attack your opinion or the bases for those opinions at trial, he may well attack your credibility, by whatever proper means he can obtain. I once saw an expert come apart on the stand when the cross-examining attorney reminded him that he had once been arrested for beating his former wife while he was under the influence of alcohol. The beating incident had nothing to do with his testimony about the case, but the domestic incident and the witness' reaction to questions about it did nothing to help his credibility.

In all of these matters, follow the guidance of your attorney.

After the Deposition

When the questioning of the deposition is complete, you may not be quite through. In most cases, the deposition transcript, once it has been completed, needs to be read by you and signed. You have an opportunity to make corrections to the transcript but, generally, not to change your answers. If you do substantially change you answers, you had better be ready to clearly explain why you changed the answer. Such changes may weaken your trial presentation. The deposition may have important use and value later in the litigation process.

Also, if your file or portions of it, or any other item in your possession, has been marked as an exhibit to your deposition, and if you have maintained possession of it, you have an obligation to maintain that material just as it was at the time of deposition. You may refer to the material, and you may even copy it, but you cannot change it.

Summary

If you are deposed, there are a few short rules that will make the process go well for you.

1. Always be truthful.

2. Follow the guidance of your attorney. Litigation is part of a lawyer's game, not an engineer's game.

3. Pause; take your time. This is not a time trial or a race.

4. Don't volunteer.

5. If you don't know or don't recall, say so. Those are good and truthful answers.

6. Remember, you are the expert on the technical subject being dealt with, or you have information the attorney needs. In effect, you are an important part of the deposition. Otherwise, they wouldn't depose you.

Chapter 10

THE TRIAL

Testimony at trial can be awesome. It is the end of the process, where a decision will be made by the court—the judge and the jury. Trials frighten most people and most engineers. They are serious. In fact, the entire justice system is a matter of profound importance. However, the engineer need not be intimidated by a requirement that he testify at trial. Some very specific rules and advice will assist him in doing so properly.

The Purpose of the Trial

The trial is the high point of the litigation process. At this time, the parties to the case have reached a situation where they agree that they cannot agree on a suitable resolution to the matter. They have then decided to submit their claims, contentions, arguments, and beliefs to a court—probably including a jury—with the expectation that the court will arrive at a proper resolution of the matter. They agree in principle to accept the final decision of the court. (They may, of course, appeal and quarrel for months or years, but in the end, the final court decision is binding to them.)

In some ways, a trial has already been in progress. The Interrogatories, the various Requests, Depositions, inspections, and all of the pre-trial activities are, in reality, the early beginnings of the trial. The trial doesn't happen before those things are reasonably well concluded. A trial can't properly be conducted until the pre-trial activities are over; to conduct a trial without the proper preparations would be a waste of time and money.

At time of trial, the preliminaries have been completed. So far as is possible, each side has collected the information it needs. Each side is ready to present its case to convince the court why its position is correct. Each side has, or should have, a good idea of the information and the strategy the other side is going to use. Ideally, there should be no surprises presented at the trial.

Further, certain pre-trial activities will have taken place, following the rules and procedures of the court. You will hear of pre-trial orders, Motions in Limine, and other legal-sounding terms. You need not concern yourself about them, with one exception—"Motions in Limine." Each side, having exchanged trial exhibits, and other details of what they will be presenting, may argue to have certain testimony or certain exhibits prohibited at trial. The reasons are technical legal reasons, but you need to be aware of any such exclusions that are granted.

For example, your attorney may argue that evidence about another accident should be excluded on a basis of irrelevancy. If it is excluded, you need to be sure that you do not speak of that accident when you are testifying. If your side has successfully argued for the exclusion, you do not want to "spill the beans," or to say it in lawyer language, "open the door on the subject."

Likewise, if your opponent has argued for and been given some exclusion, you must not speak of it. To do so would seriously damage the proceeding, and one could be subject to sanctions from the court for doing so. Further, mentioning a subject that has been excluded by the court in a Motion in Limine may well cause a mistrial. Judges and attorneys do not like that. Your attorney will guide you about such matters.

The Trial Process

Trials are guided by rules and procedures set up by the court and for the conduct of the court processes. Courts in one jurisdiction may do things in ways different from others. Federal Courts differ from state or lesser courts. However, the processes are generally close enough to be described in a single format.

The trial steps will be these:

Picking a Jury

If the trial is to be a jury trial, the choosing of a jury will follow court procedures. A jury usually is six or twelve people. There may be alternates. Jurors are chosen from a jury venue (the potential jurors for that court period) by a process that intends to obtain an unbiased and balanced jury, capable of making the determinations necessary to resolve the case. When the selection process is complete the jury for this case will be impaneled, or officially assigned the responsibility for deciding matters of fact in the case.

Opening Statements

Following a few introductory remarks usually given by the judge to show the jury what its job is to be and to introduce the case and its participants, the trial is under way.

It begins with each side presenting "opening statements." The plaintiff's attorney is usually first, followed by the defendant's attorney.

Opening statements give each attorney an opportunity to tell the jurors what the case is all about, from his client's view. The plaintiff's attorney will tell the jury what the incident was, how it happened, and what happened as a result that caused his client's loss or injury. He will tell the jury what the plaintiff contends is the cause of the loss (the defendant, of course), why the defendant is responsible, and why he should pay the plaintiff for the loss incurred. If an injury is involved, he will describe the injury and the resulting effects on his client.

Example:

"Ladies and Gentlemen of the jury, I am the attorney representing Mr. Plaintiff in this case. Mr. Plaintiff was a machine operator for the XYZ Construction Company. He ran a bulldozer 10 hours a day, 6 days a week for XYZ and had done so regularly every week, for nearly 20 years. He made his living that way, providing a home and a good life for his wife and his three children. Mr. Plaintiff was a good worker, and still wants to be. But he can't anymore.

149

"Last March, while he was on his job running the dozer for XYZ, a fellow worker ran up to his machine and got his attention. When he stopped, the fellow worker asked him to bring the dozer over to another part of the job site to hook onto a motor grader which was stuck, and to pull it out.

"Mr. Plaintiff went over there. He backed up to the front of the motor grader and waited while the co-workers tried to hook up the chain to the grader. When he looked back, he saw that the workers had placed the chain over a steering cylinder of the grader, not a good place from which to pull the grader.

"Mr. Plaintiff got off his dozer and went back to help hook the chain properly. While he was behind the dozer and between the dozer and the motor grader, the dozer suddenly, and without warning, moved backward crushing Mr. Plaintiff between the dozer and the motor grader. That incident, in a few seconds, took away all possibility that Mr. Plaintiff could continue to support his family. He lost both legs!

"You will hear that the bulldozer was designed and manufactured by the MFG Corporation. We believe, and will show you proof, that the MFG Corporation is responsible and liable for the horrible accident and the injuries to Mr. Plaintiff.

"We will show that the motion of the dozer which caused Mr. Plaintiff's injuries came because of a defect in the design of the machine. In fact, we will show there were three defects:

- defective brake designs,

- a lack of warnings that the machine could move unexpectedly, and,

- the lack of an interlock between the seat and the brake, which would have prevented Mr. Plaintiff's injuries.

"We will have an expert design engineer appear before you in this courtroom. He will describe how the accident happened, from an equipment perspective. He will also show you the simple design changes which would have prevented this injury.

150

"The plaintiff himself will tell you that he had no indication or warning that the machine could possibly move unexpectedly the way it did. He will also show you his injuries and tell you of the pain and worry it has caused him, and will cause him for the rest of his life.

"When our presentation and testimony are completed, you will see, ladies and gentlemen of the jury, that Mr. Plaintiff has been grievously injured and that those injuries and the attendant losses were the responsibility of MFG Corporation, the company that manufactured the machine by which he was injured."

The defendant's attorney, in his opening statement, will tell the jury why the defendant does not agree with the plaintiff, and what the defendant believes about the case. He will tell what he believes to be the cause of the loss or injury, differing from the plaintiff's theory. He may or may not contest the injury, if one exists, and he may comment upon the long-term expectations of that injury.

Continuing the example:

"Ladies and Gentlemen, I represent the MFG Corporation, which designed and manufactured the dozer owned by the XYZ Construction Company and which was being used by Mr. Plaintiff at the time of the unfortunate incident when he was injured.

"Mr. Plaintiff has sued the MFG Corporation claiming that certain defects in the bulldozer he was operating were the cause of his injuries, and that the MFG Corporation should be held responsible for the incident and for Mr. Plaintiff's injuries and losses. We do not agree.

"We do not contest that Mr. Plaintiff was severely injured, or that he now has problems supporting his family. We all agree that the accident has tragic results. We understand and have great empathy with the problems Mr. Plaintiff has and will continue to have.

"We do not agree, however, that any defect on the bulldozer was the cause of Mr. Plaintiff's injuries. (Here is the location of the dispute—the cause of the accident, and not whether the accident happened or whether anyone suffered a loss as a result of the accident. It does little good to suggest the accident didn't happen or that the injuries are not as serious as claimed unless that contention is provable by competent medical authority.)

"We are proud of the reputation the MFG bulldozer has made for itself, including its safety record. The chief designer of the dozer will come here to this courtroom to tell you about the machine, its brakes, other design features, and its record of safe operation. He will tell you the inside story of the development and testing of the machine. He will explain why the machine has the design features it has, and how those features make it a safe machine.

"A consulting expert will tell you about other dozers and brakes, and why the brakes on the MFG machine are the best in the industry. That expert was the chief engineer of a competitor of the MFG company. That same consulting expert will also tell you why the design suggestions of the plaintiff's expert would not have worked on the subject dozer, or on any dozer. He will consider each of the plaintiff's recommendations, one at a time, and show you why the ideas were not good ones. Some of them, he will tell you, wouldn't even work. They had been tried. Other suggestions, he will demonstrate, would not have prevented the accident that happened to Mr. Plaintiff.

"Further, an expert in accident reconstruction will appear, testifying that the incident in which Mr. Plaintiff was injured didn't happen exactly as the witnesses described it. He will show you why it was physically impossible. Further, he will show you the most likely way the incident did happen. Still further, he will show you _how_ he concluded that the cause of the incident was Mr. Plaintiff's failure to properly apply the parking brake on the machine before he dismounted to help hook the chain to the motor grader."

In their opening statements, each attorney will tell the jury what evidence he will present, what witnesses he will present, what the jury can expect to hear from that witness, and what the total evidence presented will mean. In brief, he tells the jury what they are going to see and hear in his part of the case.

Plaintiff Presents his Case

Following opening statements by each side, the plaintiff presents his case. Presentation of the case includes presentation of witnesses, evidence, and other information with which the plaintiff hopes to convince the jury that his client is right and should prevail in the case.

The plaintiff's attorney will almost certainly know ahead of time what witness he is going to present and what evidence he will offer. He will have planned his presentation so as to clearly and completely tell the jury his client's story. He will systematically present that evidence so he has a complete package to review with the jury in his final argument.

As the plaintiff presents his case, the defendant's attorney will be allowed to ask additional questions of the plaintiff's witnesses in what is called "cross-examination." Further, there may be objections and conferences at the side of the judge's bench during the testimony. There may also be presentations from depositions, either by videotape or by "reading into the record" parts of depositions. The attorney for the plaintiff may also read into the record, as evidence, admissions made by the defendant; these are shortcut ways to complete some of the evidence without having a witness on the stand to present it.

In the plaintiff's case, there will likely be all or most of the following pieces of evidence:

- A story of the accident as the plaintiff sees it,

- Medical proof of the costs and the suffering involved in the injury,

- Other proofs of the losses involved,

- Lay witness testimony verifying the story or scenario of the accident,

- Expert witness testimony as to the claimed cause of the accident,

- Expert witness testimony as to the defect or dangerous condition which caused the accident,

- Testimony as to what features or design conditions would have prevented the subject accident,

- Testimony as to the cost of the accident to the plaintiff, including medical costs, lost wages, lost earning ability, and any other element of damages allowed in the particular jurisdiction,

153

- Evidence that the defendant knew, or should have known, about the defect, lack, or dangerous condition, and

- A tying of all of the evidence into a package that suggests the defendant is responsible for the accident and therefore liable for the costs of the injury and damage.

When the plaintiff attorney has completed his presentation, he "rests." In effect, he says to the jury, "This is the case for my plaintiff-client."

Defense Presents his Case

Next, the defendant's attorney presents his case. He also follows a plan, intended to present the defendant's story and position in such a way as to convince the jury that they, not the plaintiff, have the correct position and that the jury should find in the favor of the defendant. He, too, will present witnesses and evidence. The plaintiff's attorney will also have the opportunity to cross-examine the defendant's witnesses.

In short, the defendant presents his refutation of the plaintiff's claims, and offers information to support those positions. Among the things the defending attorney will present are some or all of these things:

- Testimony about the machine, its design and background,

- Testimony about the manufacturer and his activities in the matter of safety,

- Testimony of witnesses to the incident which do not agree with the scenario of the plaintiff and his witnesses,

- Expert testimony showing why the machine was safe and not defective,

- Accident reconstruction testimony showing how the accident occurred, and especially how the defendant's scenario differs from that of the plaintiff,

- Testimony refuting suggestions of the plaintiff's experts as to what the defect of the machine was, and as to what features or attachments would have prevented the subject accident,

- Testimony disputing any or all of the medical claims,

- Testimony disputing the economic claims, and

- Any other testimony or evidence which refutes claims by the opposition.

When the defendant's case is complete, his attorney "rests." In effect, he says to the judge and the jury, "Here are the reasons and the evidence explaining why my client is not responsible and liable for the costs of the plaintiff's accident and losses."

There may be an opportunity for the plaintiff to offer rebuttal testimony. If he does, the defendant can rebut the rebuttal, if he wishes.

When each party has exhausted his presentation, they all have "rested."

Final Arguments

Then the judge says something like this to the jury, "You have now heard all of the evidence in the case. Next, each attorney will be given an opportunity to summarize that evidence and tell you why he believes that his side should prevail. In other words, each attorney will give you his final arguments. What each attorney says is not evidence. You have now heard all of the evidence. What the attorney will do is interpret that evidence, as he sees it in relationship to the matter before us."

The order of argument differs in some jurisdictions, but typically, the plaintiff's attorney will speak first, followed by the defendant's attorney, and then followed by a brief rebuttal argument by the plaintiff's attorney.

The purposes of the final arguments are to put the evidence and information that has been heard by the jury into a summary and to argue why that information supports the attorney's client. If the final arguments are presented well, you will hear the entire trial in short, capsule form.

The Charge to the Jury

The judge will then "charge" the jury. In formal fashion, he will tell the jury that they have heard the evidence in the case and that they have heard the attorneys argue their respective positions. He will tell them that they are now at the part of the process where it is the job of the jury to make decisions as to facts.

He will tell them that he is the arbiter or finder of matters concerning the law, but that they are the finders of fact. He will explain the applicable law to them, with appropriate definitions, and he will tell them what they are to determine. Usually, there will be a series of written questions for them to answer, on what may be called the Verdict Sheet. (Was the machine defective? If so, did the defect cause the accident? Was the plaintiff at any fault himself? If so, what percentage of fault do you assign to him? Should damages be paid? If so, how much?) These questions will be specifically tailored to the case at hand.

The judge may instruct the jurors on some elements of the deliberation in general, such as to use their common sense and good judgment, to be fair to all parties, and to vote their consciences. He will tell them then to go to the jury room, elect a jury foreman, and to deliberate and arrive at answers and resolutions to the case

Jury Deliberation

The jury then retires to the jury room to deliberate. This means they will consider and discuss the evidence presented during the trial, they will consider the testimony from the witnesses and any exhibits that have been admitted into evidence, and they will be guided by the charge from the judge.

Jury deliberations are difficult to predict. Sometimes they make decisions rapidly, and sometimes they take days. Sometimes they ask questions of the judge or ask for clarification or a chance to reexamine some testimony.

Eventually they arrive at a decision. They find for one side or the other; or sometimes they become deadlocked, unable to reach an agreement. They report that decision to the judge.

If the jury finds for one party or the other in the dispute, that decision will be read in open court. If the jury becomes hopelessly deadlocked, the judge, upon deciding that there is no hope for a verdict, will declare a mistrial. This says to the participants in the trial, "We have not reached a decision or verdict in this matter. You may or may not decide to start over again on a new trial."

When a resolution to the matter—or a deadlock—is reached, the jury is then dismissed.

The Verdict

The result is commonly a finding for one side or the other. If the plaintiff wins, there is usually included an award of money, which the process intends will compensate the plaintiff for his loss and injury.

If they find for the defendant, they release the defendant from responsibility and liability for the incident and the attendant losses.

Some verdicts are split or mixed. The jury may find the product defective, but not the cause of the accident. They may find the product defective but only partially responsible for the incident. They may split or divide liability.

At this point I should mention "punitive damages." Punitive damages are allowed in cases where the plaintiff claims that wanton or grossly negligent action by the defendant has led to the cause of the accident and the injuries and economic losses. In addition to the verdict award, in such cases, the plaintiff can ask for additional damages which are intended to send a message to the defendant that his negligence and gross misconduct will not be tolerated. Rules with regard to punitive damages vary among jurisdictions, but they do exist and they may greatly add to the liability in an incident, if the claim for punitive damages can be proven and is allowed by the court.

The word "verdict" comes from the Latin words meaning "to speak the truth." The jury is "speaking the truth" to the best of its ability.

That is the general scenario of a trial.

Who is in the Courtroom?

Next, you need to be introduced to the players in the trial game.

The judge is in charge of the court. He is the legal arbiter between the parties. He will see that decisions are made in matters involving legal questions, and he will conduct the trial procedure. He will sit on the judge's "bench," which doesn't look like a bench at all. The judge will usually be at the highest and most central point in the front of the room.

The judge may have several assistants in the room, chief of whom is the court clerk. That person is what amounts to the office manager of the courtroom. The clerk provides for the day-to-day operation of the courtroom and the matters that are taken up there.

A court reporter will be there to take the proceedings down for record and transcription. The reporter sits somewhere in front of the judge and near the witness box. Records of trial proceedings are recorded in detail. These records become important in the case of further disputes or appeals.

Also in the room will be a marshal, deputy, or other police officer. His job is twofold—security and order. He is to make sure the personnel in the courtroom are secure and free from any unwanted interference, and he will help maintain order in the courtroom. He also ensures no interference with the jury during the trial and during jury deliberations. He is under the direct order of the judge, and so is everyone else in the room.

A jury box is generally located at one wall or the other, to the left or to the right of the judge and a little in front of him. The jury sits there, to hear and view the evidence as it is presented.

In front of all of this are two tables at which the litigants or parties to the dispute and their attorneys sit. They face the court, to present their cases and to ask for a resolution.

There may be modifications to the above description to accommodate extra attorneys, multiple parties to the action, or others, but generally this is what you will see in courtroom.

Behind the attorneys' and litigants' tables, there is usually a fence or railing which separates the court participants from those in the audience or gallery who may be watching the proceedings. You may be in that group of observers. So may others who have business with the court, as well as members of the public who may be interested in the particular case or just in the process in general.

Appearance and Conduct in the Courtroom

Now let's talk about you. Suppose you are asked to be in court to testify, or even just to observe. There are certain matters of good taste you ought to follow. In some courts, if you don't follow them, you are almost certain to hear about it.

You should dress in a suit, dress shirt, and tie. Others may not, but you should. It makes you look more proper and businesslike. Courts and judges deserve that respect.

You should also conduct yourself in a quiet, dignified manner. Courts are serious places and you should not act otherwise. Smile, yes, but loud, bois-terous levity, no. Courtesy, certainly. That is always proper, but don't get overly friendly with others in the room.

If the judge speaks to you, in or out of the courtroom, respond to him as "your honor." He deserves that courtesy and you show respect to the court and to the justice system by answering that way. It is good practice to answer, "Yes, sir" and "No, sir," or "Yes, ma'am" and "No, ma'am" to others in the room, also.

You will generally not talk with those on the opposing side, but if you are introduced to them or if they speak to you, respond courteously and with a smile. Courtesy is never improper.

Courtesy to the jury is proper, too, but should be silent. You have no busi-ness talking to them, and to do so may be a serious breach of conduct. Don't ignore jurors or act if they are not there or are forbidden. On the other hand, don't make overt expressions toward them, either.

In normal practice, everyone in the room stands when the judge enters or leaves and when the jury enters or leaves. I once was told by a deputy in a courtroom that I didn't need to remain standing after the judge entered. I responded that I had seen a colleague censured by a judge for not remaining standing until told by the judge to be seated. The judge later told me that he appreciated my formality and respect, but that his court was less formal than many. Even so, it is better to err on the side of caution.

I suggest no gum chewing or candy eating, and no reading of magazines or newspapers while in the courtroom, either. You may find more informality, but it is better to start with care. If everyone else has his suit coat on, keep yours on, too. Business dress is proper in court.

I will note here that if you are a witness, you may well be asked to stay out of the courtroom until after you have testified. Certain rules of procedure call for witnesses not to hear the examination and cross-examination of other witnesses, at least until after they have testified and are dismissed. When this "exclusion rule" is invoked, you will be sequestered, or asked to stay in a hallway or an outer room until you are called. Make sure your attorney briefs you on these rules in your case.

Now, the marshal or court officer calls your name and you are ready to testify.

Direct Examination

Upon walking up to the front of the courtroom, you will be asked to state and spell your name to the court clerk, and you will be asked to take an oath to "tell the truth, the whole truth, and nothing but the truth." Take that oath seriously. It is a critical part of our justice system. Everyone is expected to tell the truth; unless they do, the system doesn't work properly.

You will then be seated in the witness stand. You will feel as if you are in front of and in full view of everybody. You are, and it is important that they see and hear you. One attorney, dealing with his witness in an important case, took him into the courtroom the day before the testimony, while the judge had recessed the trial for some other purpose. He put the witness in the witness stand and practiced the questions he was going to ask him on direct examination. That is an excellent way to get comfortable in the witness chair.

Try to go into the courtroom and look around before court convenes. See where the judge will be and where the jury box is, and where the attorneys sit. If you are going to demonstrate some evidence, show some model, or write on a blackboard or flip chart, know ahead of time what you are going to do and how you are going to do it. Your attorney will help you do that, and he will be pleased that you asked.

Relax and take it easy. This is a justice system and justice is for witnesses, too. You are here to give the testimony you are qualified to give, either by being a direct witness to facts or by being qualified to testify as an expert.

If you are frightened because one attorney is for you and one against you, don't let that bother you. Frequently they have lunch together. Concentrate on what you know or have expertise in. No one in the room knows more about that subject than you do. That should relax you.

Now come the questions. Your attorney will ask them first. He will let you warm up by telling a little about yourself and by getting basic information first. After you have answered about your name and address, your schooling, your work history, and your outside interests, you will feel more comfortable answering the questions that deal with the case.

Listen to the questions carefully and pause just a bit before answering. That will give you time to better frame the answer, and for one of the other attorneys to object, if he should so choose. If an attorney objects, or if the judge speaks, don't start your answer or, if you have started to answer, stop immediately. Someone will tell you when to continue.

In court, and unless your attorney advises you otherwise, the same rules apply to answering questions as in Depositions. Answer only the question; don't volunteer. Answer clearly and slowly, so the jury can hear and understand you. Don't argue, and don't express any strong emotion in your answers. Don't be cute or clever. Answer with confidence; you are the one who knows the answer. Be yourself, as much as possible.

Above all, be truthful. Any deviation from the truth is likely to result in disaster. If you don't know, that is okay, and it is the proper answer. If you don't remember, that is a good answer, too. Your attorney or the other attorney may refresh your memory by an appropriate means, if that is called for.

I have already suggested you relax as much as you can in the witness stand. That is true for your comfort. However, for the sake of good appearance, don't relax so much you slouch or lean back as if you weren't interested. A trial is serious business, and your participation is also serious. Sit up and perhaps lean a little bit forward. Face the questioner when he is asking questions, and face the jury when you answer them. This will add confidence to your response.

Your attorney will lead you through the things he wishes to cover by the order and subjects of his questions. You will have talked about the order of questions before with the attorney. That is part of his way of making you confident in your presentation and testimony.

During the questioning, you may be asked to step down to show some document or piece of apparatus to the jury or to make some calculations on a board or flip chart. Do so confidently and professionally. Speak in lay terms, so the jury understands. Remember, you are there to assist in finding a proper resolution to the dispute. You are a teacher. Act like a good one. Make certain the judge, the jury, the attorneys, and the court reporter can see and hear you.

When your attorney has completed his questions, he will indicate in some way that he is finished. Then the opposing attorney will be given an opportunity to cross-examine you.

Cross-Examination

Cross-examination sounds difficult and scary. Usually the witness about to be cross-examined has a picture of the opposing attorney, yelling and ranting and raving and accusing him of everything from telling lies to stealing the public treasury. Seldom does that happen; usually the judge won't allow it. However, having heard your direct testimony, the opposition is given a chance to ask you additional questions.

To best understand the reasons and process of cross-examination, you need to see from the attorney's point of view what he is trying to do. You are part of the presentation of your attorney—and for the benefit of your attorney's client. The opposition may not want to believe your testimony, and indeed, if the jury believes your testimony, they may well find against your opponent. Especially if your testimony is damaging to his case, he will want to reduce that damage or eliminate it if at all possible.

Of course, he can and will present his own witnesses to counteract what you say (or you may be testifying to counteract something his witness has already said). Yet, through cross-examination, he can and will attempt to reduce the effect of your testimony while you are still in the witness stand.

Following proper procedures, he can lessen the effect of your testimony—or destroy it altogether—by:

- getting you to admit you didn't tell the true story,

- getting you to admit flaws in your testimony,

- impeaching you by showing that what you said or did earlier is contrary to what you are now testifying,

- impeaching by showing other evidence to you that refutes your testimony,

- or otherwise disproving your testimony.

In addition, he will certainly bring out any bias in your relationship to the party on whose behalf you were called to testify. If you are a paid consultant, that will certainly be brought out. If you are an employee or a retiree, your dependence on the company through a retirement fund or stock holdings will be made obvious.

His objective is to make you less credible to the jury. Take heart, however. If you have told the truth, no one can show lies. If your testimony is correct and solid, you can resist any attack on it. If you don't know, or don't remember, you don't know or don't remember. Be firm and keep in mind that you are the knowledgeable one on the subject. Remember why the questions are being asked of you. <u>You know the answers</u>.

To further relieve your worry about cross-examination, you might consider the advice that a famed law professor gave to young attorneys:

1. You can and should cross-examine for only these reasons:

   - if you know the witness made an error of significance,

   - if you know and can prove the witness lied,

   - if you know the witness is faking, or bluffing,

   - if you know of bias of the witness toward one side or the other, or

   - if you have evidence—a deposition or similar prior record or statement or a piece of writing, for example—in which the witness contradicts what he said on the stand.

2. Don't give the witness a chance to repeat his testimony.

3. Don't ask any question to which you (the questioning attorney) do not already know the answer.

4. Don't argue with the witness; stick to facts, and,

5. When you are finished, stop; don't ask the witness one too many questions.

Experience shows the professor is correct in his instructions. Experience also shows that most cross-examining attorneys don't follow those rules. Few attorneys do a good job at cross-examination.

If the cross examiner gets angry or argues, let him; the jury will dislike him for it, more than likely. If he asks too many questions, the jury will get tired and bored. If the attorney rants and raves and stomps around, be calm, polite, firm, and confident in your response. Don't get cute.

I will illustrate with these two examples:

An expert had been testifying about a body of knowledge learned from an older expert in a related field. An older gentleman, apparently just a visitor to the court, walked into the room and sat in the rear row of seats. The cross-examining attorney noted the man and asked the witness, "Is Mr. X, of whom you have been speaking, here in the courtroom?" The expert answered, "God! I hope not. He has been dead for fourteen years, now." The jury laughed. They also brought back a verdict against the client-defendant for whom the expert was testifying. Don't give answers like that.

Another expert had testified in an injury case. He described a laboratory vibration test that had been conducted by the defendant as a good and effective test. On cross-examination, he was asked, "Wouldn't it be better to haul the machine on the highway over a several hundred mile trip to see what would happen?" The expert responded, "No. And I'll be glad to tell you why." The attorney objected to the response and the witness was told to restrict his yes and no answers to just that—"yes" or "no." This irked the expert, and he began answering the questions with a curt "yes" or "no," without the customary "Yes, Sir" or "No, Sir."

After eight or nine quick questions with short yes-or-no answers, the questioning attorney stepped back and scratched his head as if he didn't understand something in the answer. The expert leaned forward and said, "Counselor, you act like you don't understand my answer. Well, I'd be glad to explain it to you, but His Honor has instructed me to answer 'yes' or 'no,' and I am not going to explain it to you." Pandemonium and shouting and gavel banging reigned for fifteen minutes or so. The expert swears he will never do that again. He was lucky to escape with a whole skin. You shouldn't answer like that, either.

When the cross-examiner has finished his questions, your own attorney may ask you some additional questions, perhaps to clear up an answer you gave to one of the cross-examiner's questions. There may even be two or three or even more "redirects" and "re-crosses," but that is quite rare.

A suggestion with regard to the conduct of the witness on cross-examination was given by one attorney. It went like this: "Use the same demeanor, voice, and courtesy in answering the questions of the cross-examiner as you use in answering questions on direct examination." This is excellent advice. When you consider your place in the scheme of things in the courtroom, you realize that you are usually explaining a technical matter of some kind to the questioner and to the jury. You are a professional—and usually not in any position where you ought to be advocating or arguing your position. If the cross-examiner asks a question that seems to cast doubt upon your opinion or position, doesn't it seem more appropriate to answer him the same way you answered your own attorney? The jury will then see you as a source of credible information, and not a combatant in the matter. You need to be firm and secure in your opinions and information, but you should not need to argue about it, unless the cross-examiner gets nasty. Then, let him hang himself.

Question and Answer Rules

A list of rules generally useful in testifying in court is as follows:

1. Don't give cute or smart-aleck answers. The trial is serious business.

2. Put technical terms in lay terms, so they will be best understood. This may be a key contribution from you. You may be the only one in the courtroom who can make those translations.

Example:

A design review may not mean a lot to a jury. However, a design "audit" will tell an accountant exactly what you mean. So, also, will a design "inspection" tell the same story to a factory worker or to a railroad conductor. Try telling the jury that a design review is merely inviting someone to "look over your shoulder."

3. Don't assume your definition is the same as the questioner's. Clear up the understanding, if necessary.

Example:

I heard an attorney once define a failure as "something that broke." That may well be a failure, but there are other failures, too—including those of the people involved.

4. Don't accept a definition or understanding that varies from the generally accepted and understood definition, or that varies from one that is broadly recognized. The jury and the judge may well use the common definition, even though the special definition has been carefully explained.

5. Courteously agree on obvious good definitions. If the attorney wants to say "end for end" when you have said "reversed" or "turned around," accept those definitions. Then the jury won't have to keep interpreting your answer to the attorney's question.

6. Watch out for terms of size, time, weight, speed, etc., which are loosely defined. Insist on a number or a range of numbers. Propose a number or range of numbers yourself, to help things along. Words such as large, small, slow, fast, sharp, dull, light, dark and a host of other such words elicit images which will vary widely among speakers and listeners. They do the same among questioners and respondents—and among jurors. Use numbers and be as definite as you can.

7. Don't pontificate. You are an expert and you know more than anyone else in the room about your expertise, but do not act like you are the "Last Word."

8. Don't argue.

9. Don't ask questions, unless they are to make the question clear. Even then, try not to ask questions. Perhaps you can obtain the same result by phrasing your answer in terms of how you understand the question.

Example:

Q: "Did the mechanic give you a reasonable response?"

A: "If I understand what you mean by 'reasonable,' sir, I might detail my answer to your question. I will say that the mechanic gave me a response that might sound reasonable, but based on my knowledge of the workings of the machine, I knew that the response was not logical and could not have been correct."

(The answer could have been, "What do you mean by 'reasonable?'" However, that question response sounds like you are arguing or trying to avoid answering.)

10. Don't repeat your answers unless specifically asked to do so (or unless given the opportunity to do so on cross-examination).

11. Don't give non-answers. Answer the question if you can. If you can't answer it, say so. Don't try to bluff an answer or to avoid giving an answer. You will look bad.

12. Don't repeat planned or "school" answers. They will sound rehearsed and will impress no one. Of course you will review your expected testimony with your attorney, but don't prepare it like an amateur play.

13. Watch for such phrases as "As I already testified...," and "I already explained...." Such terms signal either unnecessary repetition or that you are getting short-tempered or tired.

14. Avoid "absolute" statements. Such overconfidence and high knowledge sounds pompous. Also, you can and will be trapped on cross-examination by little exceptions which you forgot or didn't even know about. Courts usually allow and often require experts to testify "within reasonable professional certainty," leaving room for variations, errors, and exceptions without damaging their opinions and testimony.

15. Be polite, but not overly so. Comfortable and easy politeness is impressive. Showy politeness is not.

16. Use a normal voice and manner in speaking and presenting evidence. Don't act or overemphasize words.

17. Avoid the use of extreme adjectives and other descriptors unless it is necessary to use them.

These rules are offered for your guidance. They are not infallible or universal. Your attorney may well want you to break one or more of these rules for specific reasons on particular occasions. He will tell you when. Don't try to anticipate and decide on your own.

There is a Large Range of Question and Answer Rules

Although courts are run by judges who subscribe to and follow a basic canon of laws and a general code of conduct, the witness may well experience a wide variety of rules and instructions in the courtroom about answering questions at trial. If you are a witness you will need instruction on answering before you enter the witness stand, and further, you will need to be alert to rulings of the judge and trends in the questioning as you are on the stand.

In general, listen to the question, and answer it truthfully—but no more. Don't volunteer and don't help the attorney. He is in charge of the questioning. You will, however, as you gain experience, find yourself being almost able to read the mind of a good attorney while you are on the stand—that is, if you are a good witness, too.

Judges will differ in the amount of latitude they allow a witness in answering a question. Some judges will hold the witness very tightly to answering the question and no more—not even any explanation of the answer.

Example (and I return to the story about the "smart" answer to show you where it happened):

The case involved an accident that was claimed to have happened as a result of a bolt on a handhold loosening during a long, cross-country transport of the machine on a truck. The defending company had performed a laboratory test to show the results of vibrating a bolt loose, if that is what happened.

In a cross-examination, the questioning went something like this:

Q: "Did you know of the test the defendant company ran prior to this trial today?"

A: "No, sir."

Q: "Did you suggest the little bench test to them?"

169

A: "No, sir."

Q: "Did you suggest the defendant consider hauling a sample tractor on a lowboy from Las Vegas to Minneapolis, to test the handle that way?"

A: "No, sir, and I'll be glad to tell you why."

Q: (To the Court) "Your Honor, will you please instruct the witness that he is to answer the question only and not elaborate with explanations?"

COURT: "Mr. Witness, just answer the question 'yes' or 'no' if that is possible. Don't enlarge on your answer. If there are explanations to be made, your attorney may ask those questions on redirect examination. Do you understand?"

A: "Yes, Your Honor. I'll do my best to comply and follow your instruction."

Q: "Now, we will start over again. Did you know of this bench test before today?"

A: "No."

Q: "Did you see the results of the test before today, here in this court room?"

A: "No."

Q: "Did you suggest this bench vibration test be run?"

A: "No"

Q: "And you did not know of the bench test being run until you heard of it today in this courtroom. Is that true?"

A: "Yes. I did not know about the bench test until today in this courtroom." (This answer is correct and proper, but it is misleading to some extent. Note that "Yes, I did not..." sounds almost like a contradiction. You may have to answer in this or some similar manner at times, to be certain the answer is clear and unmistakable.)

Q: "Did you suggest that a test be run hauling the tractor on a lowboy from Las Vegas to Minneapolis, as the machine which is the subject of

170

this lawsuit had been hauled, to see what might happen to the loose handle?"

A: "No."

Q: "Don't you think that would be a good test?"

A: "No."

Q: "Don't you think it would have been a better test than the little bench test the defendant ran?"

A: "No."

Q: "Don't you think the results of such a test would have helped us understand the failure that we are talking about in this accident?"

A: "No."

Q: "Don't you think you would have learned something from such a hauling test, at least?"

A: "No." (The witness really had a good reason for that answer, but under the close rule applied by the judge in this case he could do nothing but answer "yes" and "no.")

You will recognize this series of questions from my warning not to give smart-aleck answers; this series of questions led up to such a smart-aleck response. After this answer, the witness took advantage of a perplexed look on the part of the questioning attorney to remind him that he could explain, but under the instructions of the judge, he wasn't going to explain.

In another court, an expert engineering witness for the plaintiff was given almost open freedom by the judge in his answers. The following excerpt will illustrate the other extreme of the wide range sometimes allowed.

Q: "Doctor, do you have any opinions as to the cause of the accident and the injuries to Mr. Plaintiff?"

A: "Yes, I do. I have a lot of opinions and they all add up to the gross negligence of the defendant company and its engineers. They could have done several things to prevent this accident, and they should have done all of them."

Q: "Here is an internal letter about another type of machine that discusses a similar type of accident in it. Does that support your opinion?"

A: "It sure does, and I repeat again that it shows and proves gross negligence on the part of the defendant's engineers. I don't know how one of the largest manufacturing companies in the country can be so callous in ignoring this hazard. Their engineers seem to have broken every rule of good engineering and common sense in designing the machine the way they did."

Q: "How do you know the letter applies to this case? Doesn't it talk of another type of machine?"

A: "Sure it does, but a fire is a fire, wherever it happens. The defendant certainly knows fires happen, and this letter proves it. If they had done more work on the problems on this machine and provided the proper safeguards, Mr. Plaintiff wouldn't be sitting here in this court today; he would be out playing golf, which he can't do now since the horrible accident caused by the defendant's carelessness and negligence."

Q: "Do you have any recommendations as to how to avoid this problem which led to Mr. Plaintiff's injury?"

A: "Certainly! Any second-year engineering student can see that the defect exists and that there are dozens of ways to avoid the problem of the accident that happened to Mr. Plaintiff. It just happens that I have sketched up several design changes to give the defendant an idea of how he should have gone about the design. I am surprised that the defendant company, with its thousands of engineers, didn't have these same ideas. I think they did. That leads me to believe that the company overruled these ideas just to save a few pennies on the cost or maybe because they have no concern for the safety of the operator."

Q: "Have you built or tested any of these ideas?"

A: "No, but I know they will work and that they would have prevented Mr. Plaintiff's horrible and disabling injuries. Besides, the defendant isn't paying me to develop these ideas. I ought to charge them for giving them the idea here on the witness stand in the first place."

This kind of response was even allowed on cross-examination by the defendant's attorney as follows:

Q: "Did you visit the scene of the accident?"

A: "No. I didn't need to. It is obvious to anyone that the machine design is defective. Any sophomore engineering student could have done a better job concerning safety. Your client's engineers probably could have done a better job if the management of the company hadn't concentrated so much on profit and so little on the safety of the operator."

Q: "Did you inspect the machine?"

A: "I already answered that the machine was defective. I didn't need to inspect it to know that. To answer your question fully, I did not inspect the machine. Mr. Plaintiff's attorney asked me if I wanted to inspect the machine, and I told him if he wanted me to do so, I would. However, as I already stated—clearly, I hope—the design defect is obvious, and I had no need to make any inspection to know what the problem was."

Q: "Doctor, you say you have sketches of ideas which would have prevented this accident? Is that true?"

A: "I already answered that, but I'll say again that any sophomore engineering student could have made such sketches. I don't understand how your company's engineers missed these ideas. Either they were negligent or the company overruled them to save a penny or two. Either way, it was gross lack of concern for the operator, such as Mr. Plaintiff here."

Q: "Could we see the sketches, Doctor?"

A: "No you can't. Your company didn't pay me to do your work for you."

Q: "Well, Doctor, the Court may well ask you to show them."

A: "I will certainly show them to his honor or to the jury, but not to you—unless you want to pay me for the work I did."

173

Q: "Well, let's get on to something else, and we will get back to the sketches later. Doctor, how do you think the incident which led to Mr. Plaintiff's injuries happened?"

A: "That is easy. The injuries happened because the negligent engineers of your company didn't include a simple little feature on this design that would have prevented the accident."

Q: "I understand your position, Doctor, that my company was negligent, but..."

A: "I am glad you do understand what I am saying, sir. Congratulations."

Q: "Do you know any other company that manufactures machines of this type that uses any of your devices or ideas?"

A: "No, but that is entirely irrelevant. If your company had used one or all of the ideas I have, the accident would have been prevented. I still do not understand why you and your client's engineers didn't do it my way."

Seldom will a judge let a witness answer in such a manner, either on cross- or direct examination, but it does happen. Usually the questioning and responses are somewhere between the two extreme illustrations just presented.

As a witness you need to know how to answer, and I don't mean canned and prepared answers. I mean you need to know the manner, character, and expression of your answer, as well as the word or fact content of your answer. If you answer in an improper way you may hurt your client's case even if your answer is true and accurate.

Offer to explain if you feel that an explanation is appropriate. If the judge lets you do so, fine. If not, the explanation may be requested during redirect examination. For example, referring to the example about the bench test and the hauling test, the redirect may go something like this:

Q: "Mr. Witness, in cross-examination, you were asked if you had suggested that the defendant try a test hauling the machine from Las Vegas to Minneapolis on a lowboy. You responded, 'No.' Is that the correct answer?"

A: "Yes, sir."

Q: "Would you tell the court and the jury why you gave that answer?"

A: "Certainly. The roads between Las Vegas and Minneapolis have been almost 100% resurfaced since the subject machine in this accident was hauled over that same general route. I would expect the conditions of such a hauling test today to be drastically different from the hauling over five years ago. The results, then, would be subject to much question and criticism as a comparison. In my opinion the test would be meaningless."

When You are Finished

After you have satisfied the questioners, the judge will dismiss you. If you are no longer needed in the case, you may leave the courtroom. It is good advice to do so, unless you have a particular reason for staying, such as:

• the judge asks you to remain for possible later testimony,

• your attorney asks you to stay in the courtroom, or

• you have other business there, as a party or representative in the matter.

If you leave, do so quietly and courteously. If you stay, be quiet and courteous. You will be glad the testimony is completed, but don't make a big thing of it. Especially if you remain, be aware that the jury now knows who you are. Don't do anything to spoil the good impressions you have given them.

After you leave, be careful not to discuss the case or your testimony with anyone. If your attorney wants to talk about the testimony with you, he will do so at an appropriate time and place. Also, remember that a stray juror may be around. If he or she overhears you talking about the case, it could be very bad. You could give the opposing side grounds for requesting a mistrial, requesting a new trial, asking for a judgment notwithstanding the verdict of the jury, or filing an appeal.

At the End of the Trial

You may not be in the courtroom at the end of the trial, when the jury reads the verdict. However, someone will tell you what happened. If the result is good, you will hear from a happy attorney. If the result is not good, the same attorney may be less happy, but he will still call you and tell you how it came out.

If you can, ask for a little discussion or critique of your own work and involvement in the case. Even if you make that review yourself, it will help you learn from both mistakes and successes. You can learn from such a review. If you made mistakes or slips, you will benefit from knowing that.

One caution, however. It appears that almost always, when you have finished testifying, you will wish you had answered just a little bit differently. Maybe that is good. It shows you are improving, and that you are aware of and sensitive to the process.

Chapter 11

QUESTIONS

A discussion of questions would seem in order. Much of what the engineer does, in litigation, is to answer questions. All questions should be answered truthfully. Aside from that there are subtle and yet important ways in which questions are answered differently, depending on how the question is asked and in what situation it is asked.

There are no new rules in this chapter, suggesting that questions should be answered in any way other than truthfully. There are no suggestions that in one situation that answer should be "A" and in another situation, the answer should be "B." Neither do I suggest that an answer to one questioner should be different than it should be for another.

The art of asking questions, however, permits a reasonable and equivalent art of answering questions.

In this chapter, I will discuss:

- the various situations in which questions are asked,
- the various types of questions,
- the various people who ask questions,
- the questions they ask, and
- the way questioners ask questions.

Each variation of question tends to elicit or suggest answers in a particular way. You need to be aware of the ways a question can and may be varied in order to elicit a certain type of response. Some of these ideas may be of use to you.

When Questions are Asked

When you become involved in litigation, you will find questions asked of you in several differing situations.

First may well be the simple inquiry, "Do you know anything about the ABC product, or the MNO accident?" You do or you do not. If the question is asked by your supervisor, or by your corporate attorney, the inquiry probably seeks basic, starting point information. (If you suspect you will be recruited to take part in the litigation and you don't wish to be, say so. Don't fake illness or conjure up conflicting future requirements. Remember, your are to tell the truth at all times.)

If you are being asked as a potential consultant or expert witness, answer the same way—truthfully. If you are too busy to take the assignment, say so. If it conflicts with what you have already said or done, say so.

Next, the question may be asked by way of a legal inquiry, in Interrogatories or at Deposition. This situation places legal weight upon the answer and the one who answers. You must, under most circumstances, give an answer. Anything other than the truth may well involve perjury and legal consequences.

You may also be asked or assigned, by a proper company authority, to prepare answers and information responses to certain questions and requests. It is your responsibility to prepare those answers and responses in a professional and truthful way.

After you have become involved in a litigation matter, you may be asked questions almost by anyone at any time. When you are actively involved in litigation, you need to be certain that you are the one to answer the question, and that the answer is a proper response to the question.

I have discussed in some general detail, in another chapter, the matter of answering questions at deposition and at trial. This chapter covers more of those kinds of questions.

Various Types of Questions

Question types may be generally grouped as:

- specific or general,
- open or closed,
- leading or non-leading,
- formal or casual,
- polite or serious,
- rhetorical or interrogating,
- simple or complex, and,
- probing or outlining,

By type example, they may be in these forms:

Specific or General Questions

General questions are broad in apparent interest, not aimed at obtaining a certain answer or piece of information, but rather, in learning a general condition.

Examples of general questions are these:

- How is the weather?
- How is business?
- How is your health?

Such questions are best answered in general terms. They may even be questions asked out of politeness, so the answer should be polite. Answers to such questions should not be long and detailed, unless they are obviously open-ended and specifically ask for long details.

There are many jokes about doctors, dentists, lawyers, and others who are constantly bombarded with questions in an attempt to get "a little free advice." My favorite is the story of the lady who spent an hour bothering a doctor at a cocktail party about all of her little aches and pains and worries. When the doctor finally escaped the lady, he told the story of his long questioning to an attorney friend. He told his attorney friend that he had gotten tired of the constant medical questions. The attorney suggested to the doctor that he simply send the lady a bill for an office call the next day. The doctor agreed and laughed—until he got a bill for professional services from his lawyer friend two days later.

Examples of specific questions might be:

- Is it raining outside now?
- Did your company show a profit this year?
- Has your broken leg healed?

These, obviously, ask for specific answers.

Open and Closed Questions

Open and closed questions seem to be similar, but are significantly different. Open-ended questions, or open questions, ask for detailed or narrative answers. Closed-ended questions, or closed questions, by their form and nature ask for brief answers alone, not an extended discussion.

You can tell by the form of the question whether the question is open or closed.

"What is your education and work history?" is an open question, asking for as much detail in reasonable form as might be available.

"Did you graduate from college?" is a closed question, admitting to a simple yes-or-no answer.

"Tell me about your work history," is also an open invitation to describe in some detail where you have worked and what you did, along with what you may have specifically gained in knowledge and experience.

Leading and Non-leading questions

Leading and non-leading questions derive from legal definitions, and are of importance in trial testimony.

A leading question suggests the answer, and is intended to limit and control the one who answers. The leading question asks not only for a short and specific answer, but it suggests or "leads" the one who answers to give a certain answer. A leading question assumes that the questioner at least expects that he already knows the answer. He just wants to hear the answer directly from you.

Examples of leading questions:

- Didn't you run through the red light?
- You went to college, didn't you?
- Next, you went to law school. Correct?
- Isn't it true that you did commit the crime?
- Next, the rain began to fall, didn't it?

Non-leading questions do not suggest answers; they ask questions and leave the answer entirely up to the one who answers.

Examples of non-leading questions:

- Do you have any opinion as to the cause of this accident? (Even though the question asks for a yes-or-no answer, it is not leading because the question does not suggest the answer.)
- Will you describe the path of the vehicle in the accident?
- How many plates are in the master clutch?
- What is the basis of your opinion?

• Have you ever testified before?

Formal and Casual Questions

A formal question, in terms of litigation, is a question asked in a formal document, such as an interrogatory, or at a formal activity, such as a deposition or trial. Formal questions demand and deserve formal answers, thought through properly. The questions and answers are recorded and may have a major bearing on the outcome of the action. Formal questions are asked in formal situations, such as in interrogatories, during deposition, and at trial.

Casual questions are simply less formal, and asked in a casual manner. In polite conversation, they are of little import. Be careful, however, that important questions are not asked at casual times or in easy casual ways. Casual answers may become as powerful as formal answers later.

A witness in a lawsuit was politely greeted by the opposing attorney as he entered the courtroom. During pleasantries, he asked the witness, "When did you get here to Greenville?" The witness replied that he had just come from another part of the country last night. That led the opposing attorney to probe into the purpose of the trip to the other part of the country, when he later faced the witness in cross-examination. The answers were troublesome. The witness had been on vacation for three weeks. In final argument, the opposing attorney made the witness look like a playboy golfer who did nothing but travel, play golf, and testify for big money. The picture may not have been accurate, but the initial answer was, and the inferences were an easy step from that. Beware of the answers to informal or casual questions which may later become more formal answers.

The differences between polite and serious questions, although more obvious, are also important. An example follows:

I met a co-worker one morning and asked him, in a polite social way, "How are you?" He took me by the arm and filled the next hour telling me of all of his troubles, as well as those of his wife, his two children, his car, and his hunting dog. The joke was on me; he had answered that way on purpose, just to perpetrate the gag. It well illustrates the difference between a polite question and a serious question. Know which kind of question it is before you answer.

Rhetorical Questions and Interrogating Questions

The rhetorical question and the interrogating question show subtle but strong differences. The rhetorical question does not expect an answer. That is obvious from the framing and the circumstance of the question, but not necessarily from the question itself. Rhetorical questions are asked for effect— to show off, to emphasize a bad situation, to summarize a condition, or for some other reason. It may be a social question.

"Isn't that too bad?" is a rhetorical question. The speaker is trying to express sorrow or pity through a question. A witness explained an error by saying, "Well, I am only human." The attorney responded, "Aren't we all?" The response was a theoretical question. Don't try to answer rhetorical questions; you will only look like you are arguing.

An expert once had the following sequence of questions and answers in a courtroom:

Q: "Mr. Witness, what do you think of the accident that happened to my client?"

A: "It was an unfortunate incident."

Q: "Isn't that the truth?"

The questioner waited and finally yelled:

Q: "Well, give me an answer to my question, Mr. Witness!"

A: "I am sorry, sir, I didn't realize there was a question pending. Can I have the question repeated, please?"

Q: "I wish you would pay attention."

Judge: "Counselor, I think the witness did pay attention. If you look at the record, your last question, 'Isn't that the truth?' was a rhetorical question that really didn't deserve an answer. In fact, counselor, I would admonish you not to make such rhetorical comments. They disturb and clutter up the record. The witness was correct in not answering the question and in not acknowledging it as a question."

Interrogating questions are simple—they sincerely ask for an answer.

Simple and Complex Questions

Some questions are simple. They are easier to answer than complex questions. Listen carefully to all questions before you answer, but be especially aware of complex questions.

A complex question is recognized by its complex grammatical form, or by the added conditions in the questions. Hypothetical questions, as sometimes posed by attorneys, are good examples of complex questions. They have several or even many conditions, all of which must be properly recognized and integrated into the question before it can even be considered. I will illustrate with two examples, both real.

In the first example, an expert being deposed was questioned like this:

Q: "You are John J. Doe?"

A: "Yes, sir."

Q: "Are you employed?"

A: "I am."

Q: "By whom?"

A: "By J. J. Doe Consulting, Ltd."

Q: "Is that a corporation?"

A: "Yes, it is."

Q: "Is it a special professional corporation or a general corporation?"

A: "A general corporation, under the laws of Iowa."

Q: "Do you own the corporation?"

A: "Part of it."

Q: "Who else is a stockholder?"

A: "My wife, Jane."

Q: "Are you both Directors of the corporation?"

A: "Yes, we are."

Q: "Are you both officers, too?"

A: "Yes, sir."

Q: "OK. Now, as president of J. J. Doe Consulting Ltd., do you testify in lawsuits?"

A: "No, I do not."

Q: "Well, as president of your company, do you do consulting work for attorneys and manufacturers?"

A: "No, sir."

Q: "Well, as president of your company, you have done that kind of work in the past, haven't you?"

A: "No, I haven't."

Q: "As president of your company, you have never testified or consulted in product liability litigation matter. Is that true?"

A: "Yes, it is."

Q: "I don't understand. You are here today as president of J. J. Doe Consulting, Ltd., are you not?"

A: "No, sir. I am not."

Q: (Angrily) "Well, you are here today, aren't you?"

A: "Yes sir, I am—and let me help you a little to get over this barricade. I am not the president of J. J. Doe Consulting, Ltd. And while I am helping you, let me tell you that there only two of us that are officers, so if I am not president, my wife must be. You have started the last several questions with an incorrect assumption that I am the president. You may want to go back and re-ask those questions with the correct assumption or, better yet, with no assumptions at all."

Needless to say, the remainder of the deposition was not too friendly.

When you detect that a question is complex, make certain you understand it. Make sure you agree with <u>all</u> of the assumptions and modifiers, and realize that if you answer, you have tacitly accepted the complexities of the question. If you answer the question, it is assumed that you understood it."

The other example of the pitfalls of complex questioning is this:

Q: "For purposes of the following question, assume these conditions:

 • The temperature is very high, perhaps 100 degrees,

 • The ground is dry and dusty,

 • A gusty wind is blowing from the west at over 20 miles per hour, and

 • The operator of the scraper is traveling east, with the wind behind him.

Now, what is the likely condition of the air around the scraper?"

A: "The scraper is likely operating a cloud of dust."

Q: "Okay, now assume that the wind is not blowing at all. What is the condition of the air around the scraper?"

A: "I cannot really answer that question, sir, without knowing about the other circumstances."

Q: "Well, the other conditions are the same as in the first question. We only changed the wind from a gusty 20 mile per hour wind to no wind at all."

A: "OK. Thank you for clarifying that. I wasn't sure whether the other conditions remained the same or not. I would say, with no wind, and with a dry hot day, that the scraper would still be operating in a cloud of dust."

Q: "How can you say that? The wind is no longer blowing the dust along with the scraper, is it?"

A: "No, it isn't. But the scraper continually stirs up new dust as it travels. Besides, I have run scrapers in all of those conditions, and I know how the dust builds up."

Probing Questions and Outlining Questions

Another classification in question differences is even more subtle, but still important. That is the comparison between the probing question and the outlining question. Probing questions are easy—they look for answers. The probing question is aimed accurately and specifically toward a certain topic and result.

However, the outlining type of question has a subtly different purpose. In direct examination, the attorney is presenting you as part of his case before the jury. He will have certain specific information and testimony that he wants you to present to the jury. He is not, according to the rules, supposed to lead you with his questions—that is, he cannot suggest the answer to you.

Your attorney will want to present your evidence and testimony in an interesting and memorable way. To do this, he will almost certainly <u>outline</u> your testimony with his questions.

Q: "You are the designer of the ABC machine?"

Opponent: "Objection! He is leading the witness."

Judge: "Sustained! Please, counselor, don't lead your witness."

Q: "Sorry, Your Honor. It was a slip, and my opponent is correct."

Q: "Mr. Witness, are you familiar with the ABC machine which is a subject of discussion in this lawsuit?"

A: "Yes, I am."

Q: "How are you familiar with the machine?"

A: "I designed it and have operated it many times."

Q: "Tell us what the machine was designed to do."

(and after that question is answered in some narrative detail, the questioning continues):

Q: "Tell us why the machine is designed the way it is."

Q: "Are there any safety devices on the machine dealing with the brakes?"

Q: "Were other devices considered? By whom?"

Q: "Who made the final decision as to the use of the device?"

...and so on, through the specific subjects and sub-topics your attorney wants you to cover. In answering his questions, you will have told the story of the machine, its design, and its purposes in a logical order which gives the jury a good picture of the machine.

You must listen carefully. You will have discussed the process ahead of time. However, sometimes the attorney changes tactics or directions in his questioning. You need to be alert and realize that you are being directed in the questioning by the attorney's outline.

The Questioners

In brief, and as a general rule, if you are involved in a matter of litigation, talk about that subject only to the people with whom you are working on the case, and generally, only with or through the attorney in charge.

If outsiders ask questions, direct them to the attorney. If you answer, your answers may get into the wrong hands, and at the wrong time. Litigation is a matter of substantial confidentiality. Respect that by talking with only those whom you know are involved and with whom you have been asked to speak.

In court and at deposition, though, the rules will tell you that questions asked properly by certain people must be answered. That is part of the process.

To be safe, understand to whom you may talk about the subject case. Then, keep your discussions within that limit. Make certain that the person who asks you a question is within that limit before you answer.

The Questions They Ask

In a formal questioning session, you have already been told to pause before you answer. That gives an attorney who objects to the question in some way a chance to place his objection on the record. You may not even have to answer that question—at least in the form and way in which it was asked.

The rules of litigation conduct include definitions and guides to the proper questions and to the proper methods of asking questions. Attorneys take care of those detailed matters; you need not worry about them. However, you need to pause long enough before you answer to give them time to do those things.

Sometimes questions are not proper, reasonable, or even logical. At other times, the questions are inappropriate for social or legal reasons, or matters of pure courtesy. You probably do not have to answer such questions, and you shouldn't. If it is necessary for the question to be answered, you will be instructed to do so by the judge; there will be no uncertainty.

The Way People ask Questions

Also, the way people ask questions may help determine the answer, if there is one. In the formal litigation processes, the questioning ought to be reasonable. If it gets heated, slow down—try to lessen the anger with calm answers. If the questions come in rapid-fire order, slow them down with slower, more deliberate answers. You have every right to consider your answer without being hassled, and you need not be pushed or hurried.

You will sense when the questioner is annoyed with you, or is trying to force you into a bad answer, or is trying to make something where there is nothing. Don't fall into such traps.

Further, listen carefully to the way the question is asked. Are certain words emphasized? Is the meaning of the question distorted by the use of certain words or phrases? Is the same question being repeated, perhaps with slight modifications? Is there a sudden change in the way the questioner is speaking—louder or softer, slower or faster, changing subjects rapidly, going from light to serious or funny to heavy types of subjects? Any and all of these trends and changes may be important—even as important as the question itself.

Answering Questions

Likewise, there are legitimate variations in the way questions are answered depending on, as follows:

- by whom the question is answered,

- when the question is answered,

- how the question is answered,

- the reason the question is answered, and,

- if the question is answered at all.

Each variation of the answer tends to react to the variations in the way questions are asked. A question asked in anger may be answered in anger. That seems to be the normal reaction. A question asked in technical terms may be answered in technical terms. A question asked with certain assumptions—stated or tacit—may be answered as if those assumptions were true. Yet, that may not be (and usually is not) the best answer in the best form.

The Single, Simple Sentence

Before I proceed, I need to illustrate a simple principle. While a young boy, I read and studied a book in my preacher-father's library. It dealt with the process of reading written material as if one were speaking. The book was intended to train a preacher to speak written material as if he were speaking extemporaneously—or at least to sound like it.

A single sentence was used throughout the book, to show how expression, pitch of the voice, emphasis, and other speaking tricks could be use to convey specific and intentional meanings. The sentence was something like this:

My uncle was a dairy farmer in southern Michigan.

I will illustrate only by changing emphasis on words. Note that there are many other ways to modify and emphasize the meaning.

As a start, the sentence is a simple declaration of a fact. Read with no emphasis on any single word, it carries that clear message that my uncle was a dairy farmer and that his dairy farming activities were in southern Michigan.

Now, try reading the sentence with emphasis on different words, and see what happens to the meaning.

My uncle was a dairy farmer in southern Michigan.

The emphasis on the word "My" makes it sound like I am in a bragging contest. I am comparing my uncle to someone else's uncle. "My uncle was a dairy farmer in southern Michigan, but your uncle was something else...."

My uncle was a diary farmer in southern Michigan.

When I emphasize the word "uncle," I now appear to be differentiating between my uncle and some other member of my family. Perhaps you said you thought my father was a dairy farmer, and I am correcting you.

My uncle was a dairy farmer in southern Michigan.

When I emphasize the word "was," I am now focusing on the time element more than the rest of the sentence. My uncle was a dairy farmer in southern Michigan, but he gave up the farm because the profits were too low. My uncle was a dairy farmer in southern Michigan before he retired. My uncle was a dairy farmer in southern Michigan , so he understands the worries and joys of farming. Any of these might be more complete statements, or might explain why I emphasizing the word "was."

My uncle was a dairy farmer in southern Michigan.

He wasn't the only dairy farmer in southern Michigan. Maybe you think he is to get full blame or credit for something, but he was only one of many dairy farmers.

My uncle was a <u>dairy</u> farmer in southern Michigan.

He was not a wheat farmer or a hog farmer.

My uncle was a dairy <u>farmer</u> in southern Michigan.

...but he did not get involved in processing or retailing the dairy products.

My uncle was a dairy farmer <u>in southern Michigan</u>.

Now I concentrate on the place. He is not part of a dairy movement in Wisconsin because he is in southern Michigan.

With this example, you can see how a simple sentence can be slanted by emphasis on a certain word or phrase. So can other voice and personal characteristics. You might say a statement with pride or with anger. The same words have obviously different meanings when expressed in different ways.

Questions may be slanted or emphasized in the same way. As I discuss answering questions, look for that kind of shading in meaning.

Sample Questions and Varying Answers

To better explain how questions may be varied by presentation, situation, and even emotion, and how the responses may also vary for the same reasons, I will use illustrations. A set of general rules for asking and answering questions would be too long to be useful and too unclear to be understood. Experience is the best teacher. Example is the next best.

Example 1.

You are testifying in court in a lawsuit pertaining to the brakes you designed on machine ABC. You have explained the design and you have told the jury why the design is appropriate, and why other possible design choices are not as good. You have further offered the opinions that the design is not defective and that no defect of the machine, and specifically of the brakes, was the cause of the plaintiff's injury. You are now on cross-examination and the next question is:

Q: "When did you arrive at that ridiculous opinion?" (You won't have to answer that question. There will be loud shouting and gavel banging. Sit quietly. The questioner is arguing with you.)

Q: "When did you arrive at your opinions?"

A: "I probably arrived at the two opinions at different times. Can the question be rephrased, please?" (Probably it can. Ideally, he should ask and you should answer one question about one opinion at a time.)

Q: "When did you decide the brakes on the ABC machine were not defective?"

A: "I made that decision as I designed the brakes and as they were tested and developed. Further, I saw no evidence of defect as I investigated the materials and testimony in this case." (You might simply say that the brakes never were defective, from the time of design. However, your questioner is concentrating on the time, so you probably should, too, but add a measure of your own confidence and professional certainty.)

Q: "In fact, you say that the ABC machine is perfect, don't you?"

A: "I have not been asked to investigate or testify or offer opinions on the rest of the machine or on the total machine, sir. But the brakes are of good design."

(Be careful. The cross-examiner is trying to make you look like a company hack or robot. Be suspicious when your testimony is improperly stretched to cover more than the subject at hand. Also, beware of absolute words such as "perfect." Also, watch for never, always, totally, impossible, absolute, positively, and similar words which are precise and unchanging. They are used in traps.)

Q: (Sneering) "I can't believe how hard it is to get you to give good answers."

A: (Don't answer. He hasn't asked a question!)

Q: "Do you have any other words of wisdom to give to us?"

A: "I will be pleased to answer any other questions you ask specifically about the matter at hand." (Ignore the sarcasm. Respond with courtesy and professional calm. Your attorney may object to the nasty way of questioning, thus saving you from having to respond at all.)

Example 2.

You have been retained and are assisting the attorney for the plaintiff.

You enter the room to be deposed in a matter in which you have offered the opinion that a certain device, had it been on the machine involved, would have prevented the accident and injuries to the plaintiff. You are greeted by the opposing attorney for the defense.

Q: "Well, are you the man who is going to redesign our machine to make it foolproof?"

(There are a lot of tempting openings here. You might tell the man there is no such thing as a foolproof design. You might tell him that his company didn't hire you to design the machine, or it certainly wouldn't be the way it was when the plaintiff was injured. You might tell him courteously that you are serious about your opinion and that you are here to talk about it. Don't do any of those things. The correct response is:)

A: "Good morning. I am Professor Witness, and I am here for my deposition as noticed."

Example 3.

You are testifying as one of the design team who designed the machine being attacked in a products liability suit. You are on cross-examination.

Q: "You are the engineer who decided how this design was to be, are you not?"

A: "I am one of the team, and I was involved in the design decisions."

Q: "Why did you decide to sacrifice safety in the design?"

(This is an improper question. First, it assumes something—that safety was sacrificed. Second, it assumes that you made the decision to do so, and directly asks for your admission that it is true. The best response may well be to take the first assumption first.)

A: "I do not believe safety was sacrificed in our design decisions."

Q: "Well, you are the engineer who made the basic decisions, aren't you?"

(Be careful. This quick "recap" question is designed to get you to admit that you are the engineer who made the design decisions at a time the jury is thinking about whether the decisions sacrificed safety. If you merely answer, "Yes," the listener may think you are admitting to more than you understand. Give a complete answer.)

A: "I did help make the decisions, and we strongly believe the decisions were good ones, sacrificing no safety in the process."

Example 4.

You are sitting in your office and your Engineering Vice President comes in with the corporation litigation chief attorney.

VP: "Hey, Bill. We need your help on another lawsuit. Do you know anything about the hydraulic system on the GHI machine?" (The VP knows very well you do. You designed the system.)

Several answers are possible:

A: "Oh no! Not again."

or,

A: "Never heard of it."

or,

A: "I don't like litigation work, but what can I do to help?"

or,

A: "Sure I do. I designed the system. How can I help?"

Be truthful, even in the confidential privacy of your work place. Don't lie to anyone, even to yourself. If you do not like certain types or assignments, say so. Based on my experience, the chances are that you will not do good work when you are involved in things you strongly dislike.

Example 5.

The judge has just told you that questions asked by a cross-examining attorney should be answered with a "yes" or "no" if at all possible. You are cautioned to avoid long answers and explanations and told that if your attorney wishes to bring out further information or explanations, he will do so on redirect examination. The cross-examination continues.

Q: "Well, let's start over again. Mr. Witness, did you design the RST machine?"

A: "I was the team leader."

Q: "Your Honor, please make this witness stop giving speeches. My question could be and should be answered with a "Yes" or "No.""

The judge repeats his instruction to you. You are now unhappy—and perhaps rightly so—at this limitation.

A: "I will try my best, Your Honor, to answer the questions as you have instructed me."

Q: "Did you design the RST machine?"

A: "No."

Q: "Well, weren't you designated as the designer of the machine in an answer to Interrogatory # 24 answered by your attorney?"

A: "I believe so."

Q: "Did you help prepare the answer to that Interrogatory?"

A: "No."

Q: "Who did?"

A: "I do not know."

Q: "Well, I will show you the answers to the whole series of Interrogatories." (He does so. You look on the signature page and see the name of a company officer who signed the answers.)

A: "Mr. Corporate Secretary prepared and signed the answers."

Q: "OK. Now, do you still deny that you designed the RST machine?"

A: "I can't answer that question as it is stated."

Q: "I don't understand. Please explain your answer." (Finally, you get a chance to explain.)

A: "Certainly I will. I said earlier that I was not <u>the</u> designer of the RST machine. There was a group of design people assigned to that work. I was the leader of the group. I was a designer, but not <u>the only</u> designer of the RST machine. As the leader of the design group, I am familiar with the design and the design decisions made. However, it would be misleading to say that I was the designer of the RST machine."

Avoid giving incomplete or distorted answers if you can. And be patient; eventually you will be given a chance to explain your answer.

Example 6.

An engineer from a competing company was asked to testify in a case involving a pipe falling on a worker from a pipelayer, a side-boom machine. The plaintiff claimed that if the manufacturer's machine had certain design features which had been previously used on the competitive machine, the accident would have been prevented. You have been asked to testify about the feature. The attorney defending the case for the manufacturer wants to emphasize that you are from a company of substance, with a record of good and safe products of its own.

Q: "Mr. Witness, why were you called to testify in this case?"

A: "I understand the plaintiff has suggested that if the machine in this litigation had been designed with a feature similar to one found in another type of our machines, the accident wouldn't have happened."

Q: "Do you know the defendant company in this case?"

A: "Yes, sir. I worked for them about 30 years ago, for a period of 17 years. They are the leading pipelayer company in the world."

Q: "Well, is the company you work for now not a little rinky-dink company of some sort?"

A: "No, sir, not at all. We are the number one farm equipment manufacturer in the world, and we are now about number four in construction machinery in the country and about number five in the world. We are in the top 100 of the Fortune 500."

This method of questioning, and the witness' responses, made answers that were expressed with some pride and some detail that established the relative background of the witness and the industry under discussion. The informality was more interesting and memorable than boring formal questions and answers.

Example 7.

As a case develops and as testimony unfolds, an attorney may, for good reason, change his plan of questions right in the middle of the testimony.

An expert and former employee was testifying about the ways to stop a tractor in a matter of litigation that involved a roll-over. The plaintiff claimed that a loose battery box had slid out and prevented him from stopping the tractor as it backed toward his shop building, until it hit the porch and rolled over.

The former witness had found a nearly identical tractor at a monastery near the factory, and had videotaped several ways to stop the machine, even though the clutch was blocked by something. The tape clearly demonstrated those ways to stop the machine.

The witness was to testify concerning the design of the machine and concerning the lack of maintenance and improper service which let the battery box slide out. (It wasn't designed to be loose.) Then, the witness intended to show the video as a demonstration that the machine could be stopped quickly and safely in several ways, even though the machine had been improperly serviced and maintained.

After the general testimony, the time for the video arrived.

Q: "Mr. Witness, did you make a videotape for use in this testimony?"

A: "Yes, I did."

Q: "What does that tape show? Describe it to us, briefly, if you will."

A: "The tape shows a tractor just like the plaintiff used. It was built in the same month as the plaintiff's tractor. It is being used as an apple orchard utility machine on the farms of a monastery near my home. With the approval and help of the Abbot and the monk in charge of the orchards, we taped several scenarios similar to the plaintiff's incident, showing how the tractor could have been stopped and should have been stopped."

Q: "Did you videotape the work?"

A: "Yes, sir."

Q: "You are not a professional photographer, are you?"

A: "No, sir, I am not."

Q: "Who drove the tractor?"

A: "In some runs, I did. In some other runs, Father Tim, the monk in charge of the orchard, drove the tractor."

Q: "How did you drive and videotape at the same time?"

A: "Easy. I used a tripod for the camera and instructed a technician when to start and when to stop the camera."

Q: "Even though this is an amateur job, you have no qualms about showing the video to the court and to the jury, do you?"

A: "Not at all."

Q: "And would you narrate the tape—that is, describe what is happening—for the jury?"

A: "Certainly. I am prepared to do that."

Q: "Well, it is nearly noon, and in the interest of time, we won't show the tape right now. However, if the opposing attorney wishes to show the tape while he is cross-examining you, you would let him, wouldn't you?"

A: "Yes."

Q: "No further questions."

The witness had expected to show the video. For whatever good reason he saw, the attorney decided not to show the video. It may have been to shorten the trial, in deference to uneasy jurors. It may be that he decided the testimony of the witness, without the video, made the point sufficiently. It may have been a tactical move to put the video on the back of the opposing attorney. Whatever the reason, the change in plan was made on the fly, and the attorney and witness read each other well enough to carry out the change in plans with no overt signs that the tactics had changed spontaneously.

Example 8.

You are an expert witness, hired by a client to assist him with the engineering details in a lawsuit.

Q: "How much do you get paid for your testimony?"

A: "I do not testify for money. I am paid $100 per hour for my consulting time and technical assistance to Mr. Attorney in this case. When it becomes necessary for me to testify, either in deposition or at trial, I do that as part of my consulting work. I am paid for my time and for my technical expertise."

Q: "Isn't $100 per hour a little steep for this work?"

A: "It is near or slightly below the average for such consulting work. I charge all of my clients the same rate, and they continue to hire me."

Sometimes the only way an opposing attorney can attack a witness whose testimony has hurt his client's case is to try to make him look like a hired gun, getting rich in the consulting business. Don't let that happen. You are needed for your technical expertise and your ability to explain the technical matter in an understandable way. Many attorneys have signs on their walls quoting Abraham Lincoln as saying that the product of an attorney is his time. The same is true for you as an expert.

Example 9.

You are being deposed as a company representative in a matter.

Q: "How do you decide when a product is ready for production?"

(Your attorney interrupts and objects that the word "you" is not clear. Is the question being asked, "How do you as an individual decide..." or, "How does your company decide that a product is ready for production?")

Q: "How does your company make a decision that a product is ready for production?"

Your answer, as a representative for the company, is important. It will likely bind the company—that is, it will be taken as the official company answer. The answer should be well thought out. It may be brief:

A: "We determine, measured against our objectives, that the product is ready to go."

Or, it may be long and comprehensive, describing the company product philosophy, the design and development process, the testing activities, the field testing, and the interplay with marketing, certain customers, dealers, and so forth.

Example 10.

Consider this question, as it is asked at different times with differing emphasis:

Q: "What causes the crawler tractor to turn in one direction or the other?"

A: "The steering mechanism and controls."

Q: "What causes the <u>crawler tractor</u> to turn in one direction or the other?"
(He is asking about a crawler tractor steering system as it differs from the steering system of a car.)

A: "The power is disconnected from one track, causing the other track to actually 'drive around' the track without power. The turn is in the direction of the track without power."

Q: "<u>What</u> causes the crawler tractor to turn in one direction or the other?"

A: "The operator does, by pulling on one or the other steering control lever."

Q: "What causes the crawler tractor to turn in <u>one direction</u> or the other?"

A: "The operator chooses the lever on the side of the direction he wishes to turn."

The attorney will probably be more specific and less artful in asking the question. He won't generally try to shade his question to convey a more detailed request. However, you need to listen to the question carefully. If he wants a complete, detailed description, the question will ask for details. If the adverb "briefly" appears in the question, be brief.

Example 11.

Watch for repeated questions. Sometimes the attorney will not be satisfied with your answer, and he will try to get the answer he wants. He won't repeat the question identically, because that will be the subject of an objection, and the objection will likely be sustained.

You are on cross-examination. You have testified that a device claimed to be able to prevent the accident will not, in fact, work.

Q: "Mr. Witness, you said that the motion alarm would not have prevented this accident. Is that correct?"

A: "That is my testimony, yes."

Q: "Do you mean to tell this jury that a simple motion alarm on the machine wouldn't have warned the plaintiff that the machine was moving toward him?"

A: "That very accurately states my belief, and what I wish this jury to understand."

Q: "So you say that backup alarms and warnings are no good. Is that right?"

A: "No, sir. I didn't say they were no good. I said that an alarm in this incident would not have prevented the plaintiff's injuries."

Q: "So we should never put backup or motion alarms on machines. Is that right?"

A: "No, sir. That is not right, and I did not so testify."

Q: "Well, you said that a warning or motion alarm would not have prevented this unfortunate accident, didn't you?"

A: "I believe I said a motion alarm would not have prevented the accident involving Mr. Plaintiff."

Q: "Well, what did you mean by that?"

A: "Exactly as I said. That a motion alarm would not have prevented this specific accident from happening to Mr. Plaintiff."

Q: "I don't understand." (Don't respond, even after a long pause. He hasn't asked another question. He will, eventually.)

Example 12.

Sometimes even your own attorney will try to get you to improve or restate your answer. Be alert for those situations. If he asks you to restate something, he probably wants an improvement in the answer—possibly a clearer explanation.

Q: "Mr. Witness, have you been involved in the design and manufacture of DEF machines?"

A: "My company has manufactured DEF machines now for 20 years."

Q: "Have you been involved in that work?"

(He really wants you to describe your personal involvement and knowledge. That is why he emphasized the word "you" the second time around.)

A: "Yes, sir. I have worked for more than four years in the design of DEF machines and have designed major components for that type of machine. Most recently, I was the project engineer on the latest new DEF machine, the Model RST."

In some instances, your answer may be too long, or too short.

Q: "What is your education, please?"

A: (Assume your answer went into great detail about dates, schools, teachers, courses, grades, and a myriad of other things, and that you gave an educational history in detail that took 10 minutes to tell.)

Q: "Fine, Mr. Witness. Now, would you briefly review your work history?" (The emphasis and use of the word "briefly" is an open signal for you to cut back on the detail and be less long-winded. Don't put the jury to sleep talking about yourself.)

Or you may be answering with too little detail to accomplish what your questioner wants to show.

Q: "Tell of your work experience, please."

A: "I have been employed by the JKL company for the past 28 years."

Q: "Tell us a little more detail of your experience at JKL Company." (He wants to show your detailed experience and tell the court and the jury why you are qualified—and maybe the most qualified—to offer opinions in this case. Don't brag, but don't be bashful, either. This is the time for a calm professional response about your experience.)

A: "I went to work for JKL Company in 1958 when I graduated. I have held a number of positions in both Engineering and Research, where I worked on hydraulics and stress analysis of scrapers and wheel loaders, among other products. I have designed several major components for machines, and I was the Project Engineer in charge of the UVW model. I have supervised groups of engineers and technicians on various jobs, and I am now an Assistant Chief Engineer for scrapers. If I were to pick out a technical specialty, it would be the performance and reliability of hydraulic systems, and especially on scrapers."

The attorney can fill in more from this point, if he wishes, by asking additional, more specific questions to indicate to you the desired subject of further discussion.

Example 13.

If everything goes to pieces around you and everyone is yelling, be quiet. Some attorneys like to put on a show. It usually doesn't work very well. Sometimes a real argument breaks out. It is best to keep calm and not enter the fray.

You are testifying as an expert in defense of a manufacturer whose machine is claimed to be defective because of a fire that occurred on the machine, a wheel loader. Before that, the court has ruled that information on fires that occurred on other types of machines made by the defendant company will not be admitted. It is declared irrelevant. So have questions about fires on machines made by other manufacturers, including competitors to your manufacturing defendant-client. You will have been told by your attorney that those exclusions have been made. Heed that instruction.

Q: "Have you studied the circumstances around the fire that is the subject of this case?"

A: "Yes, I have."

Q: "What have you studied, and what work did you do in this case?"

A: "I have read the claims and the pleadings in this case. I have studied the Interrogatory answers and reviewed documents that have been produced in this matter. I have read several deposition transcripts in the matter, and I have inspected the machine that is the subject of this action." (Good, so far. Stop there and let your attorney guide you if he wants you to go further. From here on, the answer is not good.) "I also have studied a number· of other fire cases on other machinery, both made by HIJ company and by others. In fact, I have testified in several other fire cases..."etc., etc.

Bad news. You shouldn't talk about "other fires" unless specifically instructed by the judge or by your client-attorney to do so.

If loud arguing erupts during your answer, stop immediately and keep quiet. Even though you may have "opened the door" to let the other information in after the attorneys got a ruling to keep it out, the attorney may still be able to salvage the situation.

Before you testify, you will be told not to mention certain words or subjects. One common unmentionable is insurance. If you do mention it, you may inadvertently allow the opposition to enter certain forbidden information of evidence anyway. Improper mention of those things may cause serious difficulty for your client, and may even lead to a mistrial.

In another situation, the attorneys may begin arguing some point of law without you even realizing or understanding what is going on. Don't try to understand. Just sit and be quiet until the storm is over.

Q: "Mr. Witness, have you talked with the plaintiff during your investigation of this matter?"

A: (You pause, properly, and then, before you can begin to answer, all of the attorneys are shouting and carrying on. Why? Perhaps there was an agreement that you would not talk to the plaintiff for some reason or other. Or maybe one of the attorneys forgot to disclose to the other that you had interviewed the plaintiff. Or maybe the conversation was unintentional and social and had nothing to do with the case. Whatever,

KEEP QUIET until the fury is over. Then you will be guided to speak—sometimes even by the judge. For example, it might continue this way.)

JUDGE: "Mr. Witness, according to the agreements between the attorneys, you and others were not to have talked with the plaintiff about this case. Did you?"

A: "No, Your Honor." (if that is the truth)

or

A: "Yes, I did, Your Honor, and I will describe our conversation."

Don't lie or bluff.

Example 14.

Be polite and courteous, but don't try to guide the questioning.

These are examples of questions, they are not a series of questions.

Q: "I think we have covered everything. Did I forget anything?"

A: (How would you know if the attorney forgot anything? If you answer, perhaps in a spirit of helpfulness, you may tell him exactly what he wants to know and is trying to find out. This question appears frequently at deposition. If you need to talk to your own attorney, take a break and do so. You are not required to help the other attorney, however, except to give honest and correct answers to his questions.)

Q: "Can you think of anything else I should ask about?"

A: (You don't have to think of what he should ask.)

Q: "I will bet you are glad that this is almost finished." (You probably are, but answer professionally.)

A: "I suppose we are all tired, but I am here to answer whatever proper questions are posed to the best of my ability. I'll do so as long as it is reasonable."

Q: "I suppose you have a plane to catch."

A: "Yes, but I am prepared to do what is necessary to properly conduct and conclude this deposition."

Don't fall into a time trap or some other problem that may disclose your discomfort or inconvenience. If you have a time problem, have your attorney discuss it at the start.

Example 15.

Watch out for questions that may tend to lead you into an uncomfortable position.

Generally, the opposing attorney may try to make you look biased in favor of plaintiffs' cases or in favor of defendants' cases, depending on whose side you are on.

Q: "What percentage of your cases are for the defendant (or for the plaintiff)?"

A: "I do not know precisely, but perhaps about 90% for the plaintiff and 10% for the defendant." (If, of course, that is a reasonable estimate.)

Q: "Then you are usually working on the side of the plaintiff, is that true?"

A: "That seems to be the history of my involvement, yes."

Q: "Why do you not work more for defendants?"

A: "I have been retained frequently by plaintiffs and only infrequently by defendants."

Q: "So, your opinions and testimony usually support the side of the plaintiff. Is that true?"

A: "It may be. However, I examine a particular matter, when asked to do so, and I develop an opinion in the matter. I do not develop that opinion with the aim of supporting either the plaintiff or the defendant. It is an engineering and professional opinion, based upon my technical experience and expertise. If that opinion is useful to my attorney-client and supports the position of his client, he may well retain me to testify and express that opinion. I don't pick the sides in a dispute. They pick me."

(A similar series of responses may be made whether your involvement is heavily on one side or the other, or if your involvement is approximately 50/50.)

Q: "What percentage of your cases are for the defendant or plaintiff?"

A: "My involvement is about even. I don't know the exact relationship between them, but I would estimate that I do about the same number of cases for a plaintiff as I do for a defendant."

Q: "So, in effect, you work for whoever pays you. Is that so?"

A: "That is not so. I am paid for my time and for my expertise. I investigate and examine cases when asked to do so. I develop my professional opinion, and give that opinion to my attorney-client. If they find that opinion useful, they may retain me further, for testimony and other assistance. I don't pick my clients. They pick me."

Conclusion

There is no suggestion that an answer should be other than truthful. Knowing all of the question variations covered in this chapter should have no effect upon the truthfulness of the answer. However, there may be reasons to limit, emphasize, or reword the answer, based on the question asked and the situation in which it is asked. Delicate inflections and voice pitches, and careful wording of a question or an answer, may carry far more meaning than the mere words used.

You will find it helpful to practice answering questions, thinking carefully about each question and how it is asked.

Chapter 12

ACCIDENT RECONSTRUCTION

This chapter will consider the reasons for reconstructing an accident and the philosophical ideas involved in accident reconstruction. Except for a few examples, the detailed technology of accident reconstruction will not be studied; it is beyond the scope of this book.

In the process of litigation involving machinery and people, there are frequent disagreements as to how the accident happened. Convincing evidence and opinions, to the court and the jury, may well be a reasonable and credible accident reconstruction. That is the subject of this chapter.

Why Do We Need an Accident Reconstruction?

The existence of litigation denotes the existence of a dispute. That dispute, when it is about an accident or an injury, may well separate the two parties in their understanding as to the cause of the incident, and perhaps even as to the incident itself. In such cases, the dispute often includes a difference in belief or understanding about the scenario of the accident.

Claims may be made contending certain things happened. Those claims may be supported by testimony from witnesses, and perhaps even eyewitnesses. Certainly the injured plaintiff will have an understanding of the accident scenario.

There will be physical evidence, also. Skid marks, damage to machinery from contacts, distances rolled and moved, and other physical evidence may also be made available concerning the incident.

In the ideal situation, all of the evidence, testimony, and personal recollections fit together, in a logical and reasonable scenario. In such cases, there is seldom any dispute as to the accident scenario, although there may still be a major dispute as to the cause and liability for the loss and injury.

Things aren't always ideal, though. The story of one witness may conflict with the story of another. The story of a witness may not agree with some of the physical evidence found. Some things told in testimony may be recognized by engineers, doctors, or other experts to be physically impossible, and therefore not correct.

There doesn't need to be any intentional distortion in the testimony. Peculiar things happen in the minds of people involved in or close to traumatic happenings. They do the best they can to "record" the incident in their minds. However, as they rationalize and reason through the occurrence, they may modify their own concepts from what they thought happened to what they thought must have happened. Such are the sources of the conflicts that arise. Such rationalization often leads to testimony and evidence that doesn't fit together properly.

You cannot fault an injured worker for not knowing, in precise detail, everything that happened, how it happened, and where he and everyone else was when it happened. Neither can you fault an eyewitness for not being perfectly certain of all the details when his partner or co-worker is in a dangerous situation.

It is an unusual accident that is perfectly captured and recorded on the record—on film and in the minds of the witnesses. There are usually missing pieces to the story and there are frequent disagreements on the details of the incident, and the time and space scenarios.

Thus, there is the need for an accident reconstructionist—one who can scientifically determine and state the most probable scenarios of the accident, in terms of personal actions, time scales, space or motion scales, the starting conditions, and the final conditions of the incident.

What Goes Into a Good Accident Reconstruction?

The purpose of a good accident reconstruction is not only to understand what happened. It is important in presenting a case to a jury that the jury also be shown the most likely scenario of the incident. Of course, in a deep dispute, there may well be two or more competing "most likely scenarios." If so, the jury may be asked to choose which they believe is the most likely.

The attorney for the plaintiff may engage an accident reconstructionist to develop his concept of the incident and his opinions as to the proximate cause of the incident. He will, as a proper advocate for his client, be looking to recover damages for his client.

The attorney for the defendant will also want to know, as accurately as possible, what the incident scenario might be. From that, he may develop defenses against the claims aimed at his client's product or against the conduct of his client. In either case, the successful proof of a client's position may well rest upon a reasonable and believable accident reconstruction.

A good accident reconstruction cannot ignore any piece of evidence or testimony. Sure, some of it doesn't fit, and some of it may be wrong. Some of it may even be fraudulent, but hope and assume that the truth, so far as possible, is being told and that no evidence is contrived.

A collection of every piece of available information is the only proper starting point for the reconstruction. The reconstructionist needs to know everything he or she can about the conditions of the people, the machine, and the situation on the job site <u>before</u> the accident. This is the starting point. What was the machine doing? What were the people doing? Why? What were the conditions surrounding the site before the incident happened?

Next must be accumulated all of the information, testimony, and impressions of the people involved and the witnesses. The recollections and memories of each witness should be recorded and considered in the reconstruction. Even if the reactions or recollections differ or outright disagree, they should be considered.

Then, physical evidence, including photographs, broken parts, marks in the road or in the ground, measurements, distances, and other data, has to be collected. These become part of the story of what happened, and eventually may impact the reconstruction.

The final positions of the machine, parts, and people involved should be recorded with accuracy. In essence, this becomes the end point of the incident scenario.

Don't twist or modify any of the original information to eliminate any of the disagreements. In doing so, you may well destroy the one important piece of the reconstruction puzzle. Only a reconstructionist with a preconceived scenario of the incident will bend or twist information to make it fit. If a piece of information or testimony does not fit, it may be very important in the final analysis.

To these items of evidence and information, the reconstructionist will add the knowledge of physics, mathematics, mechanics, engineering, psychology, medicine, and other sciences to the job as needed.

The reconstructionist's job, now, is almost defined:

- to take all of the available information and to use science to determine the most likely scenario of the incident.

How is the Reconstruction Done?

To perform an accident reconstruction, the expert must, in essence, recreate the accident as it happened. One might suspect that a real reenactment of the accident would be the way to go. In a few circumstances that may be true. Further, some parts of the accident may be reenacted in real time and on real conditions. Usually, however, such a recreation is far too dangerous and costly.

You need to build what amounts to a story of the incident. You build that story on a time basis, and on a three-dimensional space basis. (Note here that "story" in regard to accident reconstruction means a description, as full and as accurate as possible, about what happened in the incident being studied and reconstructed.)

The logical starting point is to lay out all of the information, evidence, testimony, witness statements, broken parts, photographs, and anything else of significance and use what is available. In effect, you put down your story, made up of each and every piece of information available to you.

When you have made this first layout of information, several things will appear:

- some of the information will contradict other information. Some witnesses may not agree. Physical evidence may not agree with witness testimony, and so on.

- some evidence and information will be in poor definition. That is, some of the information may be general (fast, large, heavy, etc.) when more accurate information is needed (55 miles per hour, a trailer 22 feet long, 3200 pounds, etc.)

- some needed or desired evidence may be missing altogether. Marks may have been erased. Data may not have been taken. The evidence may have been misplaced, etc. Worst of all, some witnesses may be deceased or otherwise unable to respond to questions.

- some of the information may not seem correct on the surface. For example, a witness may testify that he saw a fire, but no other information suggesting a fire exists. Or another witness may say she heard a scream from an area where no other people were found or believed to have been. Maybe marks on the scene of the accident seem to denote action that is impossible or that seems not to have anything to do with the incident under investigation.

- some of the testimony may change as it is being assembled. This does not suggest faking data or fraud, although that is possible. Yet, as witnesses consider what they saw and experienced, they tend to form their impressions into logical segments of the incident. Sometimes they change their stories into what they feel "must be a more accurate story."

- some of the evidence and information doesn't seem to fit into any logical format, at least in what we suspect or begin to see as the scenario. (Note here that a good reconstructionist will delay any early or tentative thoughts on the matter until all the information is in and all of the analyses are completed.)

- sometimes the information has no outward or apparent problems, but someone still "smells a rat." The unproved gut feel of the witness or even the reconstructionist may be significant. (In truth, such "smelling of a rat" is usually an incomplete piece of logic, perhaps subconscious, that is a partial or incomplete signal that something is not right.)

In each case of incomplete or conflicting information, something needs to be done to resolve the conflict or fill in the blank. At this point, the reconstructionist will do two things:

First, he will look for other information to fill in the blank spaces and to resolve the conflicting data, at least to some usable level of certainty.

Second, he will begin to assemble the pieces into <u>possible scenarios</u>. At this stage, any possible scenario must be allowed and considered. To omit a possible scenario without good reason destroys the process and greatly lessens its probative value.

As the reconstructionist works on the two paths, a workable resolution will begin to emerge from the chaos. Some lost information will be filled in. Other conflicts will be resolved by the witnesses or by the existence of physical evidence admissible by everyone involved.

For a while, the possible scenarios will seem to multiply beyond reason. However, as the information becomes more focused, the possible scenarios will tend to reduce by self-elimination. For good and proper reason, some scenarios will dismiss themselves from possibility. Probability still is not a factor, so don't eliminate a scenario just because it seems not to be probable. If it is possible, at this stage of knowledge and understanding of the information and evidence, keep it in the game.

As missing information or blank spots are filled in, keep track of the sources and reasons for the information. As conflicts in information or testimony are resolved—at least to the satisfaction of the reconstructionist—keep the reasons and explanations for future use. You may, and probably will, have to defend and explain the reconstruction.

Finally, you end up with a list of possible scenarios. Perhaps there is only one, although that seldom happens. There could be 20 or 30 possibilities—a difficult problem, but still solvable.

Note here that, as the reconstructionist goes through the efforts of filling in missing information and resolving conflicting information, he will eliminate some of the original possible scenarios. When a scenario, under the light of the best information available, becomes impossible, it may be set aside, at least for the present. It is also possible that additional information will lead to other new scenarios. They will, of course, need to be added to the list of possibilities.

Now, with a list of possible scenarios, as complete with information and as free from conflicting information as possible, the analyst is ready to move to the next step. That step is to rate all of the possible scenarios in terms of probability. From this process, two more things will emerge.

First, according to Pareto's concepts—and verified by experience—only a very small portion of the possible scenarios will be substantially probable. This will tend to allow focus on two or three or four scenarios as the most probable.

Second, the process will show up a significant portion of the possible scenarios to be so unlikely, so low in probability, that they may be set aside or possibly discarded with little, if any, chance of error.

Evaluating the probability of a scenario happening is partially a matter of logic and partially a matter of looking at all of the factors—mechanical, physical, human, and others. One needs to go through the evaluation of probabilities of scenarios with others, exposing the logic and reasoning to critical review. If it stands up under criticism, good. If it doesn't stand the light of outside critics, then the evaluation must be reconsidered.

Note that accident reconstruction is a multidisciplinary activity. When no witness can provide information, physics or mathematics may do so. When

217

no mechanical fault is apparent, human fault may be the key. When witness evidence from two or more sources conflicts, medical information or physical data may help answer the questions.

It is also important to note that the possible scenario, if it is to be taken seriously into consideration, must follow known rules of physics and engineering. For example, no falling body can react (fall) more rapidly than that under the pull of gravity unless it has obvious external power. The transfers of energy and the movements of masses through the space and time lines must follow the accepted rules of physics, mechanics, and thermodynamics.

The reconstructionist is allowed (in fact, he had better do so) to calculate the expected paths and time lines to show that they do, indeed, follow proper rules. Violation of those accepted rules makes a scenario doubtful, if not impossible. If a scenario violates too many rules of physics or other sciences, it is a good candidate for elimination.

Note also the above general process assumes vast information and all sorts of possible unknowns and conflicts in information. If an accident happens with no witness except a deceased victim, such conditions may exist. However, usually there is a great deal of harmony in the analysis, and there is usually a rapid reduction of the "possible scenarios" to a very short list. Some of the examples that follow will show this.

It is even more likely that the reconstruction will arrive at a single major scenario, with some conflict or dispute in one detail or another.

It is time to look at the objective of the reconstruction again—to establish the scenario of the accident as accurately as possible. The work will end with either one possible scenario (and that must be the most likely one) or with a small number of possible scenarios of which one or two seem to be by far the most probable.

A Believable Accident Reconstruction

Perhaps a comment on what makes a believable accident reconstruction will aid in recognizing the end point of the study, when it is approached.

1. The good reconstruction analysis must square with the laws of physics and the rules of engineering used in the analysis. Blank spots in the information or in the analysis must be kept to a minimum and conflicts must be resolved. Otherwise, the analysis is of little value, perhaps not even as a theory.

2. The reconstruction scenario should have good agreement with the mass of the information and evidence available. Seldom does a reconstruction arrive at a completely new, different, and unexpected result. Some participants still may not like the scenario, but it should represent the mass of the available information. If it does not, it will be difficult to present to a jury as a convincing scenario.

3. The reconstruction should be explainable to lay people—jurors, for instance. If one has to understand all of the science that went into the analysis, the reconstruction may be lost.

4. The reconstruction should be as free as possible from bias and from preconceived notions and ideas. It sounds as if some of these items that make a good reconstruction might contradict each other. On one hand, the reconstruction should not be a surprise and, at the same time, a good reconstruction must be scientifically valid. This involves both careful analysis and study and also the use of good common sense. These are not in conflict. They work together for the best result.

5. As a rule, an accident reconstruction will not be a big surprise. If it is—that is, if the reconstruction varies widely from the expected pattern—it will need to be carefully and clearly explained, and delivered with patience.

6. Accident reconstructions may be disputed—they are in dispute in active litigation matters. A good reconstruction, then, will be one that will withstand any and all attacks upon it, including bias, wrong input, wrong methods, and other claims. The reconstruction must stand up to questioning from the opposition, who may well have interests other than yours. Any accident reconstruction can expect to be questioned, argued, and even attacked. When a reconstructionist presents his final result, he needs to be comfortable that the scenario will withstand attack.

Examples

Example 1.

A mine worker was injured when he was crushed between the front of a van, which was stuck, and the back of a large crawler tractor, which had backed up to the van to pull it out. While working between the van and the tractor to hook up a cable, the injured man became caught between the two.

These possible scenarios existed:

- the tractor jumped into gear and moved,
- the van moved forward into the tractor,
- someone drove the van into the tractor,
- someone drove the tractor back into the van,
- the van slid into the tractor,
- the tractor slid back into the van, or,
- the accident was faked.

Some other scenarios may exist, but are not likely. Everyone, including potential plaintiffs and potential defendants, agreed that the above list of possible scenarios was complete.

The injured man decided to file claims against the tractor manufacturer claiming the machine had, somehow, jumped into gear and backed into him. No real dispute existed among the witnesses. No one saw the tractor move except for a co-worker who was helping the injured man hook up the cable. He saw the tractor moving, and jumped out of the way, but didn't have time to warn the injured man. The injured man was also the tractor operator, who had backed into position to pull out the van. When he saw his co-worker having trouble hooking up the cable, he got off the tractor to help him.

The injured man testified that he had set the brake and placed the machine in "neutral" before he did so. It was raining. Visibility was bad, and no one heard any specific noise or change in sound before or as the tractor moved. Witnesses inside the van thought they saw the tractor move. At the end of the accident, a mine supervisor testified that the machine was in "neutral" and the brake set when he went onto the machine after the incident to move it away.

A consultant for the defendant manufacturer investigated and went forward with the list of possible scenarios above. Certain things appeared to make some of the possible scenarios less than good choices.

Following is a condensed treatment of the possible scenarios:

Regarding the first scenario, the controls of the machine did not seem to have been physically moved into powered motion condition. Of course, someone might have left the gear engaged or the brake not set. However, that disputes the testimony of the driver and the mine supervisor. The claims, and the lawsuit, concentrated upon the possibility that some defect in the design would allow the unexpected engagement and motion. Tests, records, and inspection disclosed no evidence of such action. Attempts to make the incident happen again failed completely.

Regarding the second scenario, the van was stuck and unlikely to move. Further, all witnesses inside the van agreed the van didn't move until the tractor hit it, and that no one was behind the wheel of the van. The driver of the van had been elected to get out into the rain and hook up the cable. That testimony also eliminates the third scenario, at least until other things can be proved.

Regarding the fourth scenario, no one noticed anyone on the tractor at the time of the accident.

It is almost impossible that the van slid into the tractor (the fifth scenario). It was stuck.

Maybe the tractor slid back into the van, without moving the tracks, without being in gear, and without the brakes releasing (the sixth scenario).

For the time being, at least, the idea of a fake accident (the seventh scenario) was not likely. The medical information showed the plaintiff had indeed been injured in a crushing way. Marks of the injuries coincided with the end of the tractor and drawbar and the front of the van in the stuck position.

221

At this first cut, it seems that the first and the sixth scenarios are the more probable actions.

A reexamination of the photos taken at the accident site showed that tractor had not left any track or grouser marks in the mud. Further, a reexamination of the site and the testimony of the witnesses confirmed that the tractor had "backed down an incline to where the van was stuck near the bottom of a gully." A few tests confirmed that the crawler would begin to slide with the brakes locked when parked on a 6.5 degree slope in the rain with slippery mud. The slope at the point of the accident was close to 9 degrees.

With no evidence to show that the tractor had jumped into gear or that the brakes had failed, the group agreed that the "slipping in the mud" scenario was the most likely one.

Without that agreement, of course, the matter would have eventually gone to trial where a jury would have determined which of the two scenarios, the first or the sixth, was correct.

At this point, one more objection was raised. If the locked tractor track would slide in the mud at about 6.5 degrees of slant, why didn't the tractor slide in the mud right away, when the operator stopped and applied the parking brakes? A little bit of testing showed that when the moving crawler stopped, a little mud or indentation of the track grouser in the ground would hold the machine in the stopped position for a short time—until the continually falling rain and the vibration of the idling tractor overcame the resistance of the mud or grouser indentation and began to slide in a more normal fashion.

Example 2.

A man was found dead in a driveway next to his business. Two hundred feet away, a crawler bulldozer was stopped against an aluminum building. The dozer had made marks on the building for some five feet before it stopped. The intake cover and a partially used can of ether lay on the ground some 50 feet in the opposite direction from the man's body. The man was found by members of his family when he did not come home for supper.

The investigators and police generally concluded that the victim had been standing on the track of the crawler using the ether to start the machine which had not been run for some time. He apparently was going to do some clean-up work in an area behind the shop building where he ran a small machine shop business. It was Saturday and no one else was at the shop. Apparently there were no eyewitnesses to the incident.

A consultant familiar with crawler dozers was called in to verify the incident and to agree, if possible, to the reported cause of the incident. The consultant had no reason to disbelieve any of the information.

Details of the police report stated that the tractor was not running when found, but that the throttle lever was half open and the transmission in reverse gear. All of this agrees with the reverse motion of the dozer, and the fact that the victim may have been trying to start the machine and was using ether to assist in a relatively "cold" start. In addition, the fuel tank was still over half full; the engine had not stopped by running out of fuel.

One peculiar piece of information caught the attention of the consultant. The victim's body, according to an autopsy report, had a bruise some 10 inches wide across his body, coinciding with the internal injuries which had occurred. Yet the tracks on the dozer were a full 18 inches wide. The consultant made a note to check this apparent discrepancy.

He also noted an area on the outside wall of the building some 50 feet away from the crawler impact point where other damage was apparent on the wall. An employee, he was told, had bumped the wall with his pickup truck several weeks earlier.

The consultant then listed the possible scenarios:

1. First, the victim might have been trying to start the machine, and the machine had started while he was standing on the track, throwing him behind the machine which then backed over him, then ran until it hit the aluminum building and stalled out. A lot of "end condition" evidence tended to support that scenario.

2. The victim might have fallen off the machine while running it, and he might have been injured in a similar sequence.

3. Someone else might have been at the controls of the machine during the starting process and that, in turn, led to the victim falling and being run over. In such a case, there was a missing witness.

4. Foul play. No evidence of any kind indicated any reason to suspect or look for foul play.

5. Maybe the victim was hit and run over by another person in another vehicle. In that case, one can theorize that the victim was placed in relationship to the tractor as to suggest that the tractor had run over the victim. A missing witness—and possibly more.

Other possible scenarios were more farfetched than these and justified no serious attention.

The consultant then began looking for incongruencies in the information. He found two items that were not easy to explain.

First, he looked at the point at which the tractor had hit the aluminum building wall and stalled out. The damage and the stopping point of the tractor were all well within the span between the interior steel structure of the building. The crawler had not hit any steel in the building. It had not been stalled out by the small amount of damage done to the aluminum wall of the building. This indicated to the consultant that the tractor had not stalled as it appeared to have done. If the dozer had backed into the building at about a 7-degree angle from parallel with the building wall, the tractor would have made much more damage, probably going through the building into the inside, unless it had hit a part of the steel structure. It had done neither. The damage done by the dozer backing into the building was little more than the damage done by the pickup truck earlier.

The consultant also confirmed the 10-inch bruise on the body and the 18-inch width of the tracks. It seems impossible for one to be run over with an 18-inch track and left with a 10-inch bruise. Further discussion with the medical examiner confirmed this apparent serious discrepancy.

To further study the situation, new possible scenarios were listed:

6. Someone had accidentally hit the victim with another vehicle, probably a car or a small truck, and injured him. Then, the scene had been changed to relate the body to the position of the tractor against the wall. Motive, aside from panic, was not considered. This scenario is an extension of the last scenario in the original list.

7. The accident happened as originally thought, and the medical relationship was such that an 18-inch track would only make a 10-inch bruise in going across the body. Medical experts said that this scenario was just not possible. In fact, the examiner was willing to testify that, in his opinion, the injury and bruise were not caused by the dozer passing over the victim's body.

The consultant proceeded to set up a test where he would intentionally ride a similar dozer backwards and into the wall of an aluminum building of the same make to evaluate exactly what the damage would look like in such an incident.

While the test was being prepared, the case was settled without trial. No final resolution was revealed as to the incident. However, you can see how the parts of an accident reconstruction were important to the understanding of what happened. You also see the working together of engineering data and medical information.

Example 3.

A luxurious motor home burned shortly after the owner had serviced it and parked it in a shopping mall parking lot. The home was about a year old and had relatively few travel miles on it. Damage in the engine compartment and in the rear two-thirds of the vehicle was total, for all practical purposes. The insurance company was interested in the cause. A local fire marshall, trained in fire investigation, concluded that the fire had started somewhere in the engine compartment. In the course of his investigation, he identified a fuel filter as being at or near the center of the fire. He was not able to pinpoint any ignition source for certain. Damage was so severe that no electrical or other sources could be identified.

An engine expert was called in and together with the fire marshall, they rein-spected the remains of the motor home. Based upon the reports and the testimony of the witnesses, these two likely scenarios were listed:

1. The fire was intentionally set.

2. The fire started from a fuel leak hitting a hot surface and bursting into flame, which then caught the wiring, hoses, and belts in the engine com-partment and spread to the wooden structure of the motor home itself.

The fire marshall found no indication of arson. It wasn't ruled out, mind you, but the idea was set aside for a time.

Where, then, did the fuel come from, and what ignited it? The fuel filter the marshall had noted earlier was located in the engine compartment, but reach-able from the bedroom inside the motor home so "it could be easily drained periodically to avoid fuel fouling and blockage." A review of the service records showed that the motor home had a series of problems with the fuel system, some of which were thought to be from dirty fuel. The owner him-self had drained the fuel system that very day, while the unit was being fueled up.

Looking back in the engine compartment of the unit, the two investigators noticed that the fuel filter was directly above an exhaust transfer pipe from the exhaust side of the engine to the muffler. A scenario where the filter, or a hose leading to it, was leaking and where the leaking fuel could fall down onto a hot exhaust pipe when the motor home was stopped was easy to view. Further, no hose clamps were found on the remains of the filter and hose ends, which still were on the filter.

That furnished a most likely scenario where the leak occurred at or around the filter and where the fuel leaked down onto the transfer pipe after the motor home had stopped. The owner and witnesses confirmed the fire was noted within five minutes after the unit had been parked and stopped. The parties in the matter settled soon, subscribing to the reconstructed scenario of the fire.

Example 4.

Two young men were working together one evening, clearing old junk cars out of a storage lot, using a crawler dozer to move the junk cars. It began to snow quite hard, and the two worked late to get the job finished. They were down to the last three cars when an accident happened and one of the young men was killed. The other young man had injuries on his thighs, but he survived.

The story of the survivor went like this:

"We were down to the last three cars. I was running the tractor and my partner was hooking the chain from the tractor to the car. Then we would haul the junk car to the assembly point for the truck to pick it up. As I backed up to the car—an old Lincoln—I believe my partner had some trouble trying to figure out where to hook the chain on the car. I got off the tractor to help him. While we were working between the tractor and the old Lincoln, the tractor suddenly started to move backward. I yelled and jumped to the side. The tracks ran over my upper legs, but I didn't get hurt as badly. The track ran over my partner's head. I called 911 for help."

No one seriously doubted the tragic story. Naturally the investigation focused on why the tractor moved suddenly and without warning. A suit was filed, claiming some defect in the tractor was the cause of the death. Allegedly, the unexpected motion of the tractor was caused by some design defect which would allow such motion to happen, and by a lack of warning as to the possibility of unexpected motion.

Two engineers investigated the matter. They obtained copies of all of the police photographer's pictures. When they tried to fit the survivor's story into the evidence in the pictures, taken within minutes of the incident, several things refused to fit.

There was no new damage to the front of the Lincoln which was being hooked up. Yet, according to the witness' story, the crawler had backed far enough to run over both the victim and the survivor, at least some 18 feet, according to the analysis.

227

Second, there were no track prints or other tracks in the snow in front of the Lincoln for at least 25 feet.

Third, there were tracks and footprints in the snow on both sides of the tractor as it sat after the accident, and there were footprints on one side of the tractor tracks behind the tractor. Some tracks may have been made and/or destroyed by people at the accident site immediately after the incident and before the photos were taken.

Fourth, there were tractor tracks backed up to the opposite end of the Lincoln from which the accident occurred. The witness-operator had said that they had made only one attempt to backup to the Lincoln to hook it up—obviously not an accurate statement.

It quickly became obvious that the accident had not happened as described and at the place described. Rather, the operator had apparently and probably accidentally run over his partner while backing toward the Lincoln. The tractor never got there. After discovering the accident, the operator drove forward and called 911. The story of the unintended motion probably got built up as the emergency people got to the scene and began to "wonder" what happened. A tragic incident, of course, to everyone involved—but not quite an accurate account of it.

Example 5.

An equipment operator was asked to move an earthmover on a public road to a new work site. As he did so, he hit a concrete bridge abutment and was thrown out of the machine operator's seat and onto the ground, sustaining severe injuries.

A products liability action was filed against the manufacturer of the earthmoving machine, claiming that as the operator eased up on the throttle, the engine slowed down. Further, the claim said that when the engine slowed the steering became too slow to respond, allowing the machine to hit the bridge abutment and thus injuring the operator.

There were several witnesses who testified to the same general sequence of events. The earthmoving machine was about to be passed by an automobile.

The operator slowed, apparently, and turned the machine to the right to give the auto sufficient room. It seemed to all of the witnesses that the operator never tried to straighten out the vehicle. He drove it right into the concrete abutment, from all appearances.

The earthmoving machine's steering was an electric-powered system, operating off a generator driven by the engine. The operator said he was running in road gear at top engine speed when the car started to pass him. He said he slowed (took his foot off the "throttle foot pedal") and turned the steering wheel a little to the right to give the passing car more room. When he tried to straighten the machine back out, he said the steering didn't respond, and the machine ran right into the concrete abutment.

No steering problems or defects were found on the machine by police, the OSHA inspector, or the owner of the machine after the incident. The machine continued to work from that time on with no problems or reports. Neither had there been any reports of trouble before the accident.

An engineer from the manufacturer tried to reproduce the problem. He couldn't. Then an accident reconstructionist was called in—an engineer who knew the type of machine well. The reconstructionist tried several scenarios, none of which he could reproduce physically.

Then he went out onto a finished but unconnected two-mile stretch of highway, with the approval of highway authorities, and laid out the scene of the accident with chalk on the pavement. (Of course, there was no concrete abutment to run into and no ditch to fall into.)

He found something completely missed by everyone up to that point. The machine had a direct connected transmission, which meant that there was always a direct relationship between the engine speed and the speed of the machine over the ground. When the foot was taken off the accelerator, the engine speed did not die down in a second or two as theorized. Instead, it continued to turn at the same relative speed as the machine was moving over the ground. The claim that the steering dropped off as the engine speed slowed was not accurate. Rather, it dropped off as the engine slowed down with the slowing vehicle speed. Where it took only two or three seconds for the engine to slow by itself when it was in gear and connected to the transmission, it kept running at a speed coincident with the vehicle speed. When the foot was taken off the accelerator while the vehicle was in gear and running at 25 mph, the vehicle did not slow to a stop until some 12 to 15 seconds later. Reconsidering the plaintiff's theory, the steering could not possibly deteriorate in the 2.7 seconds the reconstruction showed the accident to have taken.

Disputes over the total time of the accident still left the court and the jury with several possible scenarios on a time basis to consider. The consultant successfully, by the test and by related analyses of the various scenarios presented by the plaintiff, showed that none of these could be ascribed to a steering failure. The conclusion: the operator had merely taken his attention from his driving and lost control when the auto was passing him. Had he tried to steer back into his straight line of travel, he had more than ample engine speed to provide rapid and immediate steering.

Example 6.

A consultant was called to investigate a fatal accident. The incident involved the roll-over of a wheel loader which was being used in a farming operation to handle and load bales of hay. The victim, and owner of the machine, was "roading" or transporting the machine from a field in which he had worked back to the home farm and shop. The roading distance was some fifteen miles, through some curving and hilly but well-surfaced highway.

The operator had approached the top of a grade running about 3/4 mile and through a series of three curves. There were no eyewitnesses to the incident, although a farm family near the accident site said they heard two distinct crash sounds as they were eating their supper. They notified police and others of the accident.

The accident site was some 1200 feet from the top of the hill, and just before the machine would have entered the second of two curves on the hill. The road, at that point, had been cut through the edge of a ridge, leaving an embankment going up from each side of the highway. The machine was lying upside down, on top of the deceased operator. The machine seemed almost to have fallen in that position. There were no skid marks on the road. There were tracks off the road and onto the embankment to the right side of the road. It was obvious where the machine had hit small trees and brush. Police photos and other photographs were taken of the site and the machine.

Subsequent investigation of the machine by a consulting engineer hired by the victim's insurance company found several problems:

- The outlet hose line from the air compressor was burst. Therefore there was no air to the brakes at the time of the accident.

- The hose that had been on the compressor outlet was not the correct hose (part number or type) that should have been there.

- There were no indications of service brake failure, other than the lack of air as a result of the broken hose.

- There was no indication of any other significant problems on the machine.

- The machine was 17 years old. It had been resold three times since its original sale.

- The machine was not equipped with roll-over protection (ROPS). It did have a light canopy for weather protection.

The police and other authorities viewed the accident in this manner:

The victim was driving the machine home. He started down the hill, with which he was very familiar. As the machine began down the hill, the operator noticed that he had no brakes. As the machine sped up, he approached the second curve and, knowing he still had some downhill distance to go and another curve to negotiate, he tried to stop the machine by running into the high embankment on the right side. He chose that direction because the bank was high and very steep, and there was no chance that he could go nearly to the top of the embankment. The investigators then theorized that the machine had tipped or rolled over and rolled back onto the highway where it was found.

Lawsuits were filed claiming that a defective brake line design, a defective brake design, and the lack of a qualified roll-over protection system had directly caused the demise of the victim.

Two parties to the legal action hired accident reconstructionists. The consultant for one party was a graduate of a local police program, training policemen to evaluate auto accidents by skid marks and such evidence. He concluded that the machine could not have been moving very fast forward because there were almost no signs of skidding or scrape marks showing any motion of the machine after it became upside down.

The consultant for another party in the suit was an engineer experienced in the design and development of machinery of the type involved. That consultant inspected the site, the photos and reports, and the machine.

Two items of importance were disclosed. First, there was very little damage and almost no scraping marks on the top of the machine—that portion that was against the road at the end of the accident scenario. Second, the photos showed that the remains of the canopy were distorted to the left side of the machine as it lay on its top at the accident. At first, that didn't seem important, but as the consultant considered the accident scenario, he realized that if the machine had rolled over to the left side as it tried to climb the embankment, the remains of the canopy would have been distorted to the right side, not on the left side, where it came to rest.

With those two apparently misfit pieces of information, the consultant decided to perform his own accident reconstruction. He began his reconstruction with the original scenario theory of the accident. The concerns were the end points or conditions. It seemed illogical that the canopy should have been bent to the wrong side of the machine, if, indeed, it did roll over to the left as believed. Also, one would ask, why would a runaway machine land upside down and not continue to slide or skid forward?

The second consultant's accident reconstruction in most points verified the original scenario. Physical calculations dealing with speed and energy showed that if the machine had been coasting, against the drag of the engine in gear, from the top of the hill, the speed would have reached about 32 miles per hour at the point where the operator tried to stop the machine into the bank.

Even if the operator had (incorrectly and unsafely) put the machine in neutral and let it coast, the speed would have been only 36 to 37 miles per hour—not unreasonable.

Using the physical characteristics of energy and energy transfer, the consultant then calculated the path of the machine, up on the embankment and rolling 180 degrees and then falling back onto the pavement. The word "falling" was the missing piece of the puzzle. The machine had enough energy to run up on the bank, roll over 180 degrees, and still be 4 to 7 feet in the air—that is, it would be high enough to fall back to the ground from a height of some 4 to 7 feet in the air.

The reconstruction then looks like this:

The machine was going 32 to 37 miles per hour as it approached the curve. The operator, seeing a chance to stop the machine, tried to turn it into the bank. The machine, because of its forward speed, ran up onto the bank at an angle, using up some of the forward energy. It ran up the bank until it was some 4 to 7 feet off the surface of the road, using up some more of the energy. The fact that the right wheels went onto the bank first caused the machine to roll or rotate to the left, counterclockwise as viewed by the operator in his seat. The thrust against the bank caused the machine to be pushed back out toward the center of the road. The combinations of these things used up the kinetic energy and the machine literally dropped back onto the road, bending the canopy to the left instead of to the right as might be expected, and leaving almost no indication of forward skidding on either the road or on the top of the machine as it came to rest.

To "box in" the reconstruction, several other scenarios were checked.

What if the brakes failed part way down the hill? Did the machine have enough energy to get into its final position as shown by the police photos? Obviously, it did. The end evidence showed that. A calculation was made to determine just how fast the machine had to be rolling forward to have enough energy to get the machine into its final position. If the machine had been moving as slow as 12.5 miles per hour, the energy would have been sufficient to get the machine rolled over and still 12.5 inches above the ground to drop or free fall. The consultant picked 12.5 inches because that was the height of the canopy over the machine surfaces; it had to be at least that high, to drop instead of merely roll over. If it had been lower, the canopy would have been on the other side.

As a by-product of the reconstruction, it was clear that a standard ROPS installation would not have withstood even the 12.5-inch free drop without failing. The ROPS are designed to protect the operator in case of rollovers where contact with the ground is not lost; it is not effective in dynamic, drop load forms.

Example 7.

A finishing roller for asphalt was left by the side of a country road near where the road surfacing work had ended. A driver with a tilt semi-trailer was sent to load the machine and return it to the contractor's shop. Two hours later, the driver was found in a deep ditch under the roller, and next to the tilt trailer and truck which had obviously been placed to load the roller.

No one witnessed the incident; the man was working alone. The police investigator reported that the victim apparently had tried to load the roller onto the tilt trailer, and that he had accidentally driven it off the side of the trailer. Many excellent police photographs were taken at the scene.

To better understand the accident and why it happened, an interested insurance carrier underwrote an accident reconstruction of the event. Examining the site, the equipment, the reports, and the photos, the reconstructionist found some items of interest:

- Photos showed the truck and trailer sitting on the side of the road. The crown of the road and the soft ground near the edge of the road caused the trailer to lean to the right, toward the ditch, about 5 degrees total tilt.

- Examination of the markings on the trailer showed the machine to have been almost up on the tilt bed sufficiently to tilt the bed forward. (It was a gravity tilt bed, with no hydraulic or other power or linkage.)

- The surface of the bed was wood, with large bolt heads sticking up at intervals to hold the wooden planks in place.

- Examination of the markings on the roller made by the roller sliding on the bolt heads allowed the consultant to precisely place the roller on the bed of the trailer, and to plot the motion of the roller in respect to the bed, going up, sliding sideways, and then sliding backwards, too.

The consultant determined and proved that the roller had been driven up onto the tilt trailer bed. As it neared the point at which the trailer bed would tip forward to the travel position, the roller began to slide sideways, under the influence of the side tilt of the crown of the road by the soft shoulder. The side sliding was caused by the side tilt of the truck and the further tilting of the springs to the side under the weight of the roller. Steel will slide on steel at a coefficient of friction of about 0.11. The steel roller surface slid sideways on the steel bolt heads when the total side angle reached a little over 6 degrees.

Once the operator was in that position, he was in trouble. The roller was an articulated machine that steered by pivoting (bending) in the center of the machine. If he merely let the roller back down, it would run into the ditch. If he tried to steer the machine, he would have pulled the top (front) part of the machine off the edge of the trailer, causing him to roll over. If he tried to move still higher, even if he could have, he would continue to slide sideways toward the edge of the trailer bed.

The errors? It was obviously not a one-man job to load that roller. More than one man should have been sent to do the job. Second, a winch should have been used to help load the roller, making it unnecessary to use the power of the roller to "run up onto the tilt trailer." Third, loading and unloading machines should be done on a level surface; side tilts of the trailer create a dangerous situation which need not be included in the conditions.

Example 8.

One type of accident involves a machine backing over the victim. Back-up alarms, procedural methods, and even the job layouts are important factors in many of the backover accidents that occur.

A worker was looking in a trench to see how a sewer manhole hookup was coming. He was standing in front of a backhoe-loader, in the view of the

235

operator who was using the backhoe part of his machine to lower materials into the trench and to assist in placing and locating it. That wasn't the worker's normal workplace, but he apparently had a little breather and was interested in the job.

On the road, a wheel loader was shuttling back and forth to dig and carry fill gravel and dirt to the site from a pile some 200 feet away. As the loader approached a point even with the backhoe-loader, the workman suddenly spun around, took three or four quick steps back to the other side of the road, and found himself right behind the backing wheel loader. He fought off the loader by pushing himself away, and he had moved across the back surface of the loader, nearly to the opposite side of the loader, when he fell and the left rear wheel ran over him, killing him.

A consultant was asked to determine if any possible device or method could have prevented the accident, assuming the scenario above.

Testimony of witnesses and a reconstruction of the simultaneous motion of the wheel loader and of the victim, on a time scale, resulted in the following conclusions:

1. The back-up alarm on the machine was operating properly. Witnesses on the job heard it.

2. The victim, had he been listening, would have heard the back-up alarm at least 8 or 10 times while the loader was backing up. Yet, obviously, the back-up alarm did not cause him to change his actions. (Speculation among co-workers was that he had tried to run across the loader's path, to beat the loader.)

3. The time it took for the victim to decide to go back to his workplace, and to turn and take the 3 or 4 steps, was about 3 to 5 seconds. During that time alone he should have heard the back-up alarm twice.

4. From eyewitness testimony, confirmed by reconstruction calculations, the victim used another 1.5 to 1.75 seconds behind the loader, trying to "fight it off." The entire sequence, from the time he decided to move back to his work place until he fell behind the far left rear wheel of the loader was about 4 to 7 seconds.

5. At the time the victim decided to return to his work station, the loader was from 22 to 35 feet from the eventual impact point in the accident (3 to 5 seconds away). At the time the man began to move, the loader was only .5 to 2.5 seconds (or no more than 18 feet) away if the man strolled slowly back across and probably more like 4 to 5 feet away if he rushed, as eyewitnesses say he did.

6. One may reconstruct that if the operator had been looking straight at the worker and only at the worker, he would have had only .5 to 2.5 seconds to stop the machine. That, with normal human reaction times, and with the brake action time and the stopping time of the machine, was impossible. To even try to stop in this way would require the operator to know ahead of time that the worker was going to walk behind his machine.

The victim had literally walked right into the path of the reversing machine. Even the operator of the loader-backhoe, who was an eyewitness to the incident which happened right in front of him, testified the worker was standing right in front of the eyewitness' loader-backhoe machine; when he started to move, the eyewitness didn't have time to yell and stop the victim.

The analysis went further. Could some sort of sensor have detected the worker and stopped the machine automatically before it struck him? An analysis of the experimental devices being studied included radar, infrared detectors, sonic detectors, and other radio pulse devices. Some of these devices had the possibility of rapid detection, in the order of less than a second. Yet all of them had severe limitations in the distance behind the machine they could detect with any dependability. Twenty feet was the farthest extent, and some devices wouldn't reach that far. Further, most of the devices were undependable. They would detect things that were not people, like rocks, and were frequently stopping the machine unnecessarily. When the sensitivity was reduced to prevent the unnecessary stops, the detection of a person was questionable.

Further, assuming the device would work with high dependability, it would not detect the person until he had entered the area behind the machine. Of course, one could mount several of the devices, including one pointed to each side of the machine. Those would then stop the machine every time the machine passed a workman on the site—not a good way to enhance productivity. In the subject case, this meant that the so-called passive detection device would not know the person was there until he had actually made contact with the machine—again, far too late to prevent the accident.

Back to the real world—it is impossible to avoid hitting a person with a machine when that person literally walks into the path of the moving machine just before or at the point of contact.

Example 9.

On a pipe-laying job, the operator of a pipe layer crawler machine had picked up a 40-foot length of 10-inch water pipe. He was holding the pipe some 4 feet above the ground. The supervisor on the job crawled under the pipe to inspect the site where it was to be placed. (As an incidental note, the supervisor was also the contractor's safety officer.)

Just as the supervisor crawled under the pipe, the operator of the side boom testified that he noticed that the cable had begun to play out on the load winch. The operator said he reached out, grabbed the winch brake lever, and pulled it back to stop the winch. He said the winch stopped when the pipe was just off the ground. However, one end of the pipe had hit a couple of timbers and had snapped the other end of the pipe down, injuring the supervisor just as he was under the pipe. The pipe had dropped about 3.7 feet at that time.

Claims against the machine involved claims of defective winch latch design, allowing the latch to vibrate and fall out of engagement, letting the load winch free spool, dropping the load on the supervisor.

A reconstruction of the accident, using times for human reaction and the physical times for the load to drop, showed the following interesting findings:

- With gravity acting on the pipe load, the load would have fallen over 20 feet during the time the operator noted the unexpected movement of the winch and cable, reached for the lever, and pulled it to stop the motion.

- Considering the time it took the load to drop the 4 feet it did, the time for the operator to note the movement and react to it would have been

238

a half second—far too quickly for the operator's reaction time and actions to stop it before it hit the ground.

Conclusion: The accident just did not happen the way the operator testified. It was not caused by a latch vibrating loose and letting the winch begin to play out. The likely scenario was that the operator was only loosely holding the brake on the winch, and hadn't latched it. Then, the winch could have slipped a little, with partial winch braking, and the accident happened in approximately the way described.

Example 10.

A wheel loader with a 7.5 yard bucket capacity was being driven down an asphalt county highway at about 20 miles per hour. The operator said he took his foot off the accelerator as he passed a sign saying "STOP AHEAD— 300 FEET." As he did so, he said the engine quit, leaving him with no steering and no brakes. The operator testified that he rolled right on, through the stop sign and into the intersection. Just as he entered the intersection onto a state highway, an automobile was passing through the intersection. The loader caught the car on its bucket and carried it into the ditch across the road.

The attorney for the occupants of the auto called an engineer with earthmoving experience to analyze the accident—to find out, before they took any action, just where the fault might lie.

The engineer examined the machine and noted the following:

- No malfunctions were apparent.

- If the power were off, there would still be emergency hydraulic power for steering and emergency air for several complete braking actions. The loss of the engine did not take braking and steering away from the operator.

- Further, if the air were gone and the brakes had no air, the emergency brakes would automatically go on.

The story of the operator seemed to be in question.

239

Using a low rolling resistance of the tires on asphalt paving and assuming average mechanical efficiency for the bearings of the machine, the expert calculated that the machine—with no power and no braking—would have rolled to a dead stop in just about 200 feet beginning from the 20 mph machine speed at the time it passed the "STOP AHEAD" sign. Under the conditions described by the operator, he would have stopped before he reached the intersection.

The conclusions are quite obvious. The case was settled quickly.

Example 11.

A scraper operator complained of a crushed vertebra after running his scraper off the road and into a spill area to dump his load. He said he had hit a hole and the jarring shock of hitting the hole had caused the injury.

There were some questions about the extent of the injury, but there was injury, at least to some significant extent. The manufacturer of the scraper was sued for having a defect in the design of the scraper. That defect was claimed to be the lack of springs on the scraper to absorb the shock of hitting the hole.

An outside engineering expert was called in to assist a medical doctor in the analysis. The medical doctor established that a vertical jolt of 10 to 15 g would be necessary to cause the injury in an average person. The engineer was asked to determine the g loading at the seat when the machine went through the hole.

Unfortunately, no one measured or even saw the hole. The plaintiff claimed that at the time of the incident, not he nor anyone else attempted to measure or even look at the hole. It was supposedly covered with straw or something. Further, the incident and the injury were not reported for several days, so there was no way to determine the actual size, condition, and placement of the hole. What could be done?

The engineer, sensing the hole was not too unusual on heavy earthmoving sites, began to determine the worst possible hole—one that the wheel would drop the deepest into and then would immediately move back out of. Using the geometry of the tires on the machine, that hole size was determined. Then, using the deflection curves for the tires, the consultant determined the deflection of the tires assuming that drop occurred instantaneously—in other words, that the hole had a vertical drop and an immediate vertical rise.

At this point in the analysis, you should note that if an object is dropped and hits a surface, the *g*-force developed is equal to the distance dropped divided by the deflection of the surface which the object hits plus the deflection of the object itself. For example, if a ball drops 12 inches and the surface deflects 1 inch, a 4 *g* force on the ball is developed. If the ball drops 12 inches and the deflection is only a half inch, a 24 *g* force is developed. If the ball drops 4 inches and the deflection is 4 inches, only a 1 *g* force acts upon the ball.

In the case of the scraper tire, the maximum hole drop for the scraper was 27 inches. Using the tire deflection curves, the deflection of the tire was 8.9 inches. This amounted to a 3.0 *g* force, far less than expected to be needed to cause the injury.

With this analysis, the expert convinced his client to let him test the idea. He constructed a hole of the proper (so-called "worst case" dimensions) depth on a hard surface and began to drive an exemplar scraper through the hole. The operator said he hit the hole at something less than full speed in third gear. Beginning slowly at first, the consultant drove the machine through the hole. In steps he worked up to third gear at top speed. The hole gave a rough jolt, but nowhere near anything serious enough for injury. The tests were even videotaped.

The case was settled easily and quickly.

Example 12.

A worker in an agricultural material mixing and distributing center stepped onto the top of an augur which was covered by a fiberglass cover, bolted to the steel, U-shaped augur body. His foot slipped through the cover, and was badly injured.

All of the stress calculations of the structure, the steel body, and the bolted fiberglass cover indicate the strength to be more than enough to hold the weight of a person stepping or standing on it. Speculation was that the cover may have been loose; upon examination of photos taken at the time of the accident, it was apparent that several of the cover bolts were missing. At later examination, the missing bolts had still not been replaced. Further, photos at the time of the accident showed that the cover had been broken; it was in at least three or four pieces instead of the one ten-foot piece with which it was originally built.

To further test the theory, a consultant stood and even jumped on the cover on an exemplar conveyor section, first without the auger in it, putting the whole load on the cover, and then with the auger installed, when the cover would get additional support from the augur. All of these tests were done and video-recorded without any power being put to the augur drive.

Then the further question was asked. What would happen if a weight equal to the injured man or the consultant were put on the cover when the auger was moving under power? A test was run with the auger powered and with a weight with the area of a footprint being placed gradually down on the cover. After the weight had been placed on the cover with the auger stationary, it was not possible for the electric motor drive to start the auger with the weight standing on it.

However, when the weight was gently lowered to the cover with the auger already running, the auger began to grind away the bottom surface of the cover, breaking through the cover in about 25 seconds.

These tests showed that the injured man had not merely stepped quickly (he said he slipped) on the cover. To fail the way it did, if the cover were new and as designed, the man would have had to stand on the cover for at least a few seconds. Witnesses say that didn't happen.

The result: The auger as designed was not defective with the fiberglass cover. However, the safety rules around the auger needed to be emphasized and the walkway over the auger improved. Further, the cover had to be maintained in solid condition and properly bolted down.

Example 13.

In an underground mine, a miner was operating a mucker, or underground mining scoop, by remote control. In the work cycle, he ran the machine, which was a low clearance, front-end loader, into an area to pick up rock. Then he reversed it to back out of the area far enough for a carrier to get in front of the mucker. The rock was dumped into the carrier, which then carried the material to a hoist area.

During one cycle, the operator was crushed between his remote control machine and the wall of the tunnel. He reported to the investigators that the machine had been moved back "quite a ways" and that in moving forward to reenter the loading area, the machine suddenly "veered toward him and literally chased him to the wall where it crushed him."

Several possible scenarios were theorized:

1. The machine had malfunctioned, hydraulically or mechanically, in the steering system and caused the accident.

2. Some stray or extraneous radio signal had caused the machine to move as it did.

3. A malfunction had occurred in the transmitter control or in the receiver unit mounted on the machine, causing the incident.

4. An electric malfunction of some sort inside the interface between the machine and the electronic remote control system had happened.

5. The operator had erred in some way.

The injured operator sued everybody in sight, including the manufacturer of the mucker, the manufacturer of the remote control system, the distributor (who had installed the remote control system) and several component manufacturers and suppliers, including the manufacturer of the steering control valve in the machine.

Several consultants became involved in the investigation.

No mechanical malfunction was found in the machine after the incident, seemingly eliminating the first scenario. Yet, there had been service problems with the steering valve of the unit, placing some suspicion on that component as the culprit. Inspection of the steering valve on the accident machine showed that the valve was not broken and did not malfunction. (Further, later investigations showed that the valve was not proper for a remote-controlled machine because it could not long survive the abrupt "on-off" cycles of the remote controller. Thus the service problems.)

Likewise, no malfunction or electronic failure was found in the radio controller equipment. Further, no indications of any electronic component were ever demonstrated. Insofar as the stray signal idea, tests in the mine, required by safety authorities, showed a "stray or spurious signal" was all but impossible, virtually eliminating that scenario.

Then a study of the remote-control man/machine system, made by the operators and the consultants, indicated the real problem. As the machine cycled back and forth in front of the operator, the controls on the remote controller effectively reversed in relationship to the machine as the operator turned and continued to face the machine. The new, and generally accepted, scenario was that the operator had, without realizing it, steered the machine toward him (in the reverse control position) and had become confused and kept the machine steering directly toward him, causing the accident.

Sometimes a single factor may be the key to the solution of a situation in dispute. A few examples follow:

Example 14.

Lines-of-sight often become important in cases where visibility problems are claimed.

A truck driver at a landfill had just dumped his load and, for some unexplained reason, had stepped to a position behind the 7- or 8-foot high stack of garbage. A crawler dozer, spreading the trash, backed over the pile and injured the truck driver. Suit was filed, claiming lack of visibility from the crawler, as well as lack of a backup alarm.

Line of sight studies demonstrated that the truck driver was hidden by the pile of the load he had just dumped, and not by any lack of visibility from the tractor.

Example 15.

The malfunction of a single component may be the cause—and the only cause—of an expensive service problem with possible safety connotations.

The manufacturer of a transmission used in a service truck had changed a lubricating clearance channel in the control disc of the transmission control box. The change was not communicated to the vehicle manufacturer, who used the transmission in a refueling truck for airports. The truck used the transmission in the normal way, to propel the vehicle. While refueling an airplane, the transmission was kept engaged, but, through an auxiliary gear box, was now connected to the fuel pump for refueling and not to the drive train and wheels. In that mode, the transmission was to be held in top gear, to get the highest possible fuel pump speed. However, because of the unreported change in the control disc, the transmission "hunted" or alternated between top gear and the next lower gear. Doing this caused rapid and excess wear on the clutches of the two gear positions between which the transmission cycled, out of control. The undiscussed change caused major problems and rebuild costs.

Example 16.

In fire cases, determining the source of ignition of the fire is usually important. In a fire on a machine powered by a turbocharged diesel engine, it is easy and common to blame that ignition on the hot surface of the engine exhaust system—the hot end of the turbocharger or the exhaust manifold.

In an incident during an "off day" from work, a dozer was used to pull a pickup truck out of a muddy hole. The job was easy for the dozer; it didn't even have to pull hard. Shortly after, a broken hose sprayed hydraulic oil around the machine. The exhaust system of the machine was scarcely warmer than idle load—about 400°F on the outside where the oil might have hit. Yet, a sudden flash fire caused some burns to the operator. The exhaust system would have needed to be about 700°F to have caused the ignition.

The flash fire did no damage to the machine. The hose was replaced and the machine went back to work right away with no problems. Yet the operator, who had been soaked by the escaping fluid, suffered burns when his clothing caught fire from the flash.

Three possible ignition sources arose:

- ignition from some electrical spark,

- ignition from some dry twig or leaf or a shop rag on the manifold of the engine. Such a product would begin to smolder at about 350 to 400°F, and would have served as an ignition point for the flash.

- the glow from a hot end of a cigarette.

The operator then remembered he was smoking.

Example 17.

On occasion, a full life reenactment will disclose a fallacy in a claim.

An operator had rolled a machine onto its side while working on a rocky slope. The machine was equipped with proper ROPS (roll bars). However, the operator was injured when he tried to jump from the machine during the roll-over, and he was crushed across his legs by the roll bar. He said the machine was not equipped with seat belts—or at least, if it were so equipped, he didn't see them because they were hidden under the seat.

In an attempt to recreate the accident situation, the belts (it <u>was</u> so equipped) were placed under the seat cushion. After several attempts, it became obvious that the seat belts could not be hidden by putting them under the seat; the fastened end was clearly visible to anyone who looked at the seat.

Example 18.

The resolution of an accident scenario may well be done and aided by other than engineering sciences.

A dozer operator was clearing some brush from pasture land. He was found dead on the machine during the work day, with the machine stalled after it backed into a ditch with a steep bank slope. The operator had been injured on his forehead, and the theory of the incident said he had been hit in the forehead by a jill poke, a stick that had entered the operator's compartment of the machine and hit him.

Nothing like a jill poke was ever found at the scene or near it. Only small brush had been dug and moved. Yet, a claim against the dozer manufacturer was made alleging that the operator should have been protected by a screen or other protection completely surrounding him. That claim and question never was tried in court. A medical doctor testified that the operator had been fatally injured when he flew up out of the seat and hit his forehead on the cross bar of the ROPS. The system included seat belts, which, the operator's co-workers testified, he never used. The seat belt was not on when the victim was found. The doctor matched up the injury with the shape and position of the cross bar.

Example 19.

A farmhand was injured when the operator of a crawler tractor, after refueling, started up and struck the victim, standing on the ground, with the disc harrow implement the tractor was pulling. The incident happened at night.

The injured farmhand, who was the son of the farm owner and who had rented the machine to try it out, sued the manufacturer of the tractor, claiming several operational difficulties with the machine. Included were claims that the machine could not be "inched" or moved a short distance. They claimed it was difficult to hook up drawbar implements, because the machine would not move less than six or eight inches Further, they said the motion was "jerky."

Still further, the claims alleged that the machine could not be stopped quickly. The supposition was that after the tractor started to move, at the time of the accident, the operator could not stop the machine quickly enough to avoid hitting the farmhand.

A consultant obtained the subject tractor and implement to test the claims, and to demonstrate the claims to the attorneys.

The claims were not true. The machine could be "inched" or moved precisely as little as one quarter of an inch at a time. Further, the consultant, driving the machine, demonstrated to the attorneys that the controls were so easy to use that he could move the machine back and forth as little as a couple of inches at a time without even looking at the controls.

The consultant-driver also demonstrated at least seven ways to stop the tractor in a very short distance:

• by stepping on the brake, killing the engine and stopping the dozer in less than five feet,

• by stepping on the brake and the clutch at the same time, stopping the tractor in inches,

• by turning off the key, stopping the machine in less than three feet,

• by pushing the gear lever out of gear, stopping the machine in about four feet,

• by pushing only the clutch pedal, letting the machine "roll" to a stop in less than four feet,

• by pulling the emergency/parking brake, stopping the tractor in seven to eight feet and killing the engine, or

• by doing any combination of the above actions.

The demonstration was repeated with a video camera on the machine. There were no claims continued against the manufacturer.

Example 20.

A large mining truck in a western copper mine caught fire and burned. The cause of the fire was believed to be due to sloppy maintenance in the engine compartment; leaks were seldom fixed until they stopped the truck from operating.

The real problem, however, was the failure of a fire suppression system to activate. When the fire began and was noticed by the driver, the automatic sensor and activating system didn't work. When the driver pushed a manual button to make the suppression system work, still nothing happened.

An examination of the system after the fire showed the following:

- The dry chemical cans were still full; they had not been discharged,

- The nitrogen pressure capsules on the dry chemical cans had been punctured; the nitrogen was gone,

- The master nitrogen pressure capsule, in the truck cab, had been punctured; that nitrogen was gone, too. The same was true for an emergency manual control on the side of the truck, reachable from the ground.

Even though the nitrogen lines and the sensor wires were damaged beyond inspection in the fire, it was obvious to the consultant that the nitrogen capsules had not been properly serviced the last time the machine suppression had been checked. If there had been nitrogen in both the master capsule and the slave capsules (on the dry chemical tanks) the tanks would have been discharged. They were not.

Example 21.

A man working on his own car was fatally injured when the car fell off the jack or the jack lowered the car onto him—depending upon which scenario was correct. The hydraulic jack was impounded and carefully retained in its condition as of the accident. The plaintiff, wishing to show the jack had internal leakage problems that had let the jack drop gradually down onto the victim, asked for a chance to disassemble the jack and inspect it. All parties agreed.

However, before the disassembly, one attorney asked for the jack to be used to jack up a car. That was done, and the jack sat in that position for twenty minutes while the attorneys and consultants talked. No sign of settling or leaking was noticed.

Then, upon disassembly and inspection, several instances of poor workmanship were found on the jack and noted. Nothing was serious, but there were small defects in the castings, the seals were nicked in at least two places, and several scratches were found in the cylinder surfaces.

The plaintiff insisted that the jack was defective and that those defects, noted and photographed, had caused the victim's injury. The defendant manufacturer disagreed. The jack had performed properly and without leaking or drifting, for 20 minutes or more before the inspection.

The case never went to trial.

Chapter 13

DEFINITIONS AND TECHNIQUES EMPLOYED BY ATTORNEYS

In this chapter, I will discuss some of the definitions and apparent rules that guide attorneys. These are from my own experience and from conversations with attorneys. The definitions are expressed, for the most part, in my own words. They are not to be taken as legal advice; the definitions are not necessarily complete or precise, but they give the non-legal professional involved in litigation a sense of the meaning sufficient to aid him in giving his assistance to an attorney or to help him in his involvement in the litigation process. The definitions and, in fact, the entire book, have been reviewed by competent legal counsel.

The rules are frequently quoted, so they need not be referenced.

Definitions

First, consider some terms you will hear commonly.

Adverse Witness

An adverse witness is one who has been called to testify by the opposing attorney—not by the attorney whom he is assisting, or for whom he is consulting. Typically, a plaintiff's attorney may call an employee of the defendant company as an adverse witness—as part of the plaintiff's main case in chief. The purpose might be to show certain history or features of the product being attacked.

Answer

"Answer" is a formal term used interchangeably with the term "Response." The meaning is the same. Typical are the Responses (or Answers) to Interrogatories.

Appearance

This means that someone appears in the litigation process—in answering interrogatories, at deposition, as part of the offering of evidence, or in some other way. An attorney appears as a legal representative of one of the parties in the suit. He has a more formal meaning of the term "appearance," but you need not be too concerned with it. Your appearance is your involvement in the matter or in the litigation process. You may appear as a witness, or as a participant somewhere in the history of the product involved.

Arbitration/Mediation

You will hear that courts are overloaded and that the process of litigation and resolution of matters is slow. To bypass the courts, many litigants are resorting to various other "alternate dispute resolution" methods. Mediation is one. The mediator works with both parties, together and separately, to arrive at an agreeable resolution to the dispute. Where such resolution is possible, the process may be less costly, as well as much faster.

Arbitration is a somewhat more formal alternate resolution method. Following a set of rules agreed upon by the parties, the disputing parties will present their claims, arguments, and summarized evidence to an arbitrator or to a committee of arbitrators. The decision of the arbitrators, under some rules, is binding. In some other cases, they are completely voluntary; that is, they may be accepted or not. Sometimes a partial weight of acceptance is inferred. That means that you may reject the decision of the arbitrator, if you choose. However, if later adverse decisions develop at trial, the one who rejected the arbitration decision may be further penalized.

Balance of the Evidence

You will hear of the "balance of the evidence" when you are involved in litigation. "Balance of the evidence" refers to the information before the jury when they deliberate on the case. The jury will find facts to be as they perceive them according to the balance of the evidence, that is, according to the comparative weights of the evidence, as they see it, on each side. The jurors will have been instructed to "find for one party or the other, according to which has the heaviest weight of the evidence." This doesn't mean the most evidence or the most witnesses; it means the most believable evidence in total, as measured by the jury.

You will also hear the phrase "preponderance of the evidence." This refers to the condition of having more weight of evidence. The side with the preponderance of the evidence is the side which has more weight of evidence.

Bar

Historically, the bar is the railing between the judge and the gallery of the courtroom. "Bar" means several things, but, in a legal sense, it has three meanings of significance.

First is the location of legal activity. Bar is the generic term used to indicate that location, usually a courtroom. You will hear reference to "the question at bar" or "the prisoner before the bar."

Second, bar is a shorthand term for a grouping of attorneys in a certain area of jurisdiction. The reference is usually to a "bar association" or "the bar," referring to the organizations of attorneys in that area. In a way, there is a relationship between the first and second definitions; they overlap considerably. The "bar" (a group of attorneys in a geographic area) work "before the bar" or "at bar" in the courtroom.

Third, the verb "to bar" means to prevent or keep out. If you do not disclose an opinion or a matter in deposition or other discovery, you may well be "barred" or prevented from using that information at trial. A time-measured statute of limitations may "bar" a potential plaintiff from suing. He has waited too long before instituting the complaint, and now, he is barred from filing any action.

Bench

"Bench" has a specific meaning in legal terminology. The bench is techni-cally where the judge sits. Of course, it is not a bench in terms of furniture definition, but it is an important and focal place in litigation. The bench really is the location, person, and authority of the judge in the courtroom. Attorneys "approach the bench" when they go up front to hear from or talk to the judge in private, away from the jury and spectators in the courtroom. Bench orders are legal orders issued by the judge with the authority of his court position. If you are called before the bench, it may be serious. A bench warrant for you means you had better appear.

Best Evidence

One might think that the best evidence is the evidence that wins the case. Not necessarily, in legal terms. The term "best evidence" has to do with the acceptability and admissibility of the evidence.

The rules of evidence call, in brief, for the evidence to be presented in its best and newest form, the form that is closest to the form concerned in the par-ticular case at bar. If you have an original document, that is the "best evi-dence." If only a copy of the original document remains or exists, then that may be the "best evidence available." Test information on the actual ma-chine involved in an accident is the best evidence. Test data on a similar or exemplar machine may be good evidence, but not as good as test data on the original machine. It may be usable, but if test data on the original machine is available or possible to obtain, the court may demand that information as the best evidence.

Breach

A breach is a failure to perform or a break in a chain of action. The common form you may hear is the "Breach of Warranty" or "a breach of duty to per-form." It is the term used when the machine is alleged to have not met its promises. If you breach your duty, you have not lived up to the professional expectations you are held to in your design and other engineering work.

Burden of Proof

The burden of proof is the respective responsibilities of the parties in a lawsuit to prove (or disprove) the claims at question. In a criminal case, technically, the burden of proof is on the prosecutor or accuser. The accused may even choose not to offer any defense, and if the prosecutor doesn't prove his case, the accused will likely go free. Tactically, it is still best for the defense to offer rebuttal to the prosecutor's case. Military strategists speak of a good defense being a good offense. In the courtroom, in most cases, both parties are, in effect, on the offensive. Each is trying to establish and prove his version of the case.

In a civil case, such as a products liability matter, the resolution of the matter rests on the "balance of proof," already defined. Each side has an opportunity to present his or her evidence, testimony, and final argument. The judge will likely charge the jury to "consider the weight of the evidence. If the weight of the evidence, in your eyes, tilts in the direction of one or the other of the parties, that party should prevail. That is, if it seems to you that one party is more likely correct, or that the evidence favors that party more than the other, that party should win."

The burden of proving a products liability case, then, either for the plaintiff or for the defendant, lies upon that party. You probably won't be successful without explaining your position and offering evidence and testimony to support your position—unless your opponent is very weak in his case and arguments. As claims and counterclaims are exchanged, each side will feel the burden of needing to prove.

Care

"Care," in the form for discussion here, is merely the responsibility or charge to perform or conduct according to accepted levels of performance. If you are a designer, you exercise care in making sure the product design meets all of its requirements of performance, safety, specification, life, reliability, cost, and repairability. Maybe it has to look good, also. If you do not exercise reasonable care, according to the professional results reasonably expected of you and people in your position, you may be subject to a claim that you did not use "due or proper care." Society expects a design engineer to know more about the matter of design and to perform design work on a higher level of professionalism than it would, for example, from an operator or a lay bystander doing design work.

Likewise, society expects a journeyman operator to perform the operation processes better and more properly than it would a lay bystander, an engineer, a lawyer, or a judge. You are expected to execute your work with reasonable care, appropriate to your training and responsibilities.

Charge

You may hear a judge "charge" a jury, that is, give the jury specific instructions as to how it must proceed in deliberating the case. This meaning of the word "charge" is actually "instruct."

The judge will tell the jurors that they must follow applicable law in deliberating. He will define terms and explain what the jury is responsible for—namely, determining any facts that are in dispute. He will, more than likely, give them a series of questions regarding the facts of the incident, seeking to keep the focus of the jury on those factual disputes and reducing the tendency of emotion, sympathy, or other factors to overpower the thinking of the jury.

A "charge" may also be an accusation.

Civil Law

Civil Law is that part of the law dealing with relationships between people and other entities, rather than a person or entity and the State (which is covered in Criminal Law.)

Complaint

This is the formal name for the list of claims and the request for court intervention and judgment originally filed regarding a matter to be litigated. It is the starting paper of a lawsuit.

Due Process

"Due process" refers to the proper legal steps in a procedure. Due process tends to slow down the steps in the resolution of a disputed matter. Due process also goes far to urge and assure the proper and equitable outcomes. It seems, at times, as if the legal process is burdensome. It may be, but more often, the slow, deliberate "due process" provides good benefits that far outweigh the ills of the system.

It should also be noted that "due process" refers to the system which means to guarantee that each person or party to a legal action will get a fair and complete hearing of his position. It protects against arbitrary decisions.

Duty

"Duty," simply, is what you are supposed to do. Each of us has duties, and each of us involved in a matter of litigation will have a duty to perform properly (or to have performed properly) with regard to that matter. Duty might be termed "responsibility," with "duty" applying to legal responsibility.

A designer has a duty to use appropriate care in his work. An operator has a duty to know and follow instructions and to operate the machine correctly. Under OSHA regulations, an employer has a duty to maintain a safe workplace for his employees.

Evidence

"Evidence" refers to the information that tends to prove or disprove matters of disputed fact. Evidence may be any number of things, such as a document, marks at the scene of an accident, the condition of the machine and the person after the accident, and any number of things. Evidence may be testimony by a witness, an opinion offered by an expert witness, a physical piece of material, a map or layout of an accident site, photographs, analyses, accident reconstructions, models, and so on.

Evidence is collected and offered to prove the contentions made by one party or the other in a dispute.

Exhibit

Evidence offered and admitted at trial are termed "exhibits." They may be documents, reports, photographs, sketches on a flip chart, and so forth. Exhibits may be used for demonstration or explanation only, and not be accepted as "evidence." Because juries will understand more clearly with visual aids, exhibits are commonly used in trials.

Expert Witness

An expert witness is one who, by training, education, experience, or other special knowledge, has the ability to assist the court and the jury in understanding the technical aspects of a matter. Lay jurors are not expected to be engineers or scientists (although they may be, from time to time). Therefore an engineer who can explain and interpret the engineering and scientific details of a matter may offer opinions and explanations, if they will assist the jury and the court in determining the facts in the case.

The lay juror is not expected to understand medical details (although nurses, social workers, technicians, and doctors can be jurors). Therefore a medical doctor, nurse, or an Emergency Medical Technician may testify as an expert witness, explaining the technical details of his or her work and offering opinions in the matter.

In most circumstances, expert witnesses differ from other witnesses (fact witnesses) in that they may, after proper qualification, offer opinions.

Facts

"Facts" are things that have happened or matters that truly exist. Facts, in a lawsuit, are matters that have been agreed to by all parties or that have been substantially proven by one party or the other. Whether a fact exists or has been proven is the purpose and province of the jury, or what is sometimes called "the finder of fact." One purpose of a lawsuit and a trial are to establish as facts matters that are being disputed.

That an accident happened is a fact. That the accident was caused by a design defect is the claim of the plaintiff. If the defendant disputes that claim, the jury or court then becomes the method of establishing what is really and truly "fact."

Forensic

"Forensic" means "belonging to the law." A forensic engineer is one who applies engineering principles to the resolution of legal actions. Forensic medicine is a similar use of medical science to help resolve legal questions or issues. An engineering and medical reconstruction of an accident is a forensic use of multidisciplinary science to resolve a legal question. An autopsy, done to provide legal information, is a forensic autopsy. Investigations into accidents are forensic. A test done to duplicate or prove some contention in an accident is forensic.

If you are a forensic engineer, do you belong to the law? I would say you do, in terms of your duty to conduct your work in such a way as to lead to a proper resolution of the question or matter at hand.

Foreseeability

"Foreseeability" is a somewhat ethereal term which implies the ability of a matter, situation, condition, or action to be expected sometime in the in the future. In engineering law, the term refers to what the engineer may reasonably expect in the future with regard to the use and application of his design. If the condition is "foreseeable," the engineer is expected to have taken that condition into account in his design deliberations and decisions.

To put some fences around what is foreseeable and what is not, consider these examples:

- A design engineer should foresee that his product would be used in the way for which it is designed and built.

- Recognizing that people make errors, the engineer should probably foresee that the operator or the mechanic may make some errors.

- Based upon experience, the engineer who designs a machine might foresee that the machine would be put to uses other than those originally intended. The expansions of the use of the machine to new applications is a common happening in the field of heavy, off-road machinery. Wheel loaders are modified for use as forestry feller-bunchers. Tractors have accessories such as rippers, winches, and side booms mounted on them. Excavators are used as short cranes to lower pipe into a trench.

• You should not, as a designer, be able to foresee that an operator will misuse the machine unreasonably or irrationally. The possibilities of misuse are so broad and varied as to defy foreseeability.

• You need not foresee that the machine would be used for some crazy purpose. For example, you need not expect that a criminal will steal a motor grader and use it to crash through a customs station on an international border. (I know this happened, but I still don't have to design a motor grader to accomplish that particular activity safely and effectively.)

• You might, however, be required to foresee even intentional or unreasonable misuse, when that misuse is known to exist with some regularity or in some common fashion. For example, we know that a person can speed in an automobile—and that happens, frequently. Therefore, we have some responsibility to guard against the possible injuries from speeding (because we have made a car capable of going at that speed) even though speeding is a violation of the law.

When a matter is determined by the court to be "foreseeable," you may now have a serious duty to have taken care of that possibility in your design.

Good Faith

This term and several other terms in this list have an application to what a proper and reasonable execution of duty should be measured against. The law requires a "good faith" effort be made by the one who has a duty. An effort in good faith is an effort made to good professional standards, and in a proper professional way.

Fraud, crime, and lack of proper care are not good faith efforts. Neither, probably, are design or engineering shortcuts or guesses.

One of the facts to be determined by a jury may be whether a designer, operator, mechanic, or another person has acted in good faith. A good designer has designed the machine in good faith—that is, he has used proper and appropriate professional tools to do the best job he can.

Hearsay

The Hearsay Rule generally deals with the admissibility or inadmissibility of testimony from a witness. The rule is complicated, and I will not attempt to go into all of the technicalities. In general, witnesses may testify only to those things that they personally experienced by one of the five physical senses. A witness generally may not be allowed to tell something he heard from another.

There are several exceptions and detailed technical arguments about whether a piece of testimony is hearsay. Leave most of those arguments to the attorneys. You will be told that you may not testify in a certain manner if your testimony is determined to be hearsay.

An important exception to the hearsay rule is the expert witness, who is allowed to give opinions which are frequently based on secondhand information—reports of others, testimony of eyewitnesses and fact witnesses, and other technical and scientific sources. Those sources are approved when the sources are commonly used by the expert in his work.

In general, you may testify about what you know, and not what you have heard.

Hidden Defects

A hidden defect is one hidden from view or not easily detectable even by reasonable and common inspection of a product or component. However, that hidden defect, under doctrines of strict liability, may still be found to be the cause of an accident or injury, even though it is unreasonable or even impossible for the defect to have been detected.

This may sound frightening, but it's a part of the way of life in products liability law, at least in some jurisdictions.

Hostile Witness

A hostile witness is one who, by his actions or demeanor, demonstrates a hostile attitude toward the questioner, either on direct examination or on cross-examination. When the judge, at the request of the questioning attorney, declares the witness to be a hostile witness, he will allow certain more stringent rules of questioning aimed at allowing the attorney to better control the conduct and testimony of the witness. You are not a hostile witness merely because you are on the opposite side or because you do not agree with the questioner.

Hypothetical Question

The hypothetical question is a form of question permitted at certain times and with certain requirements during a direct or cross-examination. The hypothetical question is asked along with a statement of conditions and facts you are to assume. They are asked for specific technical, legal reasons. When you are asked a hypothetical question, listen carefully, understand all of the conditions and facts you are asked to assume, and think through the answer very carefully. If you do not understand the question or some part of it, say so. If you cannot agree with one or more of the assumptions, say so. You do not have to assume anything contrary to your own knowledge, belief, or understanding.

Impeach

With reference to the testimony of a witness, "impeach" means to show the testimony of the witness to be untrue or unbelievable. Your testimony will be presented to develop evidence to prove the case of the attorney who called you to testify. The opposing attorney, on cross-examination, has the opportunity to impeach <u>you</u>, if he can.

He can call into question your opinions, your testimony, and facts. He may try to cast doubt on the bases for your opinions or on the methods and processes you used as a scientist or an engineer. If you made a mathematical error in your calculations, the cross-examining attorney will almost certainly find it and disclose it—in front of the jury. He may attack you through contradictory things you may have done or said. He may question you about the opinions and oral and written statements of others purported to be experts in the subject.

Failing there, he may look at your biases or past relationships in an attempt to show a relationship that might make the jury less likely to believe you.

Inadmissible

Not every piece of information that might be offered at trial is admissible as evidence. The rules of litigation are complex and vary from one jurisdiction to another. That is why you use attorneys who live in the district in which the claim is made and the lawsuit filed. Testimony is admissible when it conforms to the rules governing the specific case in the specific court. When the information or evidence is outside those rules, it is inadmissible.

As an engineer or scientist, you need to know that inadmissibility has nothing to do with the quality or truthfulness of your proposed evidence or testimony. Obviously, the court will try to exclude false evidence or testimony. It may, however, exclude your testimony because, under one or more of the rules, it is "inadmissible." Those rules are drawn up as part of the attempt to provide a process that most often leads to justice and equity.

Sometimes, as an expert or a consultant, you will be asked to help find "admissible" evidence to replace evidence that has been declared "inadmissible." That is a good engineering job.

Insurance

In general, don't use this word.

In most cases, the dispute is concerning the cause or responsibility for the loss and for any injuries. Those determinations are to be made without reference or concern as to what payments may have been already made by insurance, or as to whether the injury or loss was insured against. The jury is to make the determinations of fact concerning the liability and responsibility for the incident without taking into account the possible payments by insurance companies.

This is a general rule—not a specific instruction. There may even be matters in which an insurance company is a party to the suit. Your attorney will give you specific guidance. However, unless you have specific instructions, do not mention or ask about insurance or include "insurance" in any of your answers or opinions.

Irrelevant

Relevancy is a much-discussed and argued term in litigation. It is a lawyer's term, and generally, the relevancy of a matter, fact, or piece of evidence is a legal question, to be decided by the judge and the attorneys.

You will hear, "Objection! Not relevant!" as you listen to testimony or give it. After discussion, the judge may sustain the objection and send the attorney on to some other question. Or, he may overrule the objection instruct the witness to answer. Do not let this process disturb you. The question is not whether you think the answer you are about to give is relevant. It is whether the information—the question and the answer—are relevant, that is, proper and admissible under the rules of evidence and under the procedures of the specific case.

Relevancy is determined as part of the process of getting a fair and proper hearing of the dispute. If the judge rules that a question, a potential answer, or a piece of evidence is irrelevant, he means that it does not properly belong in the matter being tried.

Examples:

- Questions about whether you have ever been arrested. (Questions about whether you have ever been convicted of a felony may be allowed.)

- Questions about your political affiliation, when you are being questioned about your part in the design of a machine.

- Questions about your work on another machine when it is not the subject of the matter at hand. (This is a close one sometimes. The judge will decide whether it is relevant.)

Judicial Discretion

This leads to an important point. The law, as it is legislated and written in court opinions, is not complete and all-encompassing. That is, it does not have rules and procedures to handle every case and dispute that comes before the court. If the law were complete, one wouldn't need trials because there would be no disputes. When a question arose, it would only be necessary to plug in the question and get the ready-made answer from the law. The process would be like plugging numbers into an engineering equation.

In actuality, there are many incomplete definitions, and there are no rules to cover certain situations. Also, there are changing conditions and developing philosophies and trends in the law. To account for these instances and to allow for the orderly process of litigation, "Judicial Discretion" is introduced.

The judge, in addition to being the director of the trial process and the referee of conduct in the trial, is the arbiter of those situations where the law does not specifically make the decision. Many legislated laws specifically refer to judicial discretion, and give the judge the right and option to make the choice in certain matters.

For example, a judge may choose to admit or not admit certain information as evidence. He may decide according to the law, but he also may use his own judgment (discretion) where the law is unclear, incomplete, or not specific. The judge can decide when an action, for example, amounts to a contempt of court. He may choose to let the jurors take notes, or he may agree to allow a witness to testify out of the normal order of procedure in order to accommodate a schedule problem.

These matters of discretion are a large part of the job of the judge. If one side or the other feels the judge has improperly used his discretion, they may appeal. However, the judge's discretion at the time must be respected and followed.

Jury Trial

Most products liability trials you see in the United States are jury trials—that is, they involve and include a jury of people to decide the facts of the matter.

If, for whatever reason, the parties in a matter choose not to have a jury to decide the factual matters, the trial is then called a "bench trial," that is, the judge (on the bench) is the sole arbiter in the case. He finds both matters of law and matters of fact. In a bench trial, the judge is often referred to as "the finder of fact and of the law."

Lay Witness

A lay witness is a common expression for a witness for the facts. The witness may be an eyewitness to the matter, or may have information related to the case. In general, the lay witness may testify only to those facts. This amounts to information the witness obtained directly through the five basic senses—sight, touch, hearing, smell, and taste. The lay witness generally will not express opinions. Also, the lay witness will not generally give hearsay testimony. In certain exceptional situations these rules may be eased for specific reasons.

In basic purpose a lay witness is used to describe and enter as evidence the known and observed factual matters surrounding the incident at trial. The facts are as he observes or knows them to be.

Liability

Liability is generally synonymous with responsibility, but it goes further. Liability is a legal responsibility to pay or provide such remedies as the court decides.

The objective of litigation is to seek a fair balancing of the hurts and costs of an incident such as an injury. The suit is filed to establish the defendant's liability for the injury or loss. When a court or a jury finds someone responsible or liable, they also determine the cost of making that plaintiff whole, or at least as properly balanced as can be obtained.

Liability includes not only the determination of responsibility, but the assessment of a money award, or of some other action to provide some approach to the balance desired.

Five jury decisions may illustrate liability better than it can be described:

266

In the first decision example, the jury found a manufacturer liable for the plaintiff's injuries and returned a verdict that the award would be one dollar. The injuries were under question. What the jury was apparently saying was that the responsibility was the manufacturer's, but that they doubted the real loss value of the injury.

In the second example, the jury found the maker of the machine responsible for the accident and returned a verdict of $23,000 to cover the medical costs and lost work time of the injury and added an additional $5,000,000 punitive damage award. The jury wanted to send a message to the manufacturer and to society that the responsibility in this case carried more than just the losses. Punitive damages are a special step juries may take under the proper circumstances and with the proper claims and evidence shown by the plaintiff.

In the third example, the jury found that the machinery manufacturer was 50% at fault and that the plaintiff was 50% at fault. They returned a verdict of $4,230,000. The claim demanded by the plaintiff had been for $2,115,000. The jury had found the plaintiff partially responsible for his own injuries, but still gave him 50% of an amount they set at $4,230,000, or $2,115,00. Juries may decide how much they want the plaintiff to get and work backward into the justification. That is not generally how they are instructed to arrive at an award, but they can do it this way.

Jurisdiction laws may further complicate the matter. In one jurisdiction, the rule was that if the plaintiff were found more than 50% liable for his own injury, he could not recover. The jury in a pedestrian accident awarded the injured plaintiff $5,000,000 and found the plaintiff 60% responsible for his injury and the machine manufacturer 40% responsible. In this situation, and under the law in effect, the plaintiff collected nothing.

In another matter in another jurisdiction, a plaintiff was awarded $1,000,000 for his injuries. The responsibility was spread in this way:

- 25% to the machine manufacturer,
- 40% to the service company that maintained the machine, and
- 35% to the property owner where the accident happened.

The service company was only able to pay $25,000 and the property owner was bankrupt and could pay nothing. Although the machine manufacturer was only found responsible for 25% of the million dollars, the manufacturer also had to pay the remainder of the portions the other two responsible parties could not pay. The manufacturer, thus, became liable for $975,000, instead of the $250,000 which the jury determined as his proper responsible share.

This kind of problem arises in jurisdictions which have some sort of "joint and several" rule.

Remember, liability may carry with it serious financial or other costs.

Litigation

"Litigation," as a term, refers to the total process of filing a lawsuit, pursuing the discovery and other pre-trial actions, the trial, and also appeals and other post-trial actions. "Litigation" is an inclusive term dealing with the entire spectrum of legal actions and court activities where the parties have a dispute.

The plaintiff litigates by "praying the honorable court" to take note of the claims and allegations presented, and by ordering the defendant to pay certain requested penalties to the plaintiff.

The defendant continues the litigation by "denying each and every claim made by the plaintiff" and by "praying the court to deny any claims by the plaintiff for redress."

Then, both parties continue the litigation until they arrive at a settlement agreement or until the court and jury return a verdict at trial and until any post-trial motions and actions are exhausted.

Mistrial

If at any time during a trial the judge determines that a fair and proper resolution can no longer be reached, he may declare a mistrial. That means the present trial is over with no result. Whether the case is retried is a matter for the attorneys and their clients to decide. There have been successive mistrials in some matters before a final trial verdict was reached.

If, after long and diligent deliberation, the jurors declare that it is not possible for them to arrive at a verdict, the judge may declare a mistrial and dismiss the jury. This is one of the more common reasons for a mistrial.

There are other reasons for mistrials, too. In a case involving a certain earthmoving machine, the plaintiff's attorney referred to the machine as a "widow maker," even after repeated and strenuous objections. This was considered inflammatory, and the judge declared a mistrial.

In another case, one attorney began to introduce evidence and information the judge had already ruled to be inadmissible. The judge, in that case, declared a mistrial.

In still another matter, an attorney, sensing that he was not winning his case, intentionally asked a witness about insurance—a strict no-no. The judge declared a mistrial (which the attorney was trying to get) but he also found the attorney to be in contempt and sentenced him to a week in jail for asking about the forbidden subject of insurance.

Negligence

Negligence is the subject of many disputes in products liability lawsuits.

A legal dictionary description of negligence is "the failure to use the ordinary amount of care that would be expected from a reasonably prudent person under the same or similar circumstances." You can see from this definition that there are at least two nouns, two adjectives, and one adverb that are not precisely defined anywhere—not to mention the phrase "same or similar circumstances."

"Negligence" is frequently one of the things that must be decided by a jury. Was the person or company negligent? Would a reasonably prudent person do the same thing? What is a "reasonably prudent" person, anyway? Thousands of pages have been written about these and other words of equal flexibility in their definitions. Yet, the dispute in a lawsuit usually centers about one or two of these words.

The engineer may be claimed to have been negligent in his design. The builder may be charged with negligence in the building of a machine. The serviceman may be charged with negligence in repairing and maintaining the machine. The operator may have been negligent in the way he applied and used the machine. Even the bystander may be accused of negligence for being in a place where he was warned not to be.

Oath

One takes an oath in legal matters to "tell the truth, the whole truth, and nothing but the truth." To take an oath means to swear to the truth of the statement you make or the information you give. If other consequences of not telling the truth do not concern you, remember that if you are caught not telling the truth under oath, you may well be guilty of perjury—a criminal act punishable by law.

Privileged Communication

A privileged communication is a transfer of information not generally discoverable by the opposing side in a matter of litigation. Generally, a conversation between a person and his or her clergyman is not discoverable under law. To disclose such information would breach the confidential relationship between a person and his spiritual counselor. Clergymen are under church rules not to make such disclosures. The law recognizes and respects that. Similar protection is recognized in some conversations between people and their medical professionals.

A similar relationship exists in legal matters. Generally, communications between an attorney and his client are privileged. The basic doctrine is that an attorney could not properly prepare to represent his client if such conversations were open and discoverable. A related class of non-discoverable material is known as "attorney work product." That is the material which contains the thinking and the ideas of the attorney for proceeding with his representation.

Use a little caution with such protection. Different jurisdictions have differing rules about confidentiality. Let the attorney determine what is and what is not privileged. Another caution is that one should not discuss with others any matters which are privileged. In doing so, he may "open the door" (waive the privilege), reducing or eliminating any privilege and protection from discovery that may have existed.

Proximate Cause

A "proximate cause" of an accident, injury, or related loss is that cause without which the incident would not have happened. The legal definition of "proximate cause" is complicated by hundreds of judicial rulings as to the relationships between cause and the resulting loss and liability. Also, thousands of words have been written on the subject.

In brief, the cause is the "proximate cause" if the incident would not have happened directly without it, and if no other intervening actions had entered the scenario.

Prudent Person

Returning to what makes a "prudent person," or better yet, a "reasonably prudent person," I cannot define it any better than I already have. However, it is important to note that there are many different "reasonably prudent" persons.

The "reasonably prudent" juror is that typical, if imaginary, juror who does what the typical juror would do in the same circumstances. (Of course, there is no such thing as the typical or average juror. That "person" is a theoretical and statistical creation from the universe of jurors.)

Likewise, the "reasonably prudent" design engineer is a design engineer who does at least what the typical or average design engineer would do according to professional standards and proper actions for such people. In other words, the prudent design engineer would be judged by his peers as having met a standard of performance that is acceptable to the profession and that represents good performance of his work according to known standards.

A "reasonably prudent" operator is one who operates his machine in a manner that measures up with what society expects of a person on that kind of job and with the training and ability that such a person needs before he can properly perform the job.

Every time one tries to describe a "prudent" person or a "reasonably prudent" person in whatever circumstance he or she may be, one ends up comparing to a generally "hypothetical" person, created from mathematical processes and sets of standards.

Juries are often asked to decide whether an action was prudent or not. Your actions should be prudent (or better) and you should be prepared to explain and show why those actions were proper and appropriate.

Puffery

The law recognizes that a certain amount of talk, aimed at getting the buyer to purchase your product, may not be completely accurate or may overstate the situation by some small amount. This is known as sales puffery. Another description is sales enthusiasm. The law seems to recognize and accept that a certain amount of that exaggeration goes on in sales activity. It comes from an old understanding that anyone involved in sales work may get excited and exaggerate a little. The law appears to allow some (undefined and unknown) amount of sales puffery. It does not permit any other puffery. Certainly, there can be little, if any, forgivable engineering puffery.

A salesman might be expected to say, "This machine is the best in the world." Maybe he is correct. If he is not, well, that may be just sales puffery. The use of common comparatives and modifiers are treated in a similar fashion— okay for the salesman but not for technical people. When the engineer says that his design is the best in the world, he is expected to produce (or, at least, be able to produce) data to sustain that claim.

Punitive Damages

Punitive damages are exemplary damages—over and above the damages intended to make the plaintiff whole—which may be granted by the jury in certain cases and under certain circumstances. In brief, punitive damages are intended to punish a grossly negligent plaintiff for wanton disregard for the safety of the plaintiff in the case. You may hear the phrase, "send the defendant a message that he can't ignore" in terms of such requests. Punitive damages may be very large and they are not based on any economic loss or injury.

The picture painted of a defendant when punitive damages are requested is something like this: The defendant just didn't care. Punitive damages are distributed according to the laws of the jurisdiction. For example, in Iowa, they go to the State. In other jurisdictions, they may go directly to the plaintiff.

Question of Fact

In a legal dispute, there are generally two types of questions—questions of fact and questions of law.

Questions of fact are those questions or unresolved disputes dealing with facts or information. Some confusion exists because frequently "questions of fact" involve opinions, too. For example: Was the design defective? Did the operator misuse the machine? Was the machine in the defective condition when it left the manufacturer? Was the use of the machine foreseeable? Was the care exercised by the manufacturer or the operator reasonable? These are questions for the "trier of fact," usually the jury.

Question of Law

A question of law is a matter of dispute concerning the applicable statutes or precedents, or a dispute concerning the process and rules of litigation procedure. In general, the judge is the decider of such matters. For example: Is the evidence admissible? Should a particular statute be applied to this matter? Which of two differing and preceding decisions should be applied to the case at hand? Is the question asked by the attorney a proper question? Does the witness have to answer the question?

Reasonable Care

Reasonable care is the care that a reasonably prudent person, properly trained and assigned to the work, would use in performing the work. A company

273

uses reasonable care when it does what other companies would prudently do in designing, developing, manufacturing, and marketing a product or machine. In all cases, the measure of reasonable care is left to the finder of fact (the jury, usually) to determine by comparing the actions at hand to the actions of a mythical "prudent company or person in the same business or doing the same work."

Your best effort should be defensible. If you do not think it is, you have a problem, and you had better do something about it. If you do not feel you can go before your boss or before a group of your customers (or before a judge and jury) and explain and defend your work and decisions, you need to rethink the matter.

Just be aware that it is a question of fact, to be decided by the jury. Was your conduct reasonable? Is the design reasonable? Were the warnings reasonable? You may have two chances at this question. First, make sure your work is reasonable and that you can explain it as such. Second, you may have to help the court and the jury understand why it was reasonable. Or if you are a plaintiff, you will look for ways to show the design and the decisions were unreasonable, and that the unreasonableness caused the loss with which you are dealing.

Red Herring

Dogs have a keen sense of smell. If you do not want a dog to keep on the trail of something or someone, drag an old fish—a red herring, perhaps—across the trail. The dog will likely be diverted, or at least slowed down for a bit.

Attorneys, judges, and juries are also susceptible to diversions and interruptions. They may be (and often are) diverted from the real issue by the dragging of some unimportant and irrelevant item across their paths.

The use of red herrings in legal activity is fallacious—that is, it is not logically a correct and proper part of the subject at hand. It attempts to divert the attention of those involved to something that is less harmful to the "dragger of the red herring." Yet, in spite of the emphasis on truth, red herrings happen in lawsuits.

Two examples:

- The plaintiff wants to talk about the strike history of a defendant company during a trial where allegations are made that a product defect caused some injury. The strike history of the company has nothing to do with the questions, either of fact or of law, before the court. Talking about the strike history is a red herring issue.

- The defendant company wants to mention the criminal history of the plaintiff, who was injured when a machine rolled over. It stretches the imagination to see what, if any, relevance the plaintiff's criminal history had on the accident. The plaintiff's criminal history is a red herring issue.

Side Bar

When an objection is made, and when the judge wishes to hear the reasons for and against the objection from both parties, he will call the attorneys to speak with him privately. These conferences usually are at "side bar," the side of the judge's bench away from and out of hearing of the jury. Side bar conferences are for the resolution of matters of law by the judge. In such conferences, he hears the objector explain why he objects, and he hears other arguments from other attorneys as to why he should sustain or overrule the objection. Other legal matters may also be so discussed. Some side bar discussions becomes so lively or carry on so long, the judge will dismiss the jury during the discussion. Some conferences, typically at the beginning and end of the day, may be in the judges office, or "chambers."

If you are a witness, sit quietly in the witness stand and wait during side bar discussions. You may be asked to answer a question. Otherwise, relax and wait quietly.

Summons

A summons is the formal legal document notifying the defendant that an action has been filed against him. It is the legal notice that a lawsuit has begun. A summons may also be used for other purposes, to order that someone appear before the court to answer certain questions.

Testimony

When you go on the witness stand, you will be asked questions, first by your own attorney or the one who engaged you, and then by the opposing attorney. (The order may be reversed at times, for example, if you are called as an adverse witness.) The sum of the answers to those questions are your testimony. You answer questions about what you saw or heard or felt, etc., if you are a fact witness. You answer questions about your opinions if you are an expert witness. Note that the answers to questions put to you at Deposition are also testimony.

Testimony must mean something to the jury and the judge. Therefore, testimony is carefully planned. The manner of presentation becomes important, because it takes place in front of a jury that is deciding between two disputing sides.

Tort

A tort, simply, is a legal wrong committed or perceived to be committed against a person or other legal entity. A products liability injury is a tort. So is a slap in the face. So is mental harassment which causes one pain or economic loss.

In products liability, the civil or tort law generally applies. The one who can be shown to have been the cause of the injury or wrong can be found liable for that wrong. If the wrong results in economic loss, injury, or other loss, the party responsible for the tort may be ordered to make payments or do other things in an attempt to make the loss whole, either in an economic sense or otherwise.

Obviously, money is not a good exchange in every case. For example, money cannot pay a widow for the loss of her husband. However, money seems to be the best medium of exchange for settling tort claims. Juries usually deal in money awards when they find a claim to be valid and a recompense needed.

Warnings

Sometimes a complaint or claim may center around the question of adequate warning. Three things may be implied:

- It may be claimed that you did not give proper instruction or warning about the operation or maintenance of the product.

- It may be claimed that you did not give proper warning of a hazard or a hazardous condition.

- It may be claimed that an appropriate warning of an impending condition was not available.

In general, if you cannot avoid a hazard or protect against a hazard, you should consider warning against it. You also need to be careful about instructions included with the product. They may well be considered as a part of the product itself.

If you can, seek to provide warning sounds or other ways of letting the operator know that a failure is approaching and may be imminent.

Weight of the Evidence

In civil cases, such as products liability cases, for example, the decision to be made on the questions of fact by the jury deal with the weight of the evidence. The judge will charge the jury to consider the evidence they have heard, and to weigh the evidence on both sides. The amount of the evidence, its impact on the situation, the credibility and relevance of the evidence, the credibility of the witnesses, and the summation and explanation of that evidence by the attorneys in their final arguments all are considered by the jury. The judge often will tell the jury that they must consider the evidence as if it were in a balance. If the weight of the evidence for one side or the other causes the balance to tip ever so slightly in favor of that side, then that is where the decision should go.

The weight of the evidence may be partially your responsibility as an engineer. If you deliver testimony, your information must be true. It should be believable, and it should be such that it will be remembered. It should deal with the questions at hand. If the jury understands and believes what you say, you have added weight to the evidence.

Work Product

This, generally, is the work of the attorney which he uses to plan and develop his case theories and his method of presentation. Any such work done by or for the attorney—at his direction—is considered to be "work product."

In a dispute, the question about whether a certain document or piece of information is work product is a question of law. The judge will decide such questions.

Techniques That Should be Used by Attorneys

There are rules which you will hear quoted by one or more of the attorneys. These rules are not binding, but they represent general guidelines to the attorney involved in litigation. In experience, these rules have developed in the lore of the law, and are quoted by those who teach and who wish to assist attorneys.

As you pass through an experience in products liability litigation, whatever your involvement may be, you will hear attorneys speak of these unofficial rules. Sometimes they will be broken and sometimes they will be kept. The techniques do not apply to you, but knowing about them may help explain why some questions are asked of you.

Never Ask One Question Too Many

Especially on cross-examination, most attorneys hear (and sometimes, follow) the rule not to ask one question too many. Some legal scholars put it this way: When you have made your point, sit down. The discussion goes on to say that if the attorney asks one question too many, in his zeal to emphasize the point, sooner or later he will get an answer that he won't like.

Two stories illustrate the point:

A witness had testified that he saw the defendant fighting with the plaintiff, and that the defendant had bitten the ear off the plaintiff. On cross-examination, the defendant's attorney appeared to have painted the witness into a corner.

Q: "How far away from the fight were you?"

A: "About a block away—a city block."

Q: "It was late in the evening, wasn't it?"

A: "Yes, sir, about 7:30 p.m."

Q: "It was beginning to get dark, wasn't it?"

A: "Yes, I suppose so."

Q: "You wear glasses, I see. Did you have them on that night?"

A: "Yes, I did."

Q: "Mr. Witness, did you actually see the defendant bite off the plaintiff's ear?"

A: "Well, no, I didn't."

(At this point, the defendant's attorney should have sat down. He didn't.)

Q: "Well, Mr. Witness, if you didn't see him bite the ear off, how can you sit here and testify that he did bite the ear off?"

A: "After he got up, I saw the defendant spit the ear out!"

The other example goes like this:

A vagrant had been struck by a city bus and killed. The city attorney, acting for the bus company, was anxious to show that the vagrant had been drinking, and that he was most likely responsible for his own accidental death. A witness, another vagrant, turned out to be the brother of the dead vagrant. Others at the scene had observed the second vagrant approach the body of the injured man and go through his pockets and then bend low over him. A young attorney for the city bus line thought he had his case solid. He speculated that the deceased man's brother had taken a bottle of liquor out of the pocket of the dead man before authorities got there. He questioned the brother (as a hostile witness) in this way:

279

Q: "Did you see your brother get hit by the bus?"

A: "Yes, I did."

Q: "You went over to him and you felt around in his pockets, didn't you?"

A: "Yes."

Q: "Then you took a bottle of whiskey out of his pocket, didn't you?"

A: "No, I didn't."

Q: "You wanted to hide the evidence that your brother had been drunk, and that he really caused his own death, didn't you?"

A: "No, sir, I removed nothing."

The attorney has now painted a picture for the jury that at least would raise some question as to the cause and liability for the incident. However, he asked one more question—to his downfall.

Q: "If you didn't take a bottle of liquor out of your brother's pocket, then what were you doing?"

A: "I was kissing my brother good-bye!"

If you are on the witness stand, be patient. Maybe your cross-examining attorney will ask you one question too many. Then, give him the answer— the one he doesn't want to hear.

Don't Fight or Argue with the Witness

I already advised you, as a witness, not to fight or argue with the attorney while he is questioning you on the stand. The rule for attorneys is that they should not argue or fight with you, either.

In cross-examination, and especially if the witness is not giving the cross-examining attorney the answers he wants to get, the attorney may become feisty or even belligerent. In the excitement of a cross-examination battle, many attorneys get caught up in the excitement and challenge and break the rule. When that happens (and it seems to happen more often than not), be calm and don't fight back. Answer questions calmly, politely, and truthfully, and you will have no trouble.

The reason for the unofficial rule on arguing or fighting with the witness is simply that such action by the attorney makes the jury tend to side with the witness. Remember, one objective of your testimony is that the jury believe what you say. If the attorney, by picking on you, makes the jury feel kindly toward you, accept that help by being calm and not joining the fight.

Keep Cross-Examinations Short

Attorneys should cross-examine only for one or more of these reasons:

- to show the witness has given information that is wrong,

- to show that the basis of the witness' testimony is bad,

- to show that the witness has contradicted himself with past statements or actions,

- to show that the witness is biased (a hired gun, for example),

- to show that the witness is not competent to give his testimony, or,

- to show in some other way that the witness is not believable.

If the cross-examining attorney can do none of these things, he should stand and say, "No questions for this witness, Your Honor." But he usually won't.

If your testimony has hurt his case, he likely will spend a lot of time hoping and trying to get you to change your story or to slip up in some way. Now you have a real benefit for telling the truth. You only need to keep answering truthfully.

One expert witness had been on the stand for three and a half days, a day and a half on direct examination and two days on cross-examination. At that point, the jury had become noticeably unhappy with the cross-examiner for going into everything about the witness except his medical condition—and he had actually asked him if he had any memory problems!

281

The attorney who had retained the expert told him, at noon, that the jury was angry at the cross-examiner for dragging the matter out, and that he, the witness, should begin responding with a little sarcasm and humor. That afternoon, the jury actually applauded when the witness remind the cross-examiner (correctly) that he had already asked about a subject four times. (Your attorney will advise you when he wants you to respond with humor or sarcasm.)

Attorneys should keep cross-examinations short, but they probably won't.

Know the Answer Before You Ask the Question

Seldom, if ever, is it good lawyering for an attorney to ask a question to which he does not already know the answer. The follow-up comment to this rule is that if there is an answer that will hurt your case, you will surely get it if you ask a question to which you do not know the answer. There are exceptions, of course. He may ask a question if he does not care what the answer is, but even that has potential problems.

The discovery process should have disclosed everything needed to conduct the trial. The trial is not the place to go fishing for information. However, if you go to court a few times, you will certainly see some attorney ask such a question, and get blasted with the answer.

A witness had testified that he saw an accident late one night in a seamy part of town. The testimony all but sewed up the case for the plaintiff. Still, the defendant's attorney felt he had to try to make the witness look bad if he could. On an impulse, he questioned this way:

Q: "Do you, Mr. Witness, often go into that part of town?"

A: "Yes, I do."

Q: "Even though it is an undesirable part of town?"

A: "Yes, sir, I do."

Q: "Do you even go on weekends, Saturdays and Sundays?"

A: "Yes, I do."

Q: "Do you go often?"

A: "Yes, I do."

Q: "Regularly?"

A: "Yes, sir."

Q: "You know, do you not, that there are many bars, criminals, prostitutes, and drug dealers in that part of town?"

A: "Yes, I do."

Q: "And you still go there, regularly and often?"

A: "Yes, I do."

Q: "Do you have friends in that part of town?"

A: "Yes."

Q: "Quite a few?"

A: "Yes, quite a few friends."

Q: "By the way, are you married?"

A: "Yes, I am."

Q: "Do you take your wife with you when you make these trips in that part of town?"

A: "No, sir, I do not."

Does the attorney quit at this spot? Certainly not. He smells a real coup.

Q: "Will you tell the jury what you are doing when you go to that part of town?"

A: "I am a minister of the Gospel, and I pastor a mission a half block away from where the accident happened."

Tell a Story—Paint a Picture for the Court and the Jury

A generally accepted rule is that the jury must remember your testimony if they are likely to decide in your client's favor. To be best remembered, a presentation—a line of witnesses and the evidence they introduce—should be molded into a continuous story, with a flow and logic that is clear and persuasive.

Still, many attorneys fail to follow that suggestion. They bore the jury. They delve into minute and technical detail. They go on and on with boring documents and apparently unimportant information. I suppose they believe they are doing a thorough job when, in fact, they are boring and losing the attention of the jury and everyone else.

The attorney should look for interesting ways to present your testimony, and fit it into the overall story your client-attorney is trying to tell. You should be able to help him. Often, visual aids and exhibits are the answer. Juries will remember more of what they saw than of what they heard.

When You Have Made Your Point—STOP

I have already discussed circumstances where this rule taught in law school is ignored. Understand this point: The weight of the evidence does not mean the number of hours or days evidence and testimony are presented. It means the believability of the testimony and its application to the case at hand. The side with the more believable story wins.

When the point has been made, the attorney should not bore the jury by repeating or emphasizing it. However, some of them will do exactly that.

Don't Assume Anything

Attorneys are taught to deal in facts. When they seem to be too concerned with details, go along with them. They must not, if at all possible, deal with assumptions. Even the assumptions given in a hypothetical question (the attorney will begin by saying, "Assume these things:") have to bear reasonable relationship to the facts of the case at hand.

If an answer is unclear, the attorney should not assume he understands it. He will ask follow-up questions. If you, as a witness, do not understand the question or instruction, you should insist on clarification.

Listen to the Answers

I have already advised you that, as a witness, you must listen carefully to the questions. Attorneys have an unwritten rule that they should listen to the answers, too.

You will be surprised, at times, when the questioning attorney, on your side or on the other side, acts like he or she didn't hear your answer. In the heat of court battle, the attorney may be following his plan exactly. However, if his witness doesn't answer exactly as he expected, the plan will be upset, perhaps badly.

Even the attorney's own witness might give an answer different from that expected. A witness was once asked by an attorney if he had ever seen a particular model of crane. He replied that he had. The attorney looked up in surprise and blurted out, "I though you told me a week ago that you had never seen one."

"I did," the witness answered, "but I saw one this morning on the way to the courthouse."

I have stated already that attorneys do not like surprises, but they still happen. It is far better for a little surprise here, during the direct examination, than to have the cross-examining opponent ask why you testified that you had not seen a machine of that model, when he saw you examining one this morning next to the hotel.

Plan, Plan, Plan

The successful lawsuit is usually characterized by a good plan. This emphasis is placed before attorneys often and regularly. Most of them plan well, too. Only an occasional attorney will "wing it" and operate without a carefully thought-out plan. He does so because the case seems open and shut (and then he usually gets surprised) or because he is lazy (and then he gets beaten in the court room).

Expect your attorney or attorney-client to spend a lot of time with you planning. It gives his best chance to win. Some of the tedium that appears in preparing a case is well spent planning time. If it takes you longer than it seems it should take, planning is probably the reason.

But what do you do when the plan needs changing? Change it, of course! If a surprise happens or something goes awry, you can change from a good plan to a modified plan much more easily and successfully if you planned well.

Don't Try to Fool the Jury or the Judge

Attorneys are cautioned by men of experience, "Don't try to fool the judge or the jury." Both will quickly spot tricks, corner-cutting, and bluffs, and neither will react well to it when it is discovered.

Again, note that these few techniques for attorneys stated above are not rules attorneys are bound to obey. They are good judgment advisories from other experienced attorneys to the new, younger attorneys. It will help you, as an engineer and as a witness involved in a products liability suit, to better understand what they are doing. By understanding the process, you will be able to assist more effectively.

Chapter 14

WAR STORIES

When attorneys meet for lunch, travel, or play golf, they tell each other "war stories." These are stories of things that have happened to the teller or to someone he knows. War stories are a little like fish stories. They are all true, but they sometimes get distorted a little in an attempt to outdo the previous storyteller.

Some war stories tell of humorous things that happened. Others may be ridiculous, and still others are so true they stand out as classics. Some stories are told to show a bad or even foolish move by a colleague or a judge.

War stories are told among lawyers because they are entertaining, but also because each of them has an important kernel of information or experience that is valuable to the teller and which may be valuable to the listener. My chapter on war stories is included in this book for the same reason. Each story has some bit of information in it that has been valuable to me and might be valuable to you.

These stories are not meant to be humorous, though some of them may be. Instead, they are intended to pass along some real life occurrences and situations, to aid the engineer in better understanding both the predictable and unpredictable natures of this business of litigation.

Each has some lesson, perhaps limited in scope and application, but nevertheless potentially useful. Some may illustrate principals already discussed in this book; some may suggest new principles that haven't yet been discussed. Any of them may be of value at some particular time in the engineer's experience in litigation.

Seventeen-Hour Deposition

An expert was called to a deposition in a case involving a fatal accident with a construction machine. Due to scheduling problems, the deposition was set for a Saturday morning, in the defending attorney's office. This is not unusual.

What he didn't know was that his own client-attorney had deposed the opposing expert witness until midnight on a Saturday a month earlier. That type of thing usually leads to "payback" time. This one did, too.

The deposition continued, with a lunch break and a few short breaks for the attorneys to "check their notes" from 9:00 on Saturday morning until 2:00 Sunday morning—a 17-hour period. The deposition continued despite the fact the expert witness was on strong medicine for a viral infection. All of the attorneys knew that.

Two attorneys collaborated in the questioning. One wrote questions on yellow sticky sheets and placed them in front of the questioner. The questioner kept asking questions as if there were no tomorrow. There were long series of questions on a single subject or point, and there were frequent moves from one subject to another.

The expert prided himself that he never was the one to ask for a break. He kept his suit coat on when everyone else in the room had taken theirs off. He kept his tie knotted properly and tight, and he refused to ask for a break until one of the attorneys asked for one.

The expert had thought up a long list of things to say at the end of the deposition. The result was good. The case was settled reasonably. However, the expert changed his requirements for deposition time and added a requirement that the deposition would not last more than eight hours in one day unless one or two more hours would be certain to complete the deposition and save future travel and expense.

The witness being deposed has the right to so limit the questioning. The deposition may take place and continue for as long as is necessary (that means until the questioner is finished), but there is no legitimate demand that the witness be questioned for an unreasonable continuous length of time.

Seldom would an attorney conduct questioning this way. If he were asked to delay questioning until the next day or even later, he almost certainly would have done so.

Don't let yourself be placed in an unreasonable or uncomfortable position at deposition. Moreover, don't place yourself in such a position, either. If you are ill or on medication, let them know. If you are tired or otherwise unable to properly deal with the deposition, tell them. The attorneys will accommodate reasonable requests.

Deposition at the Airport Gate

A matter of litigation involved attorneys from the other end of the country from where the expert lived. A decision was made to conduct the deposition near a large airport which was accessible in a reasonable way to all of the parties. This is a common decision, made to accommodate most or all of the participants. Generally, attorneys cooperate in this way.

The attorney appointed to do the questioning arrived at the airport and was met at the gate by the defense attorney and his expert witness, who was to be deposed. An argument ensued as to who was to pay for the room and who should have reserved the room for the deposition. It was all a hassling game between the attorneys, but these types of arguments do happen.

Suddenly, the court reporter showed up at the airport gate. She had been told that the deposition would be at or near that gate. To accommodate the attorneys (by keeping them close to their later scheduled departing planes) the expert agreed to be deposed at an unused gate on that same airport concourse.

The deposition was interrupted by continuing and repeated waits while plane schedules were announced and lost children were sought and executives were asked to call their offices. Such announcements badly disrupted the questioning and the answers at a deposition. Worse yet, the court reporter began to record some of the airline announcements.

This type of atmosphere is obviously not good for a deposition. The expert was so disturbed that he made a statement at the end of the deposition, and on the record, describing the conditions of the deposition location and allowing that if there were any problems with the deposition testimony, they should be blamed on the noise and interruptions, and the unreasonable decision by the attorneys to hold the deposition in that noisy place. (The attorneys, of course, objected to the statement, insisting that the witness had no right to make statements on the record; he was only to answer questions put to him by one or the other of the attorneys. However, the court reporter did record the statement, knowing that the condition caused her problems, also.)

One who takes a deposition or one who provides a witness or consultant for deposition has an obligation to provide a reasonable place for deposition. Conference rooms and attorney's offices have served well. So have motel rooms and offices at airports.

I Don't Know

You will be told that "I don't know" is a good answer if it is the truth. You do not have to be held to answer questions when you do not know the answer or you do not remember.

One vice-president of engineering for a construction machinery manufacturer was subpoenaed to testify by deposition in a case involving a machine designed and manufactured long before he joined the company.

The strategy of the deposing attorney was to ask questions of the system experts—electrical, hydraulic, structural, and others—and then ask the same questions of the vice-president and try to find discrepancies in the answers.

When the vice-president began to be questioned, he answered the first nine questions with, "I don't know." The questioner became angry and raved about how a head of engineering could know so little and be in charge of a product line. He suggested that the vice-president was obviously "sandbagging" against the possibility of a conflict between his answers and those of his assistants.

The defending attorney responded, "Wait a minute! Ask the witness how long he has been with this company and on this job."

The questioning continued something like this:

Q: "How long have you been vice-president of engineering for this company?"

A: "A little less than six months."

Q: "Congratulations! How long have you worked for the company?"

A: "A little less than six months."

Q: "Hmmm. How did you get the job as vice-president so quickly?"

A: "That was the position for which I was hired."

Q: "Oh. Well, do you know the other four gentlemen whom I deposed in this case during the last two days?"

A: "Yes, sir, I do."

Q: "Do you know anything about the model XYZ machine?"

A: "Yes, sir."

Q: "What do you know about the XYZ machine?"

A: "That is a broad question. Can you be more specific?"

Q: "Yes, I have already asked you a dozen or so specific questions, and you answered that you did not know."

A: "Those were true and correct answers, sir."

Q: "Well, how am I supposed to depose you if you do not know the answers to any of the questions?"

A: "I am giving you correct and true answers, sir."

The defending attorney interrupted and said, "Why don't you ask him if he can get the answers to the questions you would like to have answered, perhaps by tomorrow morning? He has a whole engineering department and all of the files. I'll bet he can get the answers, but I am not surprised that he doesn't know the answers right off the top of his head."

The deposing attorney agreed and asked to be given the answers to five specific questions the next morning.

The next day, the vice-president appeared in the deposition room with drawings which answered the deposing attorney's questions. The answers were not as the deposing attorney had hoped they would be. In fact, one of them was extremely damaging to the plaintiff's basic theory of the case. The deposing attorney asked no more questions and a week later the case was dropped.

I Can Prove it Didn't Happen That Way, But I Can't Prove How it DID Happen

An accident victim had slipped from the front platform of a loader while trying to wipe off the outside of his windshield. In falling, he apparently hit his head on a bolt end that was improperly installed and the injury left a clear trail of blood, marking the path of the victim's head as he fell across and through the arms of the machine and down to the ground. There were no eyewitnesses to the accident.

The victim was found an hour or so later, under the machine. He was dead. The position of the body was carefully marked and photographed. A biomechanics specialist reconstructed the fall and the path of the victim. The path was well established by the blood path from the head injury. A serious problem in the reconstruction occurred, however, near the end of the fall.

About three feet above the ground, an opening between the lift arms of the loader and the braces between the lift arms formed a square opening about 42 inches by 28 inches in dimension. The body, as found, was under that opening and about three feet back toward the center of the machine from the opening. Further, the head was on the opposite side of the opening by some 40 inches.

This indicated to the reconstructionist that there were at least three problems:

- The victim's body had to have passed through the 42 × 28-inch opening between the lift arms and the braces. To do so, it had to do one of three things: (1) it had to go through head first; (2) it had to go through feet first; or (3) it had to fold up and essentially go through the opening "center of gravity" first. The reconstructionist was unable to formulate a good working scenario with any of these possibilities.

- The victim had to turn 180 degrees, head to foot and foot to head, in the process of falling through the opening and falling the remaining three feet to the ground. This seems impossible, and could not be developed into a usable scenario.

- The position of the victim's body was not under the opening; it was about 40 inches to the rear of the opening. One possibility was some motion of the victim after the fall. This was not indicated by marks in the dirt under the machine, nor by any other trails of blood. Another possibility raised serious questions: The machine may have been moving at the time of the fall, or may have been moved after the fall.

The completion of the investigation left the consultant and the attorney with the strong position of being able to prove that the accident didn't happen according to the theories and scenario advanced by the victim's estate attorney. However, neither could the defense prove how the accident did happen. One almost had to assume that the machine was moved after the accident or was moving during the accident. No evidence was found nor eyewitnesses found to establish that motion.

The matter was settled before trial. The biomechanics consultant was told that even though they could likely prove to a jury that the accident didn't happen the way the plaintiff's attorney contended, that would not likely satisfy a jury. They would want to know how the accident did happen.

293

The Judge Down South

A trial in a mid-southern state was just being completed. The defendant had presented an expert to testify about the safety of the machine involved, and to explain that a claimed condition on the machine did not exist, and would not have caused the accident even if it had existed.

Direct testimony and cross-examination of the expert had just been completed. The time was about 4:00 in the afternoon. The judge had dismissed the jury, telling them that on the next morning, they would hear final arguments and then be given the case for deliberation.

As the attorneys for both sides were collecting their papers and checking evidence with the clerk, the judge suddenly called the expert witness to the side of the bench. The attorneys all tensed up, wondering what was going on.

The expert witness engineer cautiously, and with a little fear, approached the bench. The conversation, in low tones, went something like this:

J: "Mr. Witness, I see by your CV that you graduated from State University in 1957. Is that true?"

W: "Yes, Your Honor."

J: "You don't need to keep being formal. This is just a personal matter of interest. Did you know a certain engineer who graduated from State University that same year? I suppose it is a big school, and that you may not have know him. He is an uncle to my wife." (He named the engineer.)

W: "In fact, sir, I did know him, and I remember him very well. He graduated as a civil engineer."

J: "Right! Well, let me tell you why I asked. When I go home every night, my wife asks how my day was. I tell her a little about it, and generally, she gets bored and doesn't pay much attention. Well, tonight will be different. She likes her uncle a great deal, and when I get home tonight and she asks what happened today, I will tell her that I met and talked to a man who knows her favorite uncle. By George, she

294

will pay attention tonight. By the way, there is no reason you can't tell the attorneys what we talked about, but try to hold out on them for a while. It will have them wondering and perhaps a little scared. See how long before one of them asks you."

We all left the room. A half hour later, sure enough, one of the attorneys couldn't wait any longer and blurted out, "What on earth did the judge talk with you about?" The expert dragged out the answer a little and finally told the story. Great relief followed.

Judges are normal people. When they are friendly, they can even be fun.

At Deposition, Who is Calling the Shots?

An engineer employed by a manufacturer was acting both as the 30(b)(6) witness for the company and as an expert witness in a case involving a piece of earthmoving equipment. The claims involved inadvertent motion of the machine. The plaintiff's attorney was trying to compare the case to an automobile case he had where the car had allegedly "jumped into gear."

The case was not the same as the auto case, and the engineer was in a good position with excellent data to explain why his machine had not jumped into gear. The deposition was taken by an engineer who had turned lawyer, and he had a stack of documents which he would present and ask the engineer to explain.

At deposition, the engineer was asked dozens of questions over a period of 11 hours during two days. Two attorneys were attending the deposition for the defendant—one, a local attorney who was the defense attorney of record, and the other, the company's products litigation supervising attorney.

An interesting situation arose. The case being litigated was one of four similar cases facing the company. This case was also the first case in which the documentation would be exposed and discussed. As a matter of policy, the material was properly discoverable and the plaintiff's employee/expert witness intended to properly answer the deposition questions so the record would be built for the subsequent cases.

As questions were asked and answered, the engineer-witness thought he began to detect a difference in reaction between the attorneys on his side. When he answered some questions, the in-house attorney would flinch or raise an eyebrow. When he answered others, the outside attorney would act like he had been betrayed. The witness soon saw that the answer and reaction differences came because he was answering the questions truthfully and considering the total possible claim exposure that faced the company on that matter. Yet the local attorney was concerned only about his immediate case, and not that the witness and the company attorney were dealing with broader issues.

The deposing attorney finally noted the reactions. Observing that the opposing attorney had noticed the apparent differences in reaction between the two defending attorneys, the witness stopped and asked for a break. When he had the two attorneys on his side out in another office, he informed them that they had to find some basis of agreement, and that they must quit the face-making and flinching at the answers. He told them that the opposing attorney had noticed the reactions and "had their number." Either one or the other had to react and respond.

The engineer explained that he knew that one attorney was concerned about a group of cases and the other only about this one matter. Between them, they had to decide which was the tactical approach. He threatened that if the reactions continued, he would develop the biggest stomachache ever, and postpone the deposition until the attorneys did agree on a strategy.

They agreed somewhat reluctantly.

You have a right to not be hassled by disagreements or differences between attorneys outwardly on the same side of the matter, especially when they are on your side. Someone should be in charge.

Can You Tell What the Jury is Going to Do?

Two different cases illustrate that it is difficult to guess what the jury is going to do.

First, a fatality case in the western part of the country involved claims that a machine was defectively designed and counterclaims, by the defense, that modifications to the machine had caused the accident. The family situation was especially sad with a widow and four children in the courtroom testifying about their relationships with the deceased man.

In such cases, it is not unusual that the defendant has made an offer of settlement, and that offer has been rejected. Such was true in this case.

As the trial proceeded, the defense attorney and the company people in the courtroom felt the defense case had been effectively presented and that there was a good chance of a defense verdict from the jury. The offer to settle was repeated, however, with an additional factor—a spread was offered. One figure, $300,00, was offered as a minimum settlement, regardless of the jury verdict. Another figure, $900,000, was offered as the maximum payment, regardless of the jury verdict.

This meant that if the jury came back with anything less than a verdict of $300,000, the defendant would still pay the plaintiff $300,000. If the verdict were over $900,000, the defense would pay the plaintiff only $900,000. If the verdict were in between $300,000 and $900,000, the defendant would pay the plaintiff whatever the verdict was.

The jury, during deliberations, sent the judge a note asking if the jury could assign responsibility to both parties. (Apparently under the law of that state at that time, they could not.) This information convinced the defendants that the question was not "if" a verdict would be against them, but "how much?"

Again the plaintiff was urged by the defendant to accept the spread offer. She did not, until the court clerk announced that the jury had reached a verdict. Suddenly the attorney for the plaintiff accepted the spread offer. Apparently he had felt the same concern as had the defendant's attorney—that the case was going well for the other side.

The settlement terms were formally recorded in court before the judge, and the judge complimented the parties for having arrived at a good agreement. Then the jury reported its verdict: No liability against the defendant. Had the defendant given away $300,000? In a sense they did, but the decision to offer (and to accept) the spread deal was a business decision made before the jury said there was no liability, of course. In view of the jury note, it was a

297

reasonable decision to make. One could well assume that the jury was going to "hit" the defendant with some amount of liability.

In another case, also involving a fatality, the decedent was killed when a machine backed over him in a landfill operation. The jury was not unusual. The attorneys and the defense witness all felt positive about the case, but had the usual concerns and worries about the unknowns.

The wife of one of the people attending the trial predicted that the jury would find for the defense, and she offered to explain why she so predicted. She said the only woman on the jury was certainly going to be elected the jury foreman, and that the woman juror didn't like the deceased man's widow, plaintiff in the case, because of the way she dressed. The juror simply could not dress the same way—she was not properly shaped.

The jury found no fault nor liability on part of the defendants. The only woman juror <u>was</u> the foreman. Was the analysis correct, or was it just a lucky guess? It's impossible to say.

Sometimes you can read a jury, but usually, you can't. Some psychologists and sociologists may have developed good statistical data. For example, they may say that people with a certain education or background more often than not will do certain things or decide certain ways. The key to such advice is "more often than not." It seems unlikely, however, that a specific jury can be read in a specific case.

Surprises

There should be no surprises in the courtroom during a trial. At least, the pre-trial process attempts to prevent surprises from happening. The judge doesn't want to be surprised. None of the attorneys wants to be surprised, though any one of them will not miss an opportunity to spring a surprise on the opposition.

In practice, every question may not be asked at deposition. Every question may not be asked in interrogatories, either. As a result, and in the unfolding of the case in the courtroom, surprises do happen.

A company engineer was testifying in an accident case involving an earthmoving machine being "roaded" or moved down a city street from one work site to another. The accident happened, causing the plaintiff serious injuries. The plaintiff blamed the accident on certain steering characteristics of the machine involved.

The defendant had offered engineering testimony to rebut the contentions of the plaintiff. The trial was a long one (eight weeks, finally). The company engineer witness had been on the stand since Monday morning; it was now Thursday afternoon.

The defendant's attorney had admonished the witness that he should be courteous, professional, and calm. He had done so. During the Thursday noon break, however, the defense attorney told the engineer that the jury was getting disgusted with the long and unnecessary cross-examination, and that he, the witness, should talk back a little.

After lunch, the cross-examination continued like this.

Q: "Mr. Witness, you didn't test the machine in traffic did you?"

A: "No, sir. It wasn't necessary."

Q: "Didn't you think that you should have tested this machine in traffic so you could be sure that an accident like this couldn't happen to the poor plaintiff?"

A: "No, sir. I repeat, we had no need to test the machine in traffic."

Q: "Could you tell without testing that the machine would work properly in traffic?"

A: "Certainly. So long as it worked properly, it would work on a street or in a field or wherever."

Q: "In fact, Mr. Witness, you don't even know anything about highway traffic and what is involved, do you? You are just a construction machine man, aren't you?"

A: "That is not true, sir, and I'll explain."

299

Q: "I don't want your explanation, Mr. Witness. Just answer the questions."

Judge: "He has answered the questions, counselor. And I want to hear the explanation. Go ahead, Mr. Witness, and tell us what you know about traffic and highway matters."

A: "I drive a car, and have done so for over 25 years and many thousands of miles. In addition, I am a member of the Society of Automotive Engineers, which deals with technical matters involving automobiles and highway safety. Further, I have served as a consultant with my state's traffic safety commission, under the secretary of state and the governor."

At this point, a big silence broke out. The plaintiff's attorney went to talk with his engineering expert who was in the courtroom. After about five minutes, the impatient judge asked the attorney to continue. He did, but on a completely different line of questioning.

The defendant's lead attorney jumped to his feet demanding that the plaintiff's attorney continue on the line of questioning dealing with traffic and highway matters. Loud roaring broke out. The judge gaveled for quiet and told both attorneys to hush.

Then he explained to the defendant's attorney that he should have known his objection was improper, and that he could ask the witness whatever he wished on redirect examination. (But the jury was now wondering what the traffic safety experience was all about.)

At the recess, the defense attorney took the engineer aside and asked, "What the hell was all that talk about being a consultant to a state traffic commission about? Why didn't you tell me?" The witness said that no one had asked about it earlier.

On redirect, the witness explained his spare time commitment to reducing traffic accidents by contributing his engineering expertise to a public effort.

There were two surprises. First, the plaintiff had not brought up the possible question of compatibility of the earthmoving machine with traffic on a street.

Having brought that up with a surprise line of questioning, however, he was surprised in turn when the witness answered that he indeed had worked and was still working on such matters.

Surprises happen. When they do happen, a surprise response is sometimes effective.

Two Hours to Present Your Case

In the normal progression of affairs in a matter of litigation, the attorneys will agree with the judge, prior to the trial, that the case should take a certain length of time—or number of trial days—to complete. The court personnel and the jury need some idea of what to expect for time. So do the attorneys. Witnesses need to schedule proper time to appear and testify.

The judge will generally depend upon the participating attorneys to make those estimates. If there appears to be sandbagging or lollygagging, the judge may hurry them along, and seldom does the judge accept unreasonable time estimates or delays.

However, sometimes a schedule, situation, or even a personal desire may cause a judge to limit the time amount for a case presentation in some way. That can be a problem. It may be especially troublesome if the other side has had three or four days and the judge, needing to get the trial over with for some reason, tells your attorney that he has only two hours of direct examination time to put on his case.

Such a limitation was placed on a case involving a machine fire.

The defense had three witnesses ready—a company engineer, an outside consulting engineer, and a local college professor especially versed in certain technical details relevant to the case.

The defense attorney knew full well that the plaintiff might try to make his case through cross-examination of the defense witnesses. The plaintiff's case had not gone well up to that time. Two hours, divided between three witnesses, gave an average of 40 minutes each.

The outside consulting witness went first. He had been told that if things went well, apparently, that he might be on the stand more than 40 minutes, and perhaps as long as an hour. All three of the witnesses had been well prepared by the attorney, who knew exactly what he had to present to the jury to prevail in this matter. Given the sudden restriction of two hours, the defense attorney had to prune his presentation to fit the time. He did.

The outside engineer-witness was on the stand on direct examination about one hour and twenty minutes—far more than his average share of the time. The reason, according to the attorney, was that he was getting his case into evidence easily and comfortably. (When the machine is running right, use it.)

The company engineer and the local professor used the remainder of the time to tell their stories very briefly. The defense attorney had told the jury in opening statements that he would call the three witnesses to show certain things. He did exactly that, but not in a shared or balanced time frame.

Two points come forward. One is that if you are a witness, and if things are going well, you may keep going. Don't be surprised, and don't worry about it. If that happens to you, you are probably doing exactly the job the person asking the questions wants. And if you lose part of your time, don't let that worry you either. The trial is a game of presentations. The presentation that best convinces the jury wins. If you testify less or more as part of that presentation, so be it. You are part of a team.

You Know Something Your Attorney Doesn't Know

Suppose you are on the witness stand, and you suddenly discover something that you know but that your attorney probably doesn't know. What do you do?

You could ask for a "time out" but you probably wouldn't get it. If you did, and if you went and talked with your attorney, that would look bad to the jury and to the others in court. Furthermore, you may be asked (and probably would be asked) to disclose what you talked to your attorney about.

You could fake a coughing spell and try to sneak a little talk with your attorney. But that would be distorted and you wouldn't get away with it. You may just have to think fast and use your best judgment.

An expert engineer, on cross-examination in a products liability suit involving a construction machine, noticed that as the cross-examining attorney approached, he had a book in his hands. The expert recognized the book. He knew it contained a monograph on the subject of the trial at hand, and that the opinions expressed in that monograph were inaccurate and would be very detrimental to the case, even though the opinions expressed did not bear directly on the case. Further, he knew the material, and if he were asked to read it aloud to the jury, it would make him sound bad. Still further, he knew that some courts, at least, had admitted that very book and monograph as a "learned treatise." (He could disagree, but it might sound like sour grapes to the jury.)

The first question asked by the cross-examining attorney gave him a way out.

Q: "Mr. Witness, do you know Mr. Technology Expert?"

A: "Yes, sir, and I see you have a book there in your hands that contains an article by Mr. Technology Expert. I have seen that before, and I do not agree with large parts of his opinions."

Q: "O.K. We'll go onto something else."

During the rest of the cross-examination, the book was never used, nor was Mr. Technical Expert ever mentioned again.

The expert engineer had broken several rules generally accepted as good for testifying experts. First, he answered more than the question. Second, he volunteered information without being asked to do so. Third, he confronted the questioning attorney and, in effect, became argumentative. Fourth, he took a chance that the judge would have stopped him in midstream, making him look bad in front of the jury. Fifth, by mentioning the book, the monograph, and Mr. Technical Expert first, he took a chance that the jury would now wonder what was being withheld from them. In fact, the whole interlude was dangerous.

But it worked. The material never showed up.

After the testimony, the attorneys for whom he was consulting gave the expert a first-class lecture on following the rules, answering only what was asked, and keeping the testimony short and concise. The engineer argued that the material in the book, read from the witness stand, would have been disastrous. He never made his point with his own attorneys because they wouldn't read the monograph. The engineer was convinced that he frightened the opposing attorney from using the material. The engineer was equally convinced that discussion of the material, even though he would have openly disagreed with it, would have been bad, if not disastrous.

When the Cross-Examining Attorney Empties Out Your Briefcase

In a trial involving an earthmoving machine, and specifically some transmission features of the machine, the expert witness carried his briefcase into the courtroom and onto the witness stand during his cross-examination. The cross-examining attorney licked his chops and approached the witness.

He picked up the briefcase and actually dumped it out on the witness table, in front of the jury. "Now we will see what this witness has up his sleeve," he said.

Nothing of any consequence was in the briefcase—certainly, nothing that had anything to do with the lawsuit at hand. However, there was a small, hand-held calculator, a tablet, and a small, pocket-sized "Kraftfahr Technisches Taschenbuch," an automotive handbook written in German.

The questioning proceeded.

Q: (Holding up the German handbook) "What is this?"

A: "A Taschenbuch."

Q: "Don't get cute! Answer me in English!"

A: "I did, sir. I can translate the meaning of 'Kraftfahr Techniches Taschenbuch' if you like."

Q: "What does this title mean?"

A: "This is an automotive technology handbook."

Q: "What language is the book printed in?"

A: "It is written in German."

Q: "Do you read German?"

A: "Somewhat slowly, yes, sir."

Q: "What is in it?"

A: "It contains basic information, charts, and tables dealing with mechanical engineering in general, and specifically automotive engineering."

Q: "Where did you get this book?"

A: "It was given to me some years ago by a German engineer I met at a technical meeting in Detroit."

Q: "Why did he give it to you?"

A: "Because I asked for one."

Q: "Why did you ask for one?"

A: "I was studying German at the time, and I recognized that an engineering book written in German would be of double use to me—I could review engineering information, and at the same time, I could practice German."

Q: "What did you use from this German book in your work in this case and for this lawsuit?"

A: "Nothing, other than the book contains a lot of basic engineering information which is part of my training and experience."

Q: (To the Judge) "Your Honor, I would ask that this book be marked by the Clerk for identification, and that the witness be asked to provide English translations of any and all of the parts that pertain to this case."

Court: "Counselor, the witness has already told you that it is a book with general materials concerning mechanical and automotive engineering. If you want to examine it, get someone into the courtroom who can read German, and have him or her tell you what is in the book."

Q: "But, Your Honor, my expert witness has studied German, but he can't read this material, because it was so many years ago that he studied German."

Court: "Then, sir, you have a problem. Get on with the questioning."

If it is in the courtroom, someone may want to look at it and you may have to explain it. Be careful what you take into court in your briefcase. Have your attorney check it.

When the Cross-Examiner Checks Your Books and Your Private Papers

As an expert witness, your fee schedule, your charges in the subject case, and your accounting records in general, are all subject to discovery, by one means or another. It may sound like an infringement of personal rights, but it is not.

If you have consulted in or investigated or plan to offer opinions in a case, those kinds of records are fair game for the opposing attorney. They may or may not be allowed by the court to have those records, but they are fair game for questions at Deposition. They may be allowed as the subject of questioning on cross-examination at the trial.

In a matter of litigation involving an excavator, an outside expert had been engaged by the defending attorney. The defendant was an equipment dealer, and the original claims and suit were filed only against the dealer and not against the manufacturer. Alleged improper maintenance was the basis of the claim.

The consulting expert engineer studied the material on the incident and inspected the machine involved. He tested another similar machine and found several facts which all but eliminated the dealer as a defendant. He billed his time for that work to the attorney who was defending the case for the dealer.

Faced with the weak case against the dealer, the plaintiff's attorney expanded his claim and the suit to include the manufacturer of the machine involved. The attorney for the defense of the manufacturer contacted the same expert asking for availability. The expert told him he already was familiar with the matter, having consulted with the dealer's attorney. However, he offered that he would be pleased to continue on the case for both defendants, if it were worked out between them. It was; they agreed to co-defend the matter.

In deposition, it came out that the relationship had been as it was, separately, with both the dealer and with the manufacturer. The technical matters surrounding the accident were straightforward and not too complicated. The plaintiff's attorney asked for the expert's records and billings regarding the case—both on the present case and on the earlier work for the dealer. Copies of these were provided.

In the subject case, 90% of the cross-examination at trial involved showing the jury and the expert witness overhead view graph copies of all of his invoices to both attorneys in both parts of the case and having him explain or confirm each entry item to the jury. Copies of four invoices, over a ten-month period, went up on the screen.

Q: "Mr. Expert, is this a copy of an invoice dated March 10th and sent to Mr. Attorney as a bill for your services in this case?"

A: "Yes, sir."

Q: "Do you charge $110 dollars per hour for your services?"

A: "Yes, sir."

Q: "Isn't that a lot of money to charge?"

A: "I charge all of my clients the same rate, and they continue to hire me."

307

Q: "Do you mean to tell this court and jury that you spent four hours reading the Smith deposition?"

A: "Yes, sir."

Q: "Did it take you that long?"

A: "Yes, sir. It was 270 pages long, and I made notes as I read the deposition. You have a copy of those notes."

Q: "Did you also spend two hours examining a machine in Madison, Wisconsin, and charge that time to the client?"

A: "Yes, I did."

Q: "Why didn't you go to the dealer in Iowa to inspect a machine?"

A: "Two reasons. One, I was in Madison anyway, on another matter, and I could do this without several extra hours of travel time and expense. Second, the Iowa dealer was a party to this action, and I didn't feel it would be proper to involve that dealer in this investigation."

Q: "Do you always try to save your client's money by combining work on a single trip this way?"

A: "Certainly. It also saves me time and makes my work more planned. And, by the way, I carry a hard hat and a pair of work boots in my car, so I can stop on the road at any time and look at a machine. Sometimes I can even run it."

An on and on for about an hour with four invoices.

Note several points:

First, you must answer the questions. Short answers are best when dealing with charges and with how much money you charge and how many hours you work.

Second, if you do not have good records and keep them, you look like a sloppy professional to the jury.

Third, it is all right to expand your answer and make it more complete when you know it is truthful and your actions are proper and reasonable.

Fourth, at times it is good to try to get the questioning back to the facts of the case rather than on your charges and costs. You have made bare all of your information. It is normal for the industry, and you have nothing to hide.

The reason for this type of questioning is to attempt to show you to be a person who will testify for pay. If the opposing attorney can convince the jury that you are more interested in money than in a just outcome to this case and trial, he will have shown that you are less credible than you really are. If he can't damage your fact or opinion testimony, he may try to get at your credibility.

The expert saved one last shot for the last question.

Q: "You are getting paid for your testimony here in court today, aren't you?"

A: "No, sir. I do not sell my testimony. I develop engineering opinions and I charge proper rates for the time I spend doing professional work and arriving at the opinions. I am paid for my time, expertise, and knowledge, not for my testimony."

When Your Lawyer is Against You in the Next Case

An expert had agreed to look over a matter for an attorney-client. In the process of his preliminary examination, he noted the name of the opposing attorney in the case—an attorney for whom he was now working on another, completely unrelated matter.

He called his client in the second matter, DEF, and informed him that attorney ABC was his own client-attorney in the earlier case, still pending. Then he called the first attorney-client, attorney ABC, and told him that he now was aware of their possible involvement in the second case, against DEF.

The attorney ABC on the first case said, "I have no problem with you being against me in the second case, so long as your engineering ethics are not hurt by your involvement in both cases." (This is a good position for the attorney. In fact, it is the only proper position, barring any overt conflicts of interest.)

The second client, a manufacturer, said, "I have no problem with your involvement in both cases, so long as you are comfortable in both cases and you have solid opinions and conclusions in both cases."

The engineer-expert had four choices:

- He could drop both cases and claim a conflict. That would have been somewhat difficult in the first case, because he was already well wrapped up in the case.

- He could have turned down the second case, citing his involvement in the first case with an attorney who would be on the opposite side in the second case. However, the client in the second case urged him to take the second case, if he could.

- He could have dropped the first case, and taken the second. This would have been difficult because of his involvement in that first case so far. It may have also shown bias or preference between the two different clients.

- He could take both cases, and deal with the attorney from the first case on an arm's length basis in the second case.

The expert chose to take both cases, and he did so with the approval, and even urging, of both attorney-clients.

There were no problems. The information and opinions offered by the expert were not conflicting. (Had they been conflicting, it would have been a serious problem for the expert in both cases.) The expert gave deposition testimony in both cases. Obviously, then, the attorney-client in one case was the opposing and question-asking attorney at the deposition for the other.

The expert recognizes that there are extra cautions needed in such a situation. He cannot ever forget to whom he is talking and what the subject is. It can be done, but it is difficult.

When Your Attorney-Client gets Fired

An exciting development is to arrive at a meeting to discuss a case and find that your attorney-client has been fired by the insurance company that had hired him in the matter. To be told by the insurance company-employer and by the new attorney assigned to the case that you are OK and still on the team may give a little "comfort," as attorneys describe it, but it is still a shock.

The engineer-expert witness in such a situation finds some interesting opportunities, too. One expert had done all of the technical and product work in a case involving injury in a forestry situation. He had established his opinions, and had developed a good reconstruction of the incident which showed the injured man to be doing things improperly.

The expert had transmitted his findings and opinions orally to the fired attorney, but had not yet been deposed. The parties in the case were concentrating on depositions for discovery; the plaintiff was discovering information about the manufacturer and the product by means of discovery deposition of three key engineering employees.

The expert figured he was in an indispensable position. He had done all of the work and had all the answers, or at least the answers that a good expert should have. They couldn't fire him.

(You should know the insurance company had fired the lawyer from the case because of ideological differences between them. The differences involved such things as the kinds of questions that should be asked of plaintiff and his witnesses, and the energy with which the discovery was to proceed. It was more a matter of when to proceed than how to proceed.)

The expert, knowing nothing about the switch in attorneys, entered the meeting with an easy heart and no worries. By noon, he had plenty of worries, and some new problems to solve.

First, he had to brief the new attorney on the general scenario of the incident. The new attorney wasn't even sure who had been hurt or what had broken on the machine. Following that, the expert was asked to help the meeting group draw up a list of possible accident scenarios. This had been done once before. It is always a good way to study a case. However, the expert had a list already from which he had developed his own opinions. The new attorney insisted on a new list, whatever that might mean.

The real problem started when the others had apparently exhausted the scenario possibilities. The expert volunteered, "I have two more scenarios to add to the list." The new attorney said he didn't want the additional scenario ideas if they came from "the old list."

The expert was in trouble. He had alienated the new attorney by appearing to stick with the ideas of the first attorney on the case. Worse yet, one of the two additional scenarios was the one settled upon as the most likely accident scenario in discussions with the first attorney.

If the new attorney systematically ruled out all the scenarios on the new list—and he would certainly do that—the expert would be giving up his best advice and beliefs regarding the case. This was not proper. If, however, the expert insisted on the scenario he really believed in, the new attorney would not consider him a team player in the case.

Fortunately, someone in the meeting needed a break. During the break, the expert showed his preferred scenario, the one chosen by the first attorney as the most likely scenario, to a young legal associate of the new attorney. The associate suggested the idea to the new attorney over the drinking fountain and the new attorney reentered the meeting and "added one more possibility" —the scenario his associate had suggested over the drinking fountain.

The idea created sparks and the meeting continued as it should have—resulting in a good case presentation plan.

Your Writings Will be Read Back to You

One expert wrote a definitive paper on the subject of what is done in the engineering processes of a large manufacturing company to assure that safety is properly included in the design and development of the product. The work was done by the engineer when he was employed by the manufacturer, as a public statement for that manufacturer. (Plaintiff's experts frequently indicated that the lack of a good statement was evidence of inadequate safety emphasis. This is not true, but this paper on the subject was one way to rebut the claim of no safety plan or statement of objectives.)

The expert explained that safety was a subject that could not be separated from the design of the machine any more than the nervous system could be separated from the human body. Safety is useless, unless it is associated with or integrated into the design process of the machine.

The paper explained in detail how the process worked, and what elements were involved. It spoke of a series of "battle lines" at which the designer attacked safety hazards and it described what a good manufacturing and design organization should do to reach safety goals.

During discovery, that expert has often given a copy of that paper as one of his writings dealing with safety. It is a reasonable and proper request from the opposing attorney that he do so.

In turn, the opposing attorney frequently faces the expert in court or in deposition with questions like these:

Q: "Did you ever state a process for designing to safety goals in any of your writings?"

A: "Yes."

Q: "Isn't it true that safety is the highest and most important factor in design?"

A: "No, sir."

Q: "Didn't you say in your paper that 'there is no factor more important in design than safety'?"

A: "Yes, sir, I did."

Q: "Doesn't that mean, then, that nothing is as important as safety? That safety is Number 1?"

A: "No, sir. It means that safety is just as important as other factors such as performance, reliability, serviceability, specifications, cost, etc. It does not mean that any one of those factors can be traded off for another, or that one is less important."

Q: "I don't understand."

A: "If the product costs too much, it won't sell. If it doesn't do its work, it won't sell. If it doesn't live long enough, it won't sell. If it is too big or too heavy, it won't pass regulations, and it can't be sold. You see, all of those factors are important. Safety is Number 1, right along with performance, reliability, service life, and all of the rest. If you miss on any single factor, your product won't be successful.

"Therefore, if I trade off weight for safety, that is, if I get additional safety at the expense of making the product too heavy to sell, I lose. And if I sacrifice safety save a little cost, I will lose, too, because the public or the marketplace will soon refuse my product. I must have a balanced product, with all factors at the highest possible level, in order to be successful."

Opposing attorneys sometimes take another tack, also.

Q: "Would you agree with this statement: 'Nothing is more important than safety.'"

A: "Yes, sir."

Q: "Would you agree with this: 'The most effective way to have a safe product is to avoid the accident'?"

A: "Yes, sir."

Q: "Do you think warning of a hazard is a less effective way to avoid an accident than eliminating the hazard in design?"

A: "If eliminating the hazard is feasible, I do agree. I have to agree—I wrote those things in my paper."

If you don't tell him, he may tell you, or in court, he may try to make it appear that you were now somehow fudging on those statements. You can be sure that any written material you may have published will be used. You need to remember what you wrote. If you wrote only the truth, it shouldn't bother you.

Be Careful with Exhibits—They Can Backfire

Sometimes you may be asked to suggest, design, or prepare exhibits to be used in the courtroom during trial. Such exhibits may be charts, graphs, pictures, or documents of various types, and they may be models or sections of a machine or component, intended to be used in demonstrating or proving some contention in the case. Simple exhibits are best.

As the technical person in the case, you may be in the best position to suggest to the attorney how the exhibit can and should be constructed to demonstrate the desired feature or information. It is a rule to be careful with fancy or mechanical exhibits with moving parts. Three problems can (and do) occur in the courtroom.

1. The exhibit doesn't work

Sometimes in the interest of keeping the display or exhibit light enough to move into the courtroom, some parts are left out or made of wood, or some other shortcut is taken.

An expert sat down in a model tractor operator's station, and moved a lever only to have it come off in his hand. Of course, the jury laughed. Everyone likes to see a surprise, especially during a dull trial. What was worse, the case involved the location of a lever. In the incident, the lever didn't break, but it was alleged to have been in a position for it to be bumped. The experience did nothing to help the defense of the product.

2. The exhibit works to assist the opposition

A plaintiff's attorney had an exhibit prepared to show how easy it was for an operator to accidentally move a pin and cause a seat to drop. In fact, in the incident at trial, the claim was that the pin had accidentally vibrated out of position.

315

In court, the attorney's expert shook the exhibit slightly, to show how easily the pin would be moved. It did not move. He shook harder. It still did not move. Then he decided that the pin must have been secured in some way to keep it from coming out in shipment to the courtroom. He called for a recess to correct the problem, but the problem didn't exist. The pin was loose in the hole, but with the weight of the seat on it, it wouldn't budge. A half hour later, the expert and the attorney had to dispense with the demonstration, saying that "something apparently wasn't right with the setup." It was not an effective display. Worse, the opposition was arguing that very point—that the weight of the seat would prevent the pin motion, and that the accident couldn't have happened the way it was claimed.

3. The jury may be invited to try the demonstration display

An expert used a seat mockup to demonstrate the adjustability of the seat. He demonstrated the ease with which the seat could be adjusted.

With no warning, the judge decided the jury members might like to sit in the seat and see for themselves. They did. Seven of the twelve jurors could not even budge the seat. They were not construction machinery operators. They were housewives, jewelry salesmen, retired watchmen, and home economics teachers. They decided the seat was indeed not easy to adjust, and found against the defendant party that had built and presented the demonstration display.

One attorney, in another matter, was injured when he leaned on a demonstration setup designed to show strength. It collapsed—fortunately, after the trial was over and the jury had delivered their verdict and left.

Don't Let the Opposition Play with Your Exhibits

Exhibits, in the courtroom, are really the province of the Court—that is, the judge and the attorneys for both sides. A witness cannot take an exhibit into the courtroom and expect to use it without attorneys from both sides examining it and playing with it. There should be no surprises in the courtroom, and that applies to exhibits, too.

Yet, while the opposing attorney is examining it, someone should be there to be sure no changes are made. No accusations—just citing what happened in two situations.

In one case, a rather large exhibit had been made up and moved into the courtroom to be used as a demonstration about how a particular component system worked. A lengthy objection fuss was made over the question as to whether the exhibit was sufficiently accurate and representative as to be admitted as evidence—or even as a demonstrative exhibit.

To prove the authenticity of the exhibit, the defense attorney in the case put a company employee on the stand to testify that the exhibit had been made under his direction; that it was made of production parts; that it had been modified only to allow the exhibit, which was part of a tractor, to be moved into the courtroom; and that the exhibit was indeed what it was proffered to be.

On cross-examination, the company witness was questioned this way by the opposing attorney:

Q: "Did you say this exhibit was built at your direction and under your supervision?"

A: "Yes, sir."

Q: "Did you certify that it is indeed a good representation of the transmission control system of the Model RST tractor?"

A: "Yes, I did."

Q: "Was this exhibit inspected since it came to this courtroom, to make sure nothing had changed?"

A: (After a pause) "Yes, it was."

Q: "Did you personally inspect it?"

A: "Well, no. I didn't, but I assume someone checked it."

Q: "Interesting. Did you know two bolts were loose on the control bracket, and did you know the control yoke was loose?"

A: (Long pause.)

Q: "Obviously, you didn't. I move the exhibit not be allowed, even for demonstrative purposes."

Judge: "Now just a minute. Let me ask a couple of questions. Mr. Witness, if the bolts were replaced, and the yoke were tightened, would the exhibit be correct?"

A: "Yes, Your Honor. But first I would check to see if counsel has tampered with anything else."

(Loud clamoring, objections, and yelling.)

Judge: "That was an impertinent answer, Mr. Witness, but maybe a good one. The court will recess for 15 minutes while you recheck the exhibit."

The judge's response was too close for comfort. Apparently, however, the judge recognized at least the possibility that someone had tampered with the exhibit.

In another matter, an exhibit sitting on a courtroom table had an adjustable spring in it. If the spring were adjusted even moderately close to specifications, the component exhibit would work correctly.

The expert, preparing to testify and use the exhibit right after lunch, made one more test run with the exhibit. It didn't work. The spring had been loosened far out of adjustment. No one knew who did it.

The "one more test run" saved an embarrassing moment in the courtroom in front of the jury. If your exhibit doesn't work, the jury may well assume the component on your machine didn't work properly, either.

Let the Plaintiffs Know You Share Their Loss

First, let me insist that you do not do what I discuss in this story without being told to do so by the attorney for whom you consult or work.

One corporate engineer and expert witness who has been in court for his company perhaps two dozen times over a period of nearly 20 years had an experience which could reinforce one's belief in mankind.

He was specifically instructed, by the corporate attorney, that after the trial and the final arguments were complete, he should seek out the plaintiff (the injured person or the widow or survivor) and express sincere condolences, representing both himself and his company.

He developed an approach which went something like this (modified to fit the specific case):

> "Mrs. Plaintiff, I want to speak for myself and for my company. We sincerely regret the loss of your husband in this unfortunate accident. We have no disagreement on the nature of the loss. It is tragic. Further, what hurts you here hurts us back in Factorytown, too. We only disagree as to who is liable for the accident. We want you to know that we join you and your family in mourning this loss."

This approach should not be taken without the direction of the corporate attorney, and without asking permission of the opposing attorney to speak to the plaintiff. It should never be done if anyone objects for any reason.

The engineer-witness says the request has never been denied and the conversation has always been warm and friendly. Tears? Certainly. Sometimes the attorneys have tears, too. But the witness has met family members, clergymen, and opposing attorneys who made it abundantly clear that the gesture was appreciated. People need to remember they are people, and that they have opportunities to help other people.

When You Meet a Friend on the Other Side of the Table

It is not uncommon for a witness or an expert to meet a former employee or supervisor across the litigation table. Sometimes, they are even good friends. Still, they have adopted opposing opinions or positions in the matter under litigation. By retainer, or for the company, they have been involved in the matter where their differing opinions will come to light, and may even have a major bearing on the outcome of the case.

Is this bad? It can be, but it need not be difficult.

Such a case occurred in a matter involving an accident on an earthmoving machine. Through interrogatory answers, an engineer found that he was representing a client against a company for which his former supervisor had been retained as an expert witness.

Deposition of the engineer went something like this:

Q: "Do you know Mr. Supervisor?"

A: "Yes, I worked for him for three years."

Q: "Did you always agree, between you?"

A: "No, not always."

Q: "So, you didn't get along with him. Is that true?"

A: "No, I didn't say that. We got along fine. We just didn't always agree on everything."

Q: "Do you think Mr. Supervisor mistreated you or rated you improperly, or anything like that?"

A: "No, but I will explain. One of our disagreements was in the kind of job assignment I got. I wanted to get into management, but Mr. Supervisor thought I did better as a technical specialist, and he kept me on a special research job."

Q: "Did it cost you money, like a lower salary?"

A: "Heck, no. I probably made more money in the research job."

End of this line of questioning.

The supervisor had similar questions in his deposition:

Q: "You have heard, no doubt, that Mr. Engineer is the expert retained for our side in this dispute. Do you know him?"

A: "Yes, sir."

Q: "How do you know him?"

A: "He was a co-worker at NMO Company for about three years. He was my staff research man."

Q: "Is he a good engineer?"

A: "That is a broad question. He was my employee. Beyond that, I am not free to discuss his employment or performance. Professionally, I consider Mr. Engineer a good journeyman engineer. He is registered in this state, which also gives him some professional status."

Q: "As his supervisor, did you evaluate him, or rate him on his job?"

A: "Certainly. That was part of my supervisory responsibility."

Q: "Well, how did you rate him?"

A: "I can't discuss that. It is a private matter between Mr. Engineer and myself. You would have to get approval from him and from our former company, I believe, for us to discuss those ratings."

Q: "Wasn't Mr. Engineer dissatisfied with his job assignment?"

A: "I have already indicated that I can't answer such questions without violating Mr. Engineer's privacy. You may, I suppose, get some kind of order to force that discussion, but I am not now free to do so."

Q: "If Mr. Engineer said he wanted to be a manager, would you disagree with that?"

A: "Please, Counselor, I cannot discuss this subject further."

Q: "Well, can you tell me why the two of you have ended up on opposite sides of this dispute?"

A: "I can tell you why I am on this side of the dispute, sir. You will have to ask Mr. Engineer why he has taken the opposite view."

Q: "Well, isn't strange that you disagree on this matter?"

A: "Not at all. Reasonable thinking men often disagree. That is how things progress."

This subject came up again at trial. In each questioning at trial, the opposing expert was in the courtroom to hear the other's responses.

First, the engineer, testifying for the plaintiff:

Q: "Do you know Mr. Supervisor?"

A: "Yes, sir."

Q: "Is he sitting in the courtroom now?"

A: "Yes sir. He is right there in the front row." (Points to Mr. Supervisor.)

Q: "Did you work for him?"

A: "Yes, sir. Three years at NMO Company."

Q: "Did he treat you well?" (Objections were made and finally settled when the judge told the witness he could answer.)

A: "He treated me well, but we didn't always agree. I wanted to be a manager, but he wanted me in a technical research position."

No questions were asked about salary. The attorney already knew the answer would hurt his cause. After questioning about his opinions and the bases for them, the witness was turned over to the cross-examiner. Nothing more was said about the relationship, until Mr. Supervisor came to the stand. Then, the attorney for whom he consulted inquired in this manner:

Q: "By the way, Mr. Supervisor, the counsel for the other side made reference to the fact that his expert, Mr. Engineer, once worked for you. Is that true?"

A: "Yes, it is."

Q: "You were in the courtroom when Mr. Engineer testified, were you not?"

A: "Yes, I was."

Q: "Did you agree with the answers Mr. Engineer gave when he was talking about your relationship at the NMO Company?"

A: "Yes, I did. I don't believe I heard any answers I disagreed with, insofar as our relationship was concerned."

Q: "Why are you being so cagey about answering questions about that employer/employee relationship when you gave your deposition in this case?"

A: "The opposing counsel asked me about my rating of Mr. Engineer as an employee. I didn't disclose those ratings or talk about them because that would have been a violation of Mr. Engineer's privacy."

Q: "Well, he worked for you for three years, didn't he? You didn't fire him, did you?"

A: "He did work for me for about three years. And I did not fire him. I had no reason to do so."

Q: "Did you ever disagree with him?"

A: "Of course I did, frequently. That is the common element of engineering—disagreement and the resolution of those disagreements."

Q: "Do you know why the two of you disagree in this matter, before this court?"

A: "No sir. I know why I have my opinions and Mr. Engineer already has explained why he believes the way he does."

The trial continued with no further discussion of the employee/employer relationship between the two. The jury found in favor of one side and against the other. The two witnesses are still friends.

Take Too Many Pictures

Most experts recommend that, when an inspection of a machine or an accident site is being made, take too many pictures. What constitutes "too many" pictures? The best explanation given is that "one more picture or one more roll of pictures" is not too many.

During discovery, photos are commonly used in questioning a witness. They are also commonly used in building up the evidence of the accident and the surrounding conditions and potential causes. Perhaps better stated advice is to make sure you don't miss anything or that you don't take too few pictures.

Further, getting pictures as soon as possible after the incident is good practice. The farther away the photo is from the incident, in terms of time, the more likely the picture is to be questioned or discredited. Evidence in the picture taken long after the incident may not be evidence at all.

Police report photos and pictures taken by bystanders or witnesses to the accident may be the best. You may, however, have to deal with whomever has the pictures and how to get them. Discovery rules call for such disclosures, but sometimes they are missed in the heat of the discovery battle. Your own pictures will be the best, if they are early enough.

A professional photographer with whom I am acquainted makes a good living going to accidents (at the call of the police) and taking pictures of the site. He takes a lot of pictures, of almost everything he sees, and he frequently uses two or more cameras, to get both color and black-and-white photos. He also takes special photos, such as closeups or wide-angle shots. He makes those photos available to the police, the insurance companies, attorneys, and anyone else who may be interested.

At least twice, picture sets from that photographer have been useful in quickly and positively disposing of claims in death cases. An accident reconstructionist, in both cases, was able to reconstruct what really did happen, and to dispose of claims which were not properly founded. In another matter, a reconstructionist was able to reconstruct a case for which there were no witnesses—just from marks on the machinery which showed up and from the positions of the two machines involved.

Taking a lot of pictures has another interesting sidelight, also. If you are making an inspection and your opponent is watching you closely, you may worry and confuse him by taking a lot of pictures even though they may have nothing to do with the case. One expert on a matter had two engineers and an attorney following him around and making copious notes as to what he photographed, where he stood, and all of that sort of thing.

Later the same day, the opposing attorney had the same photos taken by his own expert. They never did figure out what the pictures were all about.

You May Not be Allowed to Testify

An expert mechanic had been retained to testify as to the proper maintenance activities concerning a certain construction machine. In brief, the mechanic was going to explain that the machine should be properly greased and oiled before it was used.

The judge, anticipating the testimony, asked to hear the testimony first, out of the hearing of the jury. He ruled, then, that the mechanic could not testify because a lay juror, with ordinary common knowledge, didn't need an expert mechanic to tell him that the machine should be oiled and greased before use.

The judge had merely ruled, at his proper discretion, that the issue of whether a machine should be oiled and greased before use was one that the jury did not need expert testimony to understand.

In another case, a judge ruled that an engineer could not testify in a case involving a dispute which boiled down to whether the operator of a machine should have shut it off before workmen worked near the cutting tool of the machine. The court ruled that a lay jury could make that decision without the help of an expert engineer's testimony.

Wait, Wait, Wait

A witness may sometimes think he is in the army. He hurries and waits, and then he hurries and waits some more. I was once given a frantic call to get to the trial city as quickly as I could; I was told I might be needed at once.

After complaining that I had waited at a hotel two and a half days before testifying after making the "panic trip," I found out what had happened. Another attorney in the case had been fined $500.00 for contempt of court because he did not have his next witness ready to go onto the stand at 4:00 p.m. during the trial. My attorney-client was taking no such chances.

Be Careful of Doing Your Engineering Work and Analysis on the Witness Stand

An expert had testified that the failure of a guard on a woodworking machine had been the fault of a manufacturing defect which started a fatigue crack that developed over a period of time. When the crack had progressed sufficiently far to distort the guard and bind the normal motion of the guard, it stuck in the open position, leading to an injury to the user.

The manufacturer defendant claimed that the crack on the guard had happened as a result of the tool being dropped, and that the crack had happened at one time, in that one drop.

The plaintiff's expert explained that the characteristics around the crack could and did prove that the crack was a fatigue failure, developing over time and starting from a sharp discontinuity in the guard profile—a manufacturing defect.

On cross-examination, the defendant's attorney handed the plaintiff's expert a box of five more failed guards, similar to the guard in the case. He said, in effect, "If you are so good at telling whether a failure crack is a crack that came from a single blow, or one that developed over time, tell us how each of these failures happened."

(The witness should have asked for ample time to examine the five additional guards away from the stare and pressure of the courtroom. He found out later that the judge would have allowed him at least overnight to study the new offerings. In fact, the judge seriously considered ruling the cross-examination request out of order, and forbidding the defendant the use of the five samples, which had not been introduced earlier.)

326

However, the witness, with careless abandon, pressed on. He told the cross-examining attorney that he could do as requested in a ten-minute recess. The recess was granted.

Four of the five guards had obvious places where they had been struck with a tool or fixture outside the guard, probably in a break test of some sort. Those were easy.

The fifth new sample had a crack that look remarkably like the trial guard on the accident tool. However, the expert, looking carefully at the guard, saw small radial cracks which identified a single impact point, and concluded that the fifth guard had been failed by a single blow, the same as the other four examples and unlike the subject of the trial.

Back in the witness stand, the expert responded that all five of the sample guards had been failed by a single blow, probably a test blow. The defendant's attorney then pointed out the similarity of the fifth sample and the guard about which the trial was concerned. He asked as follows:

Q: "Don't these two guards, sample number five and the subject guard in this case, have cracks that have very similar appearances?"

A: "They do appear to be similar in some respects, but the failures are not from the same cause."

Q: "Do you mean that although they look alike, one was a fatigue failure, over a length of time, and the other was a single impact failure?"

A: "They look somewhat alike, but if you look closely, you can see tiny radial cracks across the major crack, and if you make those tiny radial cracks, you can see they all point to a single impact point which I am convinced was the point of impact on this guard. The impact did not make a big dent, as it did on the other guards, but the sign is there if you look closely."

Q: "No further questions."

Judge: "Yes, there are. Mr. Witness, can you show me those tiny radial cracks?"

The witness did so.

Judge: "Can you mark those cracks with a red pen or something, so the jury can see them?"

They were so marked.

Judge: "Now, Mr. Witness, do I understand that you believe all five of the exemplar guards were failed by single blows of a tool or a test?"

A: "Yes, Your Honor. That is correct."

Judge: "And you state that the failure on the plaintiff's guard was a fatigue failure, starting from a manufacturing defect and continuing over a period of some time?"

A: "Yes, sir."

Judge: (To the Defendant's attorney) "Well, Mr. Attorney, are you going to tell the witness whether he is correct when he says that all five of the exemplar guards were cracked by single blows?"

Defense Attorney: "We will give you the answers when our witness testifies, Your Honor."

The answers were never given, but the jury decided the expert was correct and awarded the plaintiff damages.

It is dangerous to do such analysis on the spur of the moment. The expert in this case was correct; the Director of Testing for the manufacturer admitted that in later conversation. However, consider the chances—and consequences—of an error in front of the jury and the court.

When You are Caught with a Calculating Error

I have made calculating errors from time to time since I began school. I know how to calculate; I just do it incorrectly sometimes. When such an error happens in consulting or testifying, you can be sure the opponent will face you with it in the courtroom.

You have three choices:

- Admit the error and correct it,

- Try to explain the error and show that it was not your mistake,

- Try to show that the error was not important anyway, and really didn't matter.

A jury is not likely to understand your explanation of variances in the data or in "margins of error." They will mistrust you.

Q: "You calculated the distance to be 42 feet, didn't you?"

A: "Yes, I did."

Q: "But the distance is over 50 feet, isn't it?"

A: "Yes, but that is not important considering the probable errors in the given data and the allowable margins of error in such estimates and calculations."

Q: "But your mistake was a simple arithmetic error, wasn't it?"

A: "Sure, but it didn't substantially effect the result."

Q: "Even if you got the wrong answer to you calculation?"

A: "But it didn't make any difference. I explained that."

If you try to blame the mistake on something or someone else, the jury is not likely to believe you.

Q: "Your answer is not mathematically correct, is it?"

A: "Well, I seem to have made an error in multiplication somewhere, but it may also have been an error in the original information given to me."

Q: "Mr. Witness, I am not looking at the original information. I am looking at your multiplication of two numbers on line 7 of your calculation. That multiplication is wrong, isn't it?"

A: "Well, maybe. But I think some of the original information was wrong, too."

Q: "But you did make a mistake in multiplication, didn't you?"

It is best to face the error, admit it, and correct it. I did so in one case testimony, with this result:

Q: "You made an error in multiplying on line 7, didn't you?"

A: "Let me check it." (continuing) "Thank you, Mr. Attorney. I did make an error in multiplying."

Q: "Will you correct the calculation before we proceed?"

A: "I will. It will take a half minute or so." (continuing) "Alright, I have corrected the multiplication error."

Q: "Good. Thank you. Now we have the right answer. What, if anything, did the change in the multiplication answer on line 7 do to the final result?"

A: "It now says that the plaintiff had over 12 seconds to move from the path of the machine after the alarm sounded the first time, instead of only 9.5 seconds, as I originally and incorrectly calculated."

Q: "Oh!"

Test the Obvious

An attorney was retained by a man who was injured when a loader rolled down an incline and crushed him between a tree and the back bumper of the loader. The operator testified that he had not set the parking brake, but that he had put the bucket of the machine down on the ground when he stopped and got off the machine. He left the engine running.

Everyone assumed that the bucket, dragging on the ground, would have kept the machine from moving as it did. The defendant manufacturer used that as a fact to show that the machine could not move as the plaintiff's attorney theorized. The defendant suggested other reasons for the injury.

A consultant, hired by the plaintiff's attorney to find out how the machine actually moved, suggested testing the machine on the same slope where the accident occurred. The attorney resisted the test as unnecessary and costly. He said, "We already know that the bucket would have kept the machine from rolling."

The consultant asked, "Would it, really?"

They tested the machine. It rolled quite easily on the accident slope conditions, with the bucket down and floating; the weight of the bucket only slightly slowed the movement of the machine.

Sometimes it is worthwhile to test or even retest for the obvious. The obvious, sometimes, is not so.

Some Claims can be Refuted (or Confirmed) by Demonstration

The operator of a logging skidder, operating in a hilly terrain, ran the machine backwards down a steep slope and off the side slope, and rolled it over. Injuries resulted. The claims in the incident were that the engine had stalled or otherwise shut off, leaving the machine with no braking and/or steering control.

An engineer for the company, knowing the machine had been designed with ample emergency steering and braking power, tested the subject machine on the same slope. First, he came down the slope forward, with the engine running, demonstrating that the machine had good and safe primary steering and braking hydraulic power at engine low idle speed.

Then, he repeated the test with the engine dead, and going down the hill facing forward. He demonstrated sufficient emergency hydraulics to stop the machine seven times from a forward speed of 10 miles per hour, while making the necessary minor steering corrections.

Then, he told the defending attorney he was going to repeat the demonstration—in reverse—just as the accident situation had occurred. He drove up the slope, shut off the engine, and began to roll backward. He successfully and easily stopped the machine, using the emergency brakes, six times from 10 mile per hour rolling speed. He proved conclusively that the machine had adequate and safe emergency steering and braking ability.

No one on the work site knew the machine had that capability. Apparently at the time of the accident, the plaintiff just didn't try to stop the machine with the brake pedal. The case was quickly settled.

Noise is a Good Alarm

A worker assisting the operation of a large straddle crane in a concrete products plant was injured when he was run over by a wheel on the crane some 50 feet away from the operator. Claims were made against the manufacturer stating that the machine was defective, in that it did not have a warning alarm to tell a bystander when the distant wheel was approaching.

The attorneys involved in the case were standing around the "offending" wheel talking about whether some kind of cowcatcher or other guard device should have been installed to keep the ground man from accidentally getting under the wheel.

A consulting engineer was in the cab of the machine, inspecting the controls. He started the machine engine. Six attorneys jumped madly to get out of the way of the machine. The engineer laughed and stopped the engine. He asked the attorneys if they had heard the alarm. They all said, "No, but that engine sure barked loudly." The engineer asked if they needed ANOTHER alarm, in addition to the noise of the engine. There was no further discussion of the case.

Sometimes Testimony Comes from Unexpected Sources

A logger skidding trees on a small plot of land was hit by a sapling which he claimed knocked him out of the seat and under the rear wheel of the machine, where he was run over. Several months of discovery testimony had built the description of the accident to a point near trial.

As an afterthought, someone decided to depose the grandfather of the injured plaintiff, who was sitting nearby in a pickup truck. He had brought the plaintiff some iced tea.

The grandfather, unaware of the claims, testified that the accident happened when the plaintiff stopped the machine and got off to get his tea. The plaintiff then noticed that machine was parked on a little sapling he wanted to remove, and he tried to move the machine a little bit while standing on the ground by reaching up into the control compartment from the ground. The machine moved more than he intended, and ran over him. The new testimony stopped the case in its tracks.

Don't Be Too Sure of Yourself

One condition or feeling that the engineer-consultant must avoid is that of overconfidence. There is no such thing as a slam-dunk in the litigation game. When the attorney, his expert, or his client feels certain that they have won and cannot lose, watch out! Overconfidence has lost many cases.

First, the litigation game continues right through the trial, and even beyond. What you do and what you say about the case at any time may be critical to your success. Expect to win, yes. But don't be too sure of yourself. Cases are won by hard work and good thinking during the trial. That is what the jury or the judge sees. You may have prepared a good case, but if you do not present it well, you may be surprised by a bad outcome.

A company engineer sat on the witness stand and proudly announced that his company never made any mistakes, or not knowingly, anyway. His side lost the trial.

A professor-expert spoke to a jury about a technical subject in a condescending way. He said he knew he was correct, but that the subject was too difficult for any lay people to understand. His side lost that case, too.

A plaintiff's expert said that he had made better designs at least a dozen times. Maybe he did, but his side lost the case. No one showed any of the "better" designs to the jury, and they apparently decided that confident expert wasn't correct after all.

In a product performance suit, the jury readily told the attorneys after the case that one side had a solid case with good evidence. However, they found for the other side, because they did not like the cocksure attitude of the president of the company.

If you feel sure, and certain that you will win, recheck your position. Maybe you forgot something. That "something" you forgot may well be that the jury is going to decide who wins, not you.

Don't Get Discouraged and Give Up

A more likely thought you may have is that the whole litigation process is hopeless or that the cards are stacked against you anyway, or that you cannot possibly win even a minor argument in pre-trial hearings, let alone win the trial.

The litigation process is a continuous up-and-down game. When the claim is first made and the lawsuit first filed, the claims seem ridiculous. You are sure there is no basis for the claims and that no jury will ever find against you on such a matter. Then, the roller coaster ride begins. As the discovery develops in the case, one thing after another seems to make the case a certain winner and then a certain loser. One piece of evidence makes the defense look impossible. Another piece of evidence makes the plaintiff's position look almost untenable. Then a witness shows up with a new viewpoint as to what happened. Then a reconstructionist analyzes the matter and says, "The accident can't possibly have happened this way."

The thing to remember is not to let those up-and-down swings get too violent. And don't get too worried when you are down. Experience is that the ups and downs happen. Try to smooth them. Don't get too far up and don't get too far down. The answer comes at the end of the game, not during the game.

The same emotional swings happen, too, during a trial. That is especially true during a long, protracted trial. The swings can also occur during a deposition on a shorter cycle period.

Keep cool. Develop confidence with care. And keep working at the case.

And oh, yes. Tell the truth—always.

Chapter 15

TIPS FOR THE ENGINEER INVOLVED IN LITIGATION

In harmony with specific matters regarding discovery, depositions, and trials, here is a summary list of things for the engineer to remember and do (or to avoid doing) when involved in litigation:

- Remember, you are involved in a legal matter. You are <u>assisting</u> the attorney. Do not try to run the game.

- Always be truthful—to everyone, and especially to yourself. Don't do or say what you do not believe.

- Don't be frightened or awestruck by the legal process, the attorneys, or the courtroom. You know more than anyone else in the case about certain facts or opinions. You can assist by properly presenting what you know when you are asked.

- A good attorney will prepare you for your deposition and for your testimony, and he will listen to your thoughts and advice. Give that to him. Also listen to his direction; he is in charge.

- Follow instructions precisely and accurately. The law is a complicated process and for it to work well, procedures must be followed accurately. That applies, of course, to lawyers, but it also applies to the witness if he is to be of assistance.

- View the legal process for what it is: a flawed but still excellent and effective way for people and companies to get a good measure of equity in a dispute.

- As a professional, and as an engineer, always do your best work and use your best judgment. If you do, your product will be the best possible, and will stand up under the scrutiny of a courtroom action.

- Offer your attorney the best professional engineering advice you can. He will appreciate it. He will use some of it. What he doesn't use is not omitted because it is bad; he is looking to fill in the spaces in his case presentation, and if your advice doesn't fit or isn't appropriate for that particular situation, it may not be used.

- You may have some special skills: Creative brainstorming, expressing technical information in common lay language, a special understanding of risk and probability mathematics, artistic ability, foreign languages, psychology, personal experiences, etc., which may be of use in the litigation at hand. Offer those skills, also, and if they prove to be needed, use them.

- Be yourself, but do so in a professional way. Your appearance and your actions may well be as important as what you say. Certainly, how you say it is important. Remember, credibility is all-important. Even if you are 100% correct, and perfect in your analysis and opinions, if the judge and the jury do not believe you, you lose.

- Beware of traps—trick questions, questions with "slight misstatements," incorrect summaries of what you have already said, and questions not backed up by truth and evidence. Your attorney will protect you, but you must help, too.

- Think. Even if you already know the answer, think. Then answer.

- If you make an error or misstate something, correct it. Don't try to cover it up or explain it away. Courts and juries like honesty, and admitting a mistake is an honest action.

- Listen to advice, and use all of it that applies to your situation. Don't miss any chance to get help. Taking part in a litigation matter is not a one-man show.

- Above all, tell the truth. Truth that may hurt your client's cause is far better than falsehood that seems, at the moment, to help that cause.

When involved in litigation, you will probably make some mistakes along the way, but I hope the material in this book will help you to be successful most of the time.

INDEX

341